D1571002

...AND YOU SHALL CHOOSE LIFE...

© 2011 Kabbalah Centre International, Inc.

All rights reserved. No part of this publication may be reproduced or
transmitted in any form or by any means, electronic or mechanical,
including photocopying, recording, or by any information storage and
retrieval system, without permission in writing from the publisher, except
by a reviewer who wishes to quote brief passages in connection with a
review written for inclusion in a magazine, newspaper, or broadcast.

Kabbalah Publishing is a registered DBA of
Kabbalah Centre International, Inc.

For further information:

The Kabbalah Centre
155 E. 48th St., New York, NY 10017
1062 S. Robertson Blvd., Los Angeles, CA 90035

1.800.Kabbalah www.kabbalah.com

First Edition
February 2011

ISBN 978-1-57189-771-8

Design: HL Design (Hyun Min Lee) www.hldesignco.com

...AND YOU SHALL CHOOSE LIFE...

An Essay on Kabbalah,
the Purpose of Life, and
Our True Spiritual Work

Rav Yehuda Ashlag

EDITED BY MICHAEL BERG

Table of Contents

Foreword

It is with immense joy that we present to you, the reader, *And You Shall Choose Life*, written by the great kabbalist and Kabbalah Centre founder, Rav Yehuda Ashlag. This work was originally written as an introduction to his historic work, *The Study of the Ten Luminous Emanations*, a sixteen-part explanation of the spiritual creation of our world. It can be said that without this remarkable study, one cannot truly come to understand our world, where we came from, and where we need to go.

I remember fondly how I would study this great work with my father, Rav Berg, in the early morning hours for many years. I believe that for my brother Yehuda and me, these were the most spiritually uplifting times of our life. I know that anything I understand and anything I accomplish stems from the understanding, wisdom, and Light received during those study sessions in our house in Queens.

Rav Ashlag's *Study of the Ten Luminous Emanations* is a monumental work that takes years to learn and decades to truly master. It is one of the deepest and most complex of all kabbalistic studies. When we realize how difficult it is to come to a true understanding of this beautiful work, it gives us a greater appreciation of a statement my father's teacher (and closest student of Rav Ashlag), Rav Yehuda Brandwein, made. In one of his many letters written to his beloved student, my father, he writes: "You can only completely understand the introduction to the study written by Rav Ashlag after you have completely understood the actual study (all sixteen chapters!)."

I share this not to discourage you, the reader, but to awaken an appreciation for the book of secrets you hold in your hand now. You might ask: "If this is true, then what is the purpose of reading this introduction when we have not begun or completed the entire study, which will take years?" The answer is that while it is true that it will take many years and many readings to understand completely the great secrets and Light in this work, the little that we do pick up— even in our first reading—will awaken within us great understanding and Light.

As is true with all of Rav Ashlag's writings, the revelations in this work are obtuse and concealed for the one who does not desire wisdom and connection with the Light of the Creator. But for a person who has a true desire for wisdom, a true desire to cleave to the Light of the Creator, this work will be a wellspring of great awakening and wisdom. I have read this book countless times over the past twenty-five years, and every time I find new Light and inspiration in these words of Light. It is my hope that you, the reader, will take the time and invest the effort to extract from this powerful book the endless wisdom and Light that it contains for you.

While reading and meditating on this book, there is one verse that we should keep in mind, and it is a verse whose secret Rav Ashlag explains in this book: "Those who desire and truly seek Me shall find Me."

Blessings,

Michael Berg

Chapter One
Life Does Not Happen. Life Is a Choice

Questions about the necessity of studying the Wisdom of Kabbalah

1) At the beginning of my words, I find a great need to shatter a barrier of iron that is existing and separating us from the Wisdom of Kabbalah since the destruction of the Temple [and continues to exist] even up to our present generation. [This barrier] has put a severe and heavy load on our shoulders, and raises fears that Kabbalah may, Heaven forbid, be forgotten by the Israelites.

And whenever I start talking to the heart of someone about engaging in this [Kabbalah] study, his first question is: "Why should I know how many angels there are in Heaven and what their names are? Won't I be able to fulfill the entire Torah, with all its particulars and nuances, without all this information?"

Secondly, the person asks further: "The sages have already stated that one should first be very well versed (lit. fill up his belly) with the *Mishnah* and *Halachah*. But who would so delude himself that he has already finished studying the entire Revealed Torah, and that the only thing missing for him is the Concealed Torah?"

Thirdly, this person is afraid that he could, Heaven forbid, go astray because of this engagement [of studying Kabbalah]. After all, there are various instances of people who have strayed from the path of the Torah because they were engaged with Kabbalah. "And if this is the case", [the person asks], "why do I need this trouble? Who would be so foolish that he would put himself into danger for no reason?"

Fourthly, [the person keeps asking]: "Even those who are in favor of this study [of Kabbalah] do not permit it to anyone except holy individuals, servants of the Creator, and "not everyone who desires to take hold of the Name can just come and take." (Tractate *Berachot* 17b).

פרק ראשון

הַחַיִּים אֵינָם מִקְרֶה. הַחַיִּים הֵם בְּחִירָה

השאלות על הכרח לימוד חכמת הקבלה

א) בריש מלים, מצאתי לי צורך גדול לפוצץ מחיצת ברזל, המצויה ומפסקת בינינו לבין חכמת הקבלה, מעת חורבן הבית ואילך, עד דורנו זה, שהכבידה עלינו במדה חמורה מאד, ומעוררת פחד שלא תשתכח ח"ו חס ושלום מישראל.

והנה כשאני מתחיל לדבר על לב מי שהוא, אודות העסק בלימוד הזה, הנה הנה היא שאלתו הראשונה, למה לי לדעת כמה מלאכים בשמים, וכיצד נקראים בשמותיהם, האם לא אוכל לקיים כל התורה כולה בפרטיה ודקדוקיה בלי ידיעות הללו.

שנית ישאל, הלא כבר קבעו חכמים, שצריכים מתחילה למלאות כריסו בש"ס ששה סדרי [משנה] ובפוסקים. ומי הוא שיוכל לרמות את עצמו שכבר גמר כל התורה הנגלית, ורק תורת הנסתר חסרה לו.

שלישית, הוא מפחד שלא יחמיץ ח"ו מחמת העסק הזה. כי כבר קרו מקרים שנטו מדרך התורה בסבת העסק בקבלה. ואם כן הצרה הזאת למה לי. ומי פתי יכניס את עצמו בסכנה על לא דבר.

רביעית, אפילו החובבים את הלימוד הזה, אינם מתירים אותה אלא לקדושים משרתי אל, ו"לא כל הרוצה ליטול את השם יבא ויטול" (ברכות יז' ב').

3

Fifthly, and most important, [the person says]: "There is a rule that in every case of doubt, we should go out and see what most people do. And I can see that, all the Torah scholars of my generation hold a similar opinion to mine—and they avoid the study of the Concealed [Wisdom of Kabbalah]. They even advise those who ask them that, without any doubt, it would be much better to study a page in the *Gemarah* instead of this engagement [with Kabbalah]."

The goal and purpose of life

2) Indeed, if we would only focus our attention on answering one very well known question, I am sure that all these [other] questions and doubts would disappear from the horizon; and you would look to their place but they will be gone. This is the very small question asked by all human beings, namely: What is the purpose (lit. reason, taste) of our life? In other words, who enjoys these few years of our life, which are so costly to us in terms of all the suffering and pain that we experience in order to complete life all the way to its end? Or more precisely: Whom am I benefitting [from living my life]?

It is indeed true that scholars throughout the generations have already become weary from contemplating this [question], and needless to say, no one would even want to consider it in our generation. Yet at the same time, the question still stands with all its validity and bitterness. Because at times, it comes to us (lit. meets us) uninvited and torments our mind, bringing us to our knees in humiliation before we manage to find the well-known solution (lit. scheme)—namely, letting ourselves be thoughtlessly swept up in the streams of life, as [we have done] in the past.

By fulfilling the Torah one attains a life of goodness and truth

3) Indeed, to solve this conundrum, the Scriptures have said: "Taste and see that the Creator is good!" (Psalms 33:8). Because those

חמישית, והוא העיקר, כי קיימא לן בכל ספק נהוג לנו בכל [מקרה של] ספק, אשר פוק חזי מאי עמא דבר אשר צא וראה מה העם עושה, ועיני הרואות, שבני תורה שבדורי, כולם המה עמי בדעה אחת, ושומטים ידיהם מלימוד הנסתר, וגם מייעצים לשואליהם, שבלי שום פקפוק מוטב ללמוד דף גמרא במקום העסק הזה.

תועלת ומטרת החיים

ב) אכן, אם נשים לבנו להשיב רק על שאלה אחת מפורסמת מאד, בטוח אנכי שכל השאלות והספיקות הללו יתעלמו מן האופק ותביט אל מקומם ואינם. והיינו השאלה הזעומה הנשאלת מכל בני ירד, שהיא: מהו הטעם בחיינו. כלומר, מספר שנות חיינו הללו, העולים לנו ביוקר כל כך, דהיינו מרבית היסורים והמכאובים שאנו סובלים בעדם, בכדי להשלימם על אחריתם, הנה מי הוא הנהנה מהם. או ביתר דיוק, למי אני מהנה.

והן אמת שכבר נלאו חוקרי הדורות להרהר בזה, ואין צריך לומר בדורנו זה, שלא ירצה מי שהוא אפילו להעלותה על הדעת. עם כל זה עצם השאלה בעינה עומדת בכל תוקפה ומרירותה, שהרי לעתים היא פוגשת אותנו בלתי קרוא, ומנקרת את מוחינו, ומשפילתנו עד עפר, בטרם שנצליח למצוא התחבולה הידועה, דהיינו, להסחף בלי דעת בזרמי החיים, כדאתמול.

על ידי קיום התורה באים לחיים טובים ואמיתיים

ג) אכן, לפתרון חידה סתומה זו, דיבר הכתוב, טעמו וראו כי טוב ה' וכו' (תהילים, לג' ח'). כי מקימי התורה והמצות כהלכתן, המה הטועמים

5

who follow the Torah and perform the Precepts according to the *Halachah* are those who taste the "flavor of life" and who see and witness that the Creator is good. As our sages have said: "He has created the Worlds to benefit His created beings because it is the nature of the good to do good."

But surely, whoever has not yet tasted the life of fulfilling the Torah and the Precepts cannot understand and feel that the Creator is good according to the words of our sages who have said that the sole purpose for which the Creator has created man (lit. him) was to do benefit him. Therefore, he has no other option (lit. advice) than to fulfill the Torah and the Precepts according to the *Halachah*. This is why it is said in the Torah: "Behold, I have set before you this day life and goodness, death and evil…." (Deuteronomy 30:15)

Before the Torah was delivered, we did not have anything other than death and evil in front of us. The meaning is as follows: The sages said that evil-doers are called dead even while still alive (Tractate *Berachot*, 19b) because it is better for them to be dead than alive, since the suffering and pain that they go through to sustain their life exceeds many times over the minor pleasure that they derive in this life. And indeed, now that we have had the merit of receiving the Torah and the Precepts, we gain—by fulfilling them—that [promised] real and happy life, that gladdens their owners, as is said in the Scriptures: "Taste and see that the Creator is good!" (Psalms 33:8) And this is why the Scriptures say: "See, I have set before you this day life and goodness," (Deuteronomy 30:15) which was not in any way part of our reality before the Torah was delivered.

And that is why the Scriptures end with: "And you shall choose life, so that you and your descendants may live." (Deuteronomy 30:19) There is an apparent redundancy here: "…choose life, so that you may live." What this refers to is a life of fulfilling the Torah and the Precepts because only then is one truly alive. This is not the case [for someone] living without the Torah and the Precepts [because] that kind of life is harder than death. This is what our sages meant when they said that the wicked are called dead even when they

טעם החיים, והמה הרואים ומעידים כי טוב ה', כמ"ש חז"ל כמו שאמרו חכמינו זכרונם לברכה, שברא העולמות כדי להיטיב לנבראיו, כי מדרך הטוב להיטיב.

אבל ודאי מי שעדיין לא טעם את החיים של קיום תורה ומצוות, הוא לא יכול להבין ולהרגיש, כי טוב ה' כדברי חז"ל, אשר כל הכוונה של השם יתברך בבראו אותו, היתה רק להיטיב לו, ועל כן אין לו עצה אחרת אלא לילך ולקיים התורה והמצות כהלכתם. וז"ש וזה שכתוב בתורה (פרשת נצבים פרק ל' פסוק טו), ראה נתתי לפניך היום את החיים ואת הטוב ואת המות ואת הרע וגו'.

כלומר, בטרם נתינת התורה, לא היו לפנינו אלא המות והרע, פירוש, כמ"ש כמו שאמרו חז"ל, שהרשעים בחייהם נקראים מתים (ברכות יח' ע"ב), משום שטוב מותם מחייהם, להיות היסורים והמכאובים שסובלים בשביל השגת קיום חייהם עולה פי כמה מרובה על קצת התענוג שמרגישים בחיים הללו, אמנם עתה, שזכינו לתורה ומצות אשר בקיומה אנחנו זוכים בחיים האמתיים השמחים ומשמחים לבעליהן, כמ"ש כמו שכתוב טעמו וראו כי טוב ה' (תהילים, לג' ח') ועל כן אומר הכתוב, ראה נתתי לפניכם היום את החיים והטוב מה שלא היה לכם במציאות כלל קודם נתינת התורה.

וזהו שמסיים הכתוב, ובחרת בחיים למען תחיה אתה וזרעך (דברים, ל' טו'), שלכאורה הלשון מכופל, ובחרת בחיים למען תחיה, אלא הכוונה על החיים בקיום תורה ומצוות, שאז חיים באמת, מה שאין כן חיים בלי תורה ומצוות, המה קשים ממות, וז"ש וזה שאמרו חז"ל

are still alive. And this is the meaning of the scriptural saying: "… so that you and your descendants may live," that is to say that life without the Torah not only does not provide any joy whatsoever to its owners, but they also are not able to bring any joy to others.

[Such a person] cannot even enjoy the sons that he gives birth to because even their lives are more difficult than death, so what sort of gift is he giving to them? But he who lives with the Torah and the Precepts not only has the joy of his own life, but he is also happy to give birth to more sons and to hand down to them this good life. This is why it is said: "…that **you and your descendants** may live," because he has additional delight in the lives of his sons as he was the cause of their birth.

Man's choice together with the Creator's assistance

4) From the passage above, you should be able to understand the words of our sages concerning the saying: "Choose life," (see Rashi's commentary, Deuteronomy 30:19) which says the following: "I am instructing you to choose the part of life, as a man tells his son: Choose for yourself a beautiful part of my land. And [the man] takes [his son] to a beautiful piece of land and tells him: Choose this one! And about this, it is said: 'The Creator is my chosen portion and my cup; You support my lot.' (Psalms 16:5) [That is,] You [my Creator] have put my hand on the good lot, saying: This is what you should take." These words appear to be puzzling.

The Scripture says: "Choose life," which means that the person makes his own choice. [But] they [Rashi's commentaries] say that He [the Creator] takes him to the beautiful lot, and if that is the case, there is no choice. Not only that, they also say that the Creator [Himself] lays the person's hand on the good lot, and that is quite puzzling because if [this is] so, where is the free will of the person?

With the following explanation, you will understand these words in their correct meaning. Because it is very true and correct that the

רשעים בחייהם נקראים מתים, כמבואר. וז"ש וזה שאומר הכתוב למען תחיה אתה וזרעך, כלומר שחיים בלי תורה, לא לבד שאין בהם הנאה של כלום לבעלים, אלא גם אינו יכול להנות לאחרים.

כלומר אפילו בבנים שמוליד אין לו נחת, להיות גם חיי הבנים האלו קשים ממות ואיזו מתנה הוא מנחיל להם. אמנם החי בתורה ומצוות לא רק שזכה ליהנות מחייו עצמו, הוא שמח עוד להוליד בנים ולהנחילם מהחיים הטובים הללו וז"ש וזה שכתוב למען תחיה אתה וזרעך, כי יש לו תענוג נוסף בחיים של בניו, שהוא היה הגורם להם.

בחירת האדם ביחד עם הסיוע מהשם יתברך

ד) ובאמור תבין דברי חז"ל על הכתוב ובחרת בחיים הנ"ל (עיין שם בפירוש רש"י ז"ל רבי שלמה יצחקי זכרונו לברכה, דברים ל' י"ט), וז"ל וזה לשונו אני מורה לכם, שתבחרו בחלק החיים כאדם האומר לבנו בחר לך חלק יפה בנחלתי, ומעמידו על החלק היפה, ואומר לו את זה ברור לך. ועל זה נאמר, ה' מנת חלקי וכוסי אתה תומך גורלי (תהלים ט"ז ה'), הנחת ידי על הגורל הטוב, לומר את זה קח לך, שלכאורה הדברים תמוהים.

כי הכתוב אומר ובחרת בחיים, שהמשמעות היא, שהאדם בוחר מעצמו, והם אומרים, שמעמידו על החלק היפה, אם כן כבר אין כאן בחירה. ולא עוד אלא שאומרים, אשר השם יתברך מניח ידו של אדם על גורל הטוב, וזה מפליא מאד, דאם כך היכן הבחירה שבאדם.

ובמבואר תבין דבריהם כמשמעם, כי אמת הדבר ונכון מאד, שהשם יתברך בעצמו מניח ידו של אדם על גורל הטוב, דהיינו על ידי שנותן

Creator Himself lays the hand of a man on the good lot, that is, by giving him a life of contentment and pleasure within a material life full of suffering and pain, and empty of any substance; [a material life] that a person would inevitably detach himself and run away from, the first moment he gets a glimpse (lit. peers through the lattice, [Song of Songs 2:9]) of a place of peace, so that he could flee from this life that is more difficult than death. Thus, there is nothing greater for a person than the Creator laying the hand of a man on the good lot.

The matter of a person's choice is only to strengthen himself because surely a lot of work and effort is required until a person can purify his body to the point of being able to fulfill the Torah and perform the Precepts properly, namely, not for his own enjoyment but to give pleasure to his Maker. This is called *Lishma*, For Its Own Sake, because only in this manner can one gain the life of happiness and pleasantness that accompanies the fulfilling of the Torah. And surely, before reaching this purity, there definitely is free will to persevere in the path of good, using all sorts of means and schemes. [A person] should do whatever he can (lit. his hand finds the strength to do) until the job of purification is done, so that he will not, Heaven forbid, crumble mid-way under the weight of his load.

Engaging with the Torah and the Precepts out of sorrow or out of joy

5) **Through** the above commentary, you can understand the words of our sages in Tractate *Avot* (6:4): "This is the path of the Torah: A morsel with salt shall you eat. You shall also drink water by measure, and shall sleep upon the ground, and live a life of sorrow, and in the Torah shall you labor. If you do so, 'happy shall you be and you shall be well.' (Psalms 128:2) Happy shall you be'—in this world; and 'you shall be well'—in the World to Come."

We should question their words. What is the difference between the wisdom of the Torah and all other worldly branches of knowledge,

לו חיי נחת ועונג, בתוך החיים הגשמיים המלאים יסורים ומכאובים וריקנים מכל תוכן, שבהכרח נעתק האדם ובורח מהם, בזמן שיראה לו אפילו כ"מציץ מן החרכים" (שיר השירים, ב, ט) איזה מקום שלוה, להימלט שמה מהחיים האלו הקשים ממות, שאין לך הנחת ידו של אדם מצדו ית' גדולה מזו.

ודבר הבחירה של האדם היא רק לענין החיזוק, כי ודאי עבודה גדולה ויגיעה רבה יש כאן, עד שיזכך גופו ויוכל לקיים התורה ומצוות כהלכתם, דהיינו לא להנאת עצמו אלא כדי להשפיע נחת רוח ליוצרו, שנקרא "לשמה", שרק באופן זה, זוכה לחיי אושר ונועם המלווים עם קיום התורה, ובטרם שמגיע לזכוך הזה, נוהג ודאי בחירה להתחזק בדרך הטוב בכל מיני אמצעים ותחבולות, ויעשה כל מה שתמצא ידו לעשות בכחו, עד שיגמור את מלאכת הזכוך, ולא יפול חס ושלום תחת משאו באמצע הדרך.

עסק התורה והמצות מתוך צער או מתוך אושר

ה) ועל פי המתבאר, תבין דברי חז"ל במסכת אבות (פרק ו' משנה ד'), "כך היא דרכה של תורה, פת במלח תאכל, ומים במשורה תשתה, ועל הארץ תישן, וחיי צער תחיה, ובתורה אתה עמל, אם אתה עושה כן, אשריך וטוב לך (תהילים, קכח' ב'), אשריך בעולם הזה, וטוב לך בעולם הבא".

ויש לשאול על דבריהם אלו, מה נשתנתה חכמת התורה, משאר חכמות העולם שאינן צריכות לסיגופים הללו ולחיי צער, אלא

which do not require this kind of asceticism and a life of sorrow? In those other branches, study (lit. effort) itself is completely sufficient to attain them. [But with regards to] the wisdom of the Torah, even if we put a lot of effort into [studying and deciphering] it, this is still not enough to acheive it. The only way this [can be achieved] is through asceticism, such as "a morsel with salt, etc. and the life of sorrow, etc."

And the end of these words is even more perplexing because they say: "If you do thus, happy shall you be in this world, and you shall be well in the World to Come." While it is possible that all will be well with me in the World to Come, how can I say that in this world, when I engage in self-mortification with regard to eating and drinking and sleep, and I live in great sorrow: "Happy shall you be in this world." Can this be called a happy life in the context of this world?

6) Indeed, the commentary above indicates that the [purpose of] studying (lit. being engaged with) the Torah and properly carrying out the Precepts is, in the strictest sense, is to give pleasure to our Maker and is not [meant] for our own enjoyment. We cannot get to this level except through much work and great effort in purifying our body. And the primary method (lit. first scheme) for accomplishing this is to get into the habit of never receiving anything for our own enjoyment, even with regard to things that are permitted and necessary for the sustenance of our body, such as food, drink, sleep, and other similar requisites. Thus, we should refrain completely from even the pleasure that inevitably ensues (lit. comes) from providing for our own sustenance, to the point that we are literally living a life of sorrow.

And then, once we have already gotten into this habit and our body has no desire to receive any pleasure for itself, we can start studying (lit. engaging with) the Torah and carrying out the Precepts in the manner [discussed above], that is, to give pleasure to our Maker and not for our own pleasure. (This is true if we do not wonder about the former words, as was said in the *Tosafot* for Tractate *Rosh Hashanah*, page 4, starting with the words: For the purpose..., see

העמל לבד מספיק לגמרי בחכמות הללו לזכות בהן, וחכמת התורה אף על פי שאנו עמלים בה במדה רבה, עדיין אינו מספיק לזכות בה, זולת על ידי הסיגופים של פת במלח וכו' וחיי צער וכו'.

וסיומם של הדברים מפליא עוד יותר, שאמרו "אם אתה עושה כן אשריך בעולם הזה וטוב לך לעולם הבא", כי בשלמא מובן מאליו בעולם הבא אפשר שיהיה טוב לי, אכן בעולם הזה בעת שאני מסגף עצמי באכילה ושתיה ושינה ואני חי בצער רב, יאמרו על חיים כאלו, אשריך בעולם הזה, הכאלו, חיים מאושרים יקראו, במובן שבעולם הזה?

ו) **אמנם** לפי המבואר לעיל, אשר עסק התורה וקיום המצוות כהלכתן בתנאם החמור, שהוא, בכדי להשפיע נחת רוח ליוצרו ולא לצורך הנאתו עצמו, אי אפשר לבא לזה, אלא, בדרך העבודה הגדולה וביגיעה רבה בזכוך הגוף, והתחבולה הראשונה היא, להרגיל עצמו שלא לקבל כלום להנאתו, אפילו בדברים המותרים והמוכרחים שבצרכי קיום גופו, שהם אכילה ושתיה ושינה, וכדומה מהכרחיים, באופן שיסלק את עצמו לגמרי מכל הנאה המלווה לו אפילו בהכרח, בדרך ההספקה של קיום חייו, עד שחיי צער יחיה פשוטו כמשמעו.

ואז, אחר שכבר התרגל בזה, וכבר אין בגופו שום רצון לקבל הנאה כל שהיא לעצמו, אפשר לו מעתה לעסוק בתורה ולקיים המצוות גם כן בדרך הזה, דהיינו בכדי להשפיע נחת רוח ליוצרו ולא להנאת עצמו במשהו (אא"כ אלא אם כן שאינו תוהה על הראשונות כמ"ש כמו שכתוב **בתוספות** מסכת רה"ש ראש השנה **דף ד' ד"ה** דבור המתחיל [במילה]

there; and also, there is a secret there, as was said by Maimonides, and nothing further should be said here). And when we finally merit this, we then merit tasting the happy life, full of every kind of goodness and pleasure, untainted by any blemish of sorrow—the kind of life that is revealed through engagement with the Torah and the Precepts *Lishma* (For Its Own Sake).

As Rav Meir says (Tractate *Avot* 6a): "Whoever engages himself in the Torah for its [own] sake merits many things; and not only so, but he is worthy of enjoying the entire world, etc. ... And the secrets of Torah are revealed unto him; and he becomes like a strong fountain, etc." Study that well. And of this person the Scriptures say: "Taste and see that the Creator is good!" (as discussed above, verse 3) because he who tastes the flavor of engaging with the Torah and the Precepts For Its Own Sake gains the merit to see for himself the Purpose of Creation, which is solely to bring goodness to its created beings since it is the nature of good to bestow goodness. And he is happy and enjoys the years that the Creator has bestowed upon him, and "he is worthy of enjoying the entire world."

7) **Now** you can understand both sides of the coin in how to engage with the Torah and the Precepts. The first side is the Way of the Torah, that is, the extensive preparation that a man must go through to purify his body before he merits to actually fulfill the Torah and the Precepts. And [even] then, he will, of necessity, study (lit. engage with) the Torah and the Precepts *lo Lishma* (Not For Its Own Sake), but rather for a mixture of [reasons that include] personal pleasure. This is because he has not yet managed to refine and purify his body from its desire to receive pleasure from the vanities of this world.

During this period, he must live a life of sorrow and must labor in the Torah, as is said in the *Mishnah*. Indeed, after he has finished [his preparation] and has completed the Way of the Torah, and has already refined his body and is now qualified to fulfill the Torah and the Precepts For Its Own Sake, [namely] in order to give pleasure to his Maker, then he moves to the other side of the coin: a life of

בשביל ע"ש עיין שם ועוד יש סוד בדבר כמ"ש הרמב"ם ואכמ"ל כמו
שכתב הרמב"ם, רבי משה בן מימון ואין כאן מה להוסיף), וכשזוכה בזה אז זוכה
לטעום את החיים המאושרים המלאים מכל טוב ועונג בלי פגם של
צער כל שהוא, המתגלים בעסק התורה והמצוה לשמה.

כמו שרבי מאיר אומר (פרקי אבות פ"ו פרק ג, פסוק א) כל העוסק בתורה
לשמה זוכה לדברים הרבה, ולא עוד אלא שכל העולם כולו כדאי לו
וכו', ומתגלין לו רזי תורה ונעשה כמעין המתגבר וכו' עש"ה עיין שם
היטב ועליו הכתוב אומר, טעמו וראו כי טוב ה' כמבואר לעיל בסעיף
ג, שהטועם טעם העוסק בתורה ומצות לשמה, הוא הזוכה ורואה
בעצמו את כונת הבריאה, שהיא רק להיטיב לנבראיו, כי מדרך
הטוב להיטיב, והוא השש ושמח במספר שנות החיים שהעניק לו
השם יתברך, וכל העולם כולו כדאי לו.

ז) עתה תבין את שני הצדדים, שבמטבע של העסק בתורה ומצות.
כי כיצד הא' הוא דרכה של תורה, כלומר, ההכנה הרבה, שהאדם צריך
להכין את טהרת גופו, בטרם שיזכה לעצם קיום התורה והמצות,
ואז בהכרח שעוסק בתורה ומצות שלא לשמה, אלא בתערובות
של להנאתו עצמו, שהרי עדיין לא הספיק לזכך ולטהר את גופו,
מהרצון לקבל הנאות מהבלי העולם הזה.

ובעת הזאת, מוטל עליו לחיות חיי צער ולעמול בתורה, כנ"ל
במשנה. אכן אחר שגמר והשלים את דרכה של תורה, וכבר זכך
גופו, ומוכשר לקיים התורה והמצות לשמה בכדי להשפיע נחת רוח

pleasure and great peace, which is what Creation intended by "to benefit His created beings." This is the happiest life in [both] this world and the World to Come.

From the wisdom of the Torah one gains all the happiness in the world; not so from other types of wisdom

8) We have thus made clear the big difference between the wisdom of the Torah and other kinds of wisdom. Attaining other kinds of wisdom does not improve life in this world at all, as they do not offer even the slightest relief to a person for the pain and suffering that he suffers throughout his life. For this reason, he does not need to purify his body; [basically] the work and effort that he invests to gain such other wisdom is enough, much the same way that any other worldly goods are obtained through effort and work. This is not the case, however, with the Torah and the Precepts because their entire purpose is to prepare the person to be ready to receive all the goodness that is included in the Purpose of Creation: "to bestow goodness upon His created beings." For this reason, he [who wishes to study the Torah and the Precepts] certainly needs to refine his body so that it will be worthy and befitting for this Divine good.

9) This also clarifies the saying of the *Mishnah* that "If you do thus, happy shall you be in this world." They [the sages] were purposely accurate to teach us that the happy life of this world is available only to those who have completed the Way of the Torah. This means that austerity in food, drink, and sleep as well as a life of sorrow; all spoken of previously (lit. here) are practiced only when one is on the Path of the Torah, which is why they specifically said: "This is the Way[1] of the Torah, etc." And after you have completed this path of Not For Its Own Sake, with austerity and a sorrowful life, the *Mishnah* concludes: "You shall be happy in this world,"

---

1. In Hebrew, the same word is used for both "path" and "way."

16

ליוצרו, הרי הוא בא לצד השני של המטבע, שהוא חיי עונג ושלוה רבה, שעליה היתה כונת הבריאה "להיטיב לנבראיו", דהיינו החיים המאושרים ביותר שבעולם הזה ועולם הבא.

בחכמת התורה זוכה להאושר שבעולם, מה שאין כן בשאר חכמות

ח) והנה נתבאר היטב, ההפרש הגדול בין חכמת התורה לשאר חכמות העולם, כי שאר חכמות העולם, אין השגתן מטיבה כלל את החיים שבעולם הזה, כי אפילו הספקה בעלמא סתם הנאה לא יתנו לו, בעד המכאובים והיסורים שהולך וסובל במשך ימי חייו, על כן אינו מוכרח לתקן גופו, ודי לו בעמל שנותן בעדם, כמו כל קניני העולם הזה הנקנים על ידי יגיעה ועמל עליהם, מה שאין כן עסק התורה והמצות, שכל ענינם הוא להכשיר את האדם, שיהיה ראוי לקבל כל אותו הטוב שבכונת הבריאה "להיטיב לנבראיו", על כן ודאי שצריך לזכך גופו, שיהיה ראוי וכדאי לאותו הטוב אלה"י.

ט) גם נתבאר היטב מה שאומרת המשנה, אם אתה עושה כן אשריך בעולם הזה (פרקי אבות.ג, א), כי בכונה גמורה דייקו זאת, להורות, כי חיי העולם הזה המאושרים, אינם מוכנים אלא רק למי שהשלים את דרכה של תורה, באופן, שענין הסיגופים של אכילה שתיה שינה וחיי צער, האמורים כאן, המה נוהגים רק בעת היותו בדרכה של תורה, כי על כן דייקו ואמרו "כך היא דרכה של תורה וכו'", ואחר

because you will have gained the same happiness and goodness that was included in the Purpose of Creation, and you shall be worthy of enjoying "the entire world," referring to this world and even more so to the World to Come.

Those who engage with the Torah and the Precepts For Its Own Sake merit the Concealed Light

10) And this is what is written in the *Zohar* (Genesis A 37:351) about the verse, "And the Creator said, 'Let there be Light,' and there was Light" (Genesis 1:3): "'Let there be Light'—for this world; and 'there was Light'—for the World to Come." Meaning that during the Act of Creation, [the created beings] were created in their final form and full stature, as our sages said; that is, in their final purpose of complete perfection and glory. And according to this the Light that was created on day one emerged in all its complete perfection, which included life in this world in utter refinement and pleasure to the extent that is expressed in the words: "Let there be Light."

But to prepare space for free will and labor, He [the Creator] hid [the Light] for the righteous of future days, as the sages said (*Beresheet Rabbah*). This is why they said in their pure language: "Let there be Light for this world." Yet, [the Light] did not remain in this way, but became instead: "And there was Light for the World to Come," meaning that those who engage with the Torah and the Precepts For Its Own Sake shall gain the Light only in the future, referring to the future that is expected to come once the refinement of their body in the Way of the Torah has been completed. Then they would be eligible for the great Light even in this world, as the sages said: "You shall see your [afterlife] world in your lifetime." (Tractate *Berachot* 17a)

שגמר דרך זו של שלא לשמה בחיי צער וסיגופים, מסיימת המשנה,
אשריך בעולם הזה, כי תזכה לאותו האושר והטוב שבכונת הבריאה,
וכל העולם כולו יהיה כדאי לך, דהיינו אפילו העולם הזה, ומכל שכן
לעולם הבא.

העוסקים בתורה ובמצות לשמה זוכים לאור הגנוז

י) וז"ש וזה שכתוב בזוהר (סולם, בראשית א', שנ"א) על הכתוב
(בראשית א,ג): ויאמר אלקים יהי אור ויהי אור "יהי אור לעולם הזה ויהי
אור לעולם הבא". פירוש, כי מעשה בראשית בצביונם נבראו ובכל
קומתם נבראו, כמ"ש כמו שאמרו חז"ל, דהיינו בתכלית שלימותם
ותפארתם. ולפי זה, האור שנברא ביום א' יצא בכל שלימותו, הכולל
גם חיי העולם הזה בתכלית העידון והנועם, כפי השיעור המתבטא
בהמלות יהי אור.

אלא כדי להכין מקום בחירה ועבודה, עמד וגנזו לצדיקים לעתיד
לבא, כדברי חז"ל (בראשית רבה). על כן אמרו בלשונם הצח "יהי אור
לעולם הזה" אמנם לא נשאר כן אלא "ויהי אור לעולם הבא",
כלומר, שהעוסקים בתורה ובמצות לשמה, זוכים בו רק לעתיד
לבוא שפירושו, בזמן העתיד לבא אחר גמר הזדככות גופם בדרכה
של תורה, שכדאים אז לאור הגדול ההוא גם בעולם הזה, כמ"ש כמו
שאמרו חז"ל עולמך תראה בחייך (ברכות יז' ע"א).

The "Light in the Torah" instead of sorrow and austerity

11) Indeed, we find and see in the words of the sages of the *Talmud* that they have made the Way of the Torah easier for us, more so than the sages of the *Mishnah*, because they said: "A person should always engage with the Torah and the Precepts, even if it is Not For Its Own Sake, because out of [engaging with them] Not For Its Own Sake, he will come to [engage with them] For Its Own Sake, (Tractate *Sanhedrin* 105b) since the Light in the Torah brings one back to the right path.

Thus, they have provided us with a new method to replace the austerity of Tractate *Avot* in the *Mishnah* that was mentioned above. "The Light is in the Torah," which has enough power in it to make a person return to the right path and to bring him to study (lit. engage with) the Torah and the Precepts For Its Own Sake. [The sages of the *Talmud*] did not mention austerity—only that being engaged with the Torah and the Precepts is sufficient [in and of itself] for its Light to make him return to the right path, and to enable him to engage with the Torah and the Precepts in order to give pleasure to his Maker, and not at all for his own pleasure. This is what is meant by [studying the Torah and fulfilling the Precepts] Not For Its Own Sake.

ה"מאור שבתורה" במקום צער וסיגופים

יא) אמנם אנו מוצאים ורואים בדברי חכמי התלמוד, שהקלו לנו את דרכה של תורה יותר מחכמי המשנה, כי אמרו "לעולם יעסוק אדם בתורה ובמצות אפילו שלא לשמה ומתוך שלא לשמה בא לשמה" (סנהדרין קה, ע"ב) והיינו, משום שהמאור שבה מחזירו למוטב.

הרי שהמציאו לנו ענין חדש במקום הסיגופים המובאים במשנה אבות הנ"לשהוא "המאור שבתורה", שיש בו די כח להחזירו למוטב ולהביאהו לעסק התורה והמצות לשמה, שהרי לא הזכירו כאן סיגופים, אלא רק שהעסק בתורה ומצות בלבד, מספיק לו אותו המאור המחזירו למוטב, שיוכל לעסוק בתורה ומצות בכדי להשפיע נחת רוח ליוצרו, ולא כלל להנאת עצמו, שהוא הנקרא "לשמה".

Chapter Two
Do Not Take It Personally

The boundary of studying the Torah Not For Its Own Sake

12) But one should seemingly reflect on their words [above]. After all, we have found a number of people studying and for whom engagement with the Torah did not do much good to merit that the Light in the Torah [will transform them into individuals who engage with the Torah] For Its Own Sake. Engaging with the Torah and the Precepts Not For Its Own Sake means that one believes in the Creator, in the Torah, and in reward and punishment, and that he engages with the Torah because the Creator has commanded it, yet he also incorporates his own benefit together with giving pleasure to his Maker.

But if, after all his effort in engaging with the Torah and the Precepts, he realizes that by his intense study (lit. great engagement) and great effort, he has not gained any pleasure and personal benefit, he regrets having struggled for so long. This is because he deceived himself from the start, thinking that he, too, would also get some enjoyment out of his effort. This example is called Not For Its Own Sake (as mentioned in the *Tosafot* [of Tractate] *Rosh Hashanah*, page 4, starting with the words: "For the purpose..."). Nevertheless, our sages have permitted to start engaging with the Torah and the Precepts Not For Its Own Sake because from [studying the Torah] Not For Its Own Sake, a person will come to For Its Own Sake, as was explained.

Those who lack trust, Heaven forbid, do not merit the Light of the Torah

Undoubtedly, if this person who is engaged with the Torah and the Precepts has not yet gained trust in the Creator and His Torah, but,

פרק ענ״ו
אל תקח את זה באופן אישי

גדר לומדי התורה שלא לשמה

יב) אבל יש להרהר לכאורה אחר דבריהם אלו, הלא מצאנו כמה לומדים, שלא הועיל להם העסק בתורה, שיזכו על ידי המאור שבה לבוא לשמה. אמנם, ענין העסק בתורה ומצות שלא לשמה, הפירוש, שהוא מאמין בהשם יתברך ובתורה ובשכר ועונש, והוא עוסק בתורה מחמת שהשם יתברך צוה לעסוק, אבל משתף הנאת עצמו עם עשיית הנחת רוח ליוצרו.

ואם אחר כל טרחתו בעסק התורה והמצות, יודע לו שלא הגיעה לו על ידי העסק והטורח הגדול הזה שום הנאה ותועלת פרטית, הוא מתחרט על כל שיגע, מטעם שאינה הַטְרִיחַ את עצמו מתחילתו, שכסבור שגם הוא יהנה מטרחתו, כגון זה, שלא לשמה נקרא (כמ״ש כמו שכתוב בפירוש בתלמוד בתוספות רה״ש ראש השנה דף ד׳ ד״ה דבור המתחיל [במילה]: בשביל). ואף על פי כן התירו חז״ל את תחילת העסק בתורה ומצות גם שלא לשמה. מטעם, שמתוך שלא לשמה בא לשמה, כמבואר לעיל.

מחוסרי אמונה ח״ו אין זוכים להמאור שבתורה

אמנם בלי ספק, אם העוסק הזה לא זכה עדיין לאמונת השם יתברך ותורתו, אלא מתגורר בספיקות חס ושלום, לא עליו אמרו חז״ל

Heaven forbid, [still] dwells in his doubts, he is not the person our sages [referred to when they] said that from Not For Its Own Sake he shall come to For Its Own Sake. Nor is he the person of whom it is said (in *Midrash Rabbah* in the opening of Lamentations (*Eichah*), and in the Jerusalem *Talmud*, Tractate *Hagigah* 1:7) that out of engaging with the Torah, [he shall merit that] its Light within the Torah shall bring him back to the right path, because the Light of the Torah shines only for those who master trust.

Moreover, the strength of this Light is in proportion to the strength of the person's trust. And for those who, Heaven forbid, lack trust, the opposite is true. As it is said: "For those who take the left path, it will be like a potion of death," (Tractate *Shabbat* page 8) because they receive darkness from the Torah and their eyes go blind.

13) And the sages have already drawn a nice parable in this regard, commenting on the verse: "Woe to you who desire the day of the Creator! What would you have the day of the Creator for? It is darkness, and not light." (Amos 5:18) This is like the rooster and the bat that were waiting for the light. The rooster said to the bat, "I am waiting for the light because the light is mine, but what do you need light for?" (Tractate *Sanhedrin*, page 98b). Study that well!

It is obvious that for those who study the Torah but did not merit the [experience] that from [their engagement with the Torah] Not For Its Own Sake emerged [an engagement with it] For Its Own Sake, because they lack trust, Heaven forbid. Therefore, they have not received any Light from the Torah, and accordingly, they walk in darkness and "they die, but without wisdom." (Job 4:21)

But those who merited complete trust are promised by the words of the sages that even if they engage with the Torah Not For Its Own Sake, the Light of [the Torah] shall put them back on the right path. And so they shall merit, even without going through austerity and a life of pain, to engage with the Torah For Its Own Sake, which brings a life of happiness and goodness in this world and the World to Come, as mentioned above. And the Scriptures say about them: "Then you shall take delight in the Creator, and I will make you ride upon the heights of the earth, etc." (Isaiah 58:14)

שמתוך שלא לשמה בא לשמה, ולא עליו אמרו (במ"ר במדרש רבא בפתיחתא בהקדמה דאיכה [ובתלמוד] ירושלמי מסכת חגיגה פ"א ה"ז פרק א' הלכה ז'), שמתוך שמתעסקים בה המאור שבה מחזירם למוטב, כי המאור שבתורה אינו מאיר אלא לבעל אמונה.

ולא עוד אלא שמדת גודל המאור הזה, היא כמדת תוקף אמונתו, אבל למחוסרי אמונה חס ושלום, היא להיפך, כמ"ש כמו שכתוב למשמאילים בה סמא דמותא סם מות (מסכת שבת פ"ח פרק ח'), כי מקבלים חושך מהתורה ונחשכות עיניהם.

יג) וכבר משלו חכמים משל נאה על ענין זה, על הפסוק (עמוס ה, יח): הוי המתאוים את יום ה' למה זה לכם יום ה', הוא חושך ולא אור. משל לתרנגול ועטלף שהיו מצפים לאור, אמר לו תרנגול לעטלף, אני מצפה לאורה שאורה שלי הוא, ואתה למה לך אורה (סנהדרין דף צ"ח ע"ב עמוד ב'), ודו"ק והתבונן ודייק מאד.

ומובן היטב, שאותם הלומדים שלא זכו מתוך שלא לשמה לבא לשמה, היינו משום שהם מחוסרי אמונה חס ושלום, ועל כן לא קבלו שום מאור מהתורה, ועל כן בחשכה יתהלכון, וימותו ולא בחכמה (איוב, ד' כא).

אבל אותם שזכו לאמונה שלמה, מובטחים בדברי חז"ל, שמתוך שמתעסקים בתורה אפילו שלא לשמה, המאור שבה מחזירם למוטב, ויזכו, גם בלי הקדם של יסורים וחיי צער, לתורה לשמה המביאה לחיי אושר וטוב בעולם הזה ובעולם הבא כנ"ל. ועליהם הכתוב אומר (ישעיהו נח, יד): אז תתענג על ה' והרכבתיך על במתי ארץ וגו'.

"His Torah is his trade": the diligence in studying the Torah is in proportion to one's trust in God

14) Associated with the above mentioned issue I once translated a saying of our sages: "His Torah is his trade," (Tractate *Shabbat,* 11a) [meaning that] the way that [a person] engages with the Torah shows his level of trust (*emunato*) because "his trade" (*umanuto*) is spelled [in Hebrew] with the same letters as "his trust" (*emunato*). This is analogous to a person who has trust in his friend and lends him money. Perhaps he trusts his friend with one pound, but if the friend asks for two pounds, he would refuse. Or perhaps he trusts his friend with up to one hundred pounds, but not more than that. Or perhaps he would even trust his friend and lend him half of his possessions, but not all of his possessions. It may even be possible that he would trust his friend with all of his possessions, without any shadow of fear. This final [example] of trust is considered complete trust, but the former examples of trust are considered incomplete trust or partial trust, whether it [the trust] is less or more.

Similarly, one person allocates for himself, according to the degree of his trust in the Creator, but one hour of his day to engage with the Torah and with [spiritual] work. Another person allocates two hours, according to the degree of his trust in the Creator. But the third does not waste even one hour of his free time without engaging with the Torah and with [spiritual] work. This means that only the latter [third] person has complete trust because he trusts the Creator with all his possessions, unlike the others, whose trust is not yet complete. But we should not elaborate too much on it.

With absence of trust, Light turns into darkness

15) And it has become clear that one should not expect that engaging with the Torah and the Precepts Not For Its Own Sake would [necessarily] bring him to engaging with them For Its Own Sake. For only when [a person] knows in his soul that he has gained proper trust in the Creator and His Torah, then the Light in the

"תורתו אומנותו" השקידה בתורה לפי מדת אמונתו בה'

יד) ומעין ענין הנ"ל פירשתי פעם את מליצת חז"ל, "מי שתורתו
אומנותו" (שבת י"א א) אשר בעסק תורתו ניכר שיעור אמונתו: כי
אומנתו אותיות אמונתו. בדומה לאדם, שמאמין לחבירו ומלווה לו
כסף, אפשר שיאמין לו על לירה אחת, ואם ידרוש ממנו שתי לירות,
יסרב להלוות לו. ואפשר שיאמין לו עד מאה לירות, אבל לא יותר
מזה. ואפשר שיאמין לו אפילו להלוות לו את חצי רכושו, אבל לא
את כל רכושו. ואפשר גם כן שיאמין לו על כל רכושו בלי שום צל של
פחד. ואמונה זו האחרונה, נחשבת לאמונה שלימה, אבל באפנים
הקודמים נבחנת לאמונה בלתי שלמה, אלא שהיא אמונה חלקית,
אם פחות אם יותר.

כך, אדם אחד מקצה לו מתוך שיעור אמונתו בה', רק שעה אחת
מיומו לעסוק בתורה ובעבודה. והשני מקצה לו שתי שעות, לפי
מדת אמונתו בה', השלישי אינו מזניח אפילו רגע אחד משעת
הפנאי שלו מבלי לעסוק בתורה ובעבודה. הוי אומר, שרק האחרון
אמונתו שלמה היא, שהרי מאמין להשם יתברך על כל רכושו, מה
שאין כן הקודמים, עדיין אין אמונתם שלמה לגמרי, כמובן, ואין
להאריך בכגון זה.

בהעדר האמונה נהפך האור לחושך

טו) והנה נתבאר היטב, שאין לו לאדם לצפות שהעסק בתורה
ומצות שלא לשמה יביאהו לשמה. רק בזמן שידע בנפשו שזכה
באמונת השם יתברך ותורתו כראוי, כי אז המאור שבה מחזירו
למוטב, ויזכה ליום ה' שכולו אור. כי קדושת האמונה מזככת את

Torah returns him back to the right path. [Then] he shall merit the "day of the Creator," which is all Light, because the holiness of trust purifies one's eyes so that they can enjoy [the Creator's] Light. Then the Light in the Torah returns him back to the right path.

Indeed, those who lack trust are similar to bats that cannot see the light of the day. The light of the day becomes severe darkness for them, more [severe] than the darkness of the night because they get their nourishment during the darkness of the night. [It is] likewise with those who lack trust: Their eyes are blinded by the Light of the Creator, and therefore the Light becomes darkness for them and the potion of life becomes for them the poison of death. And these are the people of whom it is said: "Woe to you who desire the day of the Creator! Why would you want the day of the Creator? It is darkness, and not Light." For as we said earlier, one has first to accomplish full trust [to merit the Light].

Other things that amount to engaging with the Torah Not For Its Own Sake

16) And what has been said so far explains the query of the *Tosafot* (Tractate *Ta'anit*, page 5, 'And all…'). It is said there: "Whoever engages with the Torah For Its Own Sake, the Torah becomes for him a potion for life, etc., [but] whoever engages with the Torah Not For Its Own Sake, the Torah becomes for him a potion of death". And [the *Tosafot*] raised a question: But it is said that one should always engage with the Torah, even when it is Not For Its Own Sake, because out of engaging with it Not For Its Own Sake, one finally starts engaging with it For Its Own Sake, see above. Now according to what has been explained, it [the answer of the *Tosafot*] should be divided simply.

Here, [in the first case, we are speaking] about someone who engages with the Torah for the sake of learning the Torah, and he believes in reward and punishment yet [this person] incorporates

העינים של האדם שתהנינה מאורו יתברך, עד שהמאור שבתורה
מחזירו למוטב.

אמנם מחוסרי אמונה, דומים לעטלפים, אשר לא יוכלו להסתכל
באור היום, כי נהפך להם אור היום לחושך נורא יותר מחשכת ליל,
כי אינם ניזונים אלא בחושך הלילה. כן מחוסרי אמונה, עיניהם
מתעוורות כלפי אור ה', על כן נהפך להם האור לחושך, וסמא דחיי
נהפך להם לסמא דמותא וסם החיים נהפך להם לסם המות, ועליהם אמר
הכתוב הוי המתאוים את יום ה', למה זה לכם יום ה', הוא חושך ולא
אור (עמוס ה, יח). אלא שצריכים מקודם להשתלם באמונה שלמה,
כמבואר.

עוד בגדרי תורה שלא לשמה

טז) ובאמור מתורצת קושית התוספות (תענית דף ז' ד"ה דבור
המתחיל [במילה] וכל) דאמרין שאומרים שם, כל העוסק בתורה לשמה
תורתו נעשית לו סם חיים וכו', וכל העוסק בתורה שלא לשמה
נעשית לו סם המות, והקשו, והלא אמרין והרי אמרו לעולם יעסוק
אדם בתורה אע"ג אף על גב שאינה לשמה, שמתוך שלא לשמה בא
לשמה, ע"ש עיין שם. ולפי המבואר, יש לחלק בפשטות.

כי כאן, בעוסק בתורה לשם מצות לימוד התורה עכ"פ על כל פנים,
להיותו מאמין בשכר ועונש, אלא שמשתתף הנאתו ותועלתו עצמו,
עם הכונה דלעשות נחת רוח ליוצרו, על כן המאור שבה מחזירו

29

his own enjoyment and benefit with his intention of giving pleasure his Creator, then the Light of the Torah shall bring him back to the right path and he will end up engaging with the Torah For Its Own Sake. Here [the other case], however, is of someone who engages with the Torah not for the purpose of fulfilling the commandment of studying the Torah—because he does not believe in reward and punishment sufficiently (lit. to such a degree) that he will try hard enough—so that all the effort he makes is only for his own benefit, and because of that, [the Torah] becomes like a potion of death for him, since its Light becomes darkness for him, as explained.

Trust is strengthened through exertion in the Torah

17) And therefore, before commencing his study, the learner has to commit himself to strengthening his trust in the Creator, in His Providence, and in reward and punishment, as the sages said: "Your employer is bound to pay you the worth of your efforts." (Avot, 2:13) So he must direct his effort towards being for the purpose of fulfilling the Precept of [studying] the Torah, and in this way, he will merit enjoying its Light. And his trust will also become stronger and greater by virtue of that Light, as it is said: "It will be a cure to your flesh and a remedy to your bones." (Proverbs 3:8) And then he will be assured in his heart that from Not For Its Own Sake, he shall come to [studying the Torah] For Its Own Sake.

In this way, even someone who knows that he has not yet merited having trust, Heaven forbid, nevertheless [also knows] there is still hope for him through [his] engaging with the Torah. Because if he focuses his heart and mind on gaining trust in the Creator through the Torah, there is no greater way to fulfill the Precepts, than this one, as our sages said (Tractate *Makkot*, 24): "Habakkuk came and condensed them all to one (principle): 'The righteous shall live by his trust (*emunato*).'" (Habakkuk 2:4)

Not only that, but he has no other alternative, as we have learned (Tractate *Baba Batra*, 16a): "Rabba said: Job wanted to exempt the entire world from the Judgment, and he said to Him, Master of the

למוטב, ובא לשמה. וכאן, בעוסק בתורה שלא לשם מצות לימוד התורה, כי אינו מאמין בשכר ועונש בשיעור הזה, עד שבשבילה יתיגע כל כך, אלא רק לשם הנאתו עצמו מתיגע, ועל כך נעשית לו סם המות, כי האור שבה נהפך לו לחושך, כמבואר.

על ידי יגיעה בתורה מתחזקת האמונה

יז) ולפיכך מתחייב הלומד בטרם הלימוד, להתחזק באמונת השם יתברך ובהשגחתו בשכר ועונש, כמ"ש כמו שאמרו חז"ל, נאמן בעל מלאכתך שישלם לך שכר פעולתך (אבות, ב' יד), ויכוון את היגיעה שלו, שיהיה לשם מצות התורה, ובדרך הזה יזכה ליהנות מהמאור שבה, שגם אמונתו תתחזק ותתגדל בסגולת המאור הזה, כמ"ש כמו שכתוב, רפאות תהי לשרך ושקוי לעצמותיך (משלי ג', ח). ואז יהיה נכון לבו בטוח, כי מתוך שלא לשמה יבא לשמה.

באופן, אפילו מי שיודע בעצמו שעדיין לא זכה חס ושלום לאמונה, יש לו תקוה גם כן על ידי עסק התורה, כי אם ישים לבו ודעתו לזכות על ידה לאמונת השם יתברך, כבר אין לך מצוה גדולה מזו, כמ"ש חז"ל (מסכת מכות כ"ד ע"א), בא חבקוק והעמידן על אחת: צדיק באמונתו יחיה (חבקוק ב, ד).

ולא עוד אלא, שאין לו עצה אחרת מזו, כמו שאיתא שמובא (במסכת ב"ב בבא בתרא דף ט"ז ע"א) אמר רבא, ביקש איוב לפטור את כל העולם כולו מן הדין, אמר לפניו, רבונו של עולם, וכו' בראת צדיקים

Universe…. You have created the righteous; You have created the evil ones; who can stand in Your way?" And Rashi commented on this verse: "You have created the righteous through the good inclination; You have created the evil ones through the evil inclination; and therefore, no one can survive Your [judgment], because who can stop [the sinners]? The sinners have no [free] choice."

[Rabba continues]: "And what did Job's friends tell him? 'But even you are undermining piety and hindering conversation before the Creator' (Job 15:4). The Creator created the evil inclination [but] created the Torah as an antidote." Rashi's commentary on this verse says: "He created the Torah, which in itself is the antidote because it erases the thoughts of transgressions, as the [*Talmud*] says 'If you meet this villain, pull him to the *Beit Midrash*, if he is made of stone, he will melt….' (Tractate *Kiddushim*, 30) Therefore, they [the sinners] are not left without [free] will because after all, they can save themselves." See that [Tractate] and study it well.

The Light [that is] in the Torah is the antidote to the evil inclination

18) And it is clear that [these sinners] cannot exempt themselves from the Judgment if they say that in spite of receiving this antidote, they still have sinful thoughts—that is, they still dwell in doubt, Heaven forbid, and the evil inclination has not dissolved yet. [Surely] the Creator, who created the evil inclination and gave it its validity, also knew how to create the cure and the antidote that are bound to exhaust the evil inclination and completely wipe it out.

And if a person has engaged with the Torah and still was not able to remove the evil inclination from himself, this can only be [for one of two reasons:] either he neglected to expend the due effort and toil required for engaging with the Torah, as it is said "I did not toil and I did find, do not believe!" (Tractate *Megillah* 6b) Or he actually fulfilled the required "amount" of toil but was neglectful as far as

בראת רשעים מי מעכב על ידך, ופירש"י ופירש רש"י שם, בראת צדיקים על ידי יצר טוב, בראת רשעים על ידי יצר הרע, לפיכך אין ניצול מידך, כי מי יעכב, אנוסין הן החוטאין.

ומאי אהדרו ליה חבריה דאיוב ומה ענו לו חבריו של איוב, (איוב ט"ו, ד') אף אתה תפר יראה ותגרע שיחה לפני אל, ברא הקדוש ברוך הוא יצר הרע, ברא לו תורה תבלין. ופירש"י ופירש רש"י שם, ברא לו תורה שהם תבלין, שהיא מבטלת את "הרהורי עבירה", כדאמר בעלמא כמו שאומר העולם, (במסכת קידושין דף ל) אם פגע בך מנוול זה משכהו לבית המדרש, אם אבן הוא נימוח וכו', הלכך לאו אנוסין ננהו ולכן הם לא אנוסים, שהרי יכולין להציל עצמן, ע"ש ודו"ק עיין שם, התבונן ודייק.

המאור שבתורה תבלין ליצר הרע

יח) **וזה** ברור שאינם יכולים לפטור את עצמם מן הדין, אם יאמרו שקבלו התבלין, הזה, ועדיין יש להם הרהורי עבירה. כלומר, שמתגוררים עוד בספיקות חס ושלום, ועדיין היצר הרע לא נמוח, כי הבורא ב"ה שברא אותו ונתן לו ליצר הרע את תוקפו, ברור שידע גם כן לברוא את התרופה והתבלין הנאמנים להתיש כחו של היצר הרע, ולמחותו כליל.

ואם מי שהוא עסק בתורה ולא הצליח להעביר היצר הרע ממנו, אין זה, אלא או שהתרשל לתת את היגיעה והעמל המחויב ליתן בעסק התורה, כמ"ש כמו שכתוב: לא יגעתי ומצאתי אל תאמין (מגילה ו, ע"ב), או יכול להיות שמילאו את "כמות" היגיעה הנדרשת, אלא שהתרשלו ב"איכות", כלומר, שלא נתנו דעתם ולבם במשך זמן העסק בתורה,

its "quality." This means that he did not pay attention nor did he focus his intention [suitably] during his engagement with the Torah to merit drawing the Light of the Torah, which instills trust in the heart of the person. Instead, he engaged with the Torah unmindful of the essence required from the Torah, which is the Light that leads to trust, as was said above.

And although it was his intention at the start, his mind wandered away from it during the course of his study. In any event, a person should not exempt himself from the judgment [consequences], claiming that he [was given] no choice, because our sages demand [responsibility] quoting: "I [the Creator] have created the evil inclination but also created the Torah as its antidote," and if there was any exception in this, then Job's query would have been legitimate, Heaven forbid. Study that well.

Clarifying Rav Chaim Vital's saying that sometimes only the Wisdom of Kabbalah should be studied

19) And by all the explanation up to this point, I have countered (lit. removed) a great complaint that has been voiced with astonishment in reaction to the words of Rav Chaim Vital in his introduction to the *Sha'ar Ha'akdamot* (Gate of Introductions) of the Ari [and] also in the introduction to the book *The Tree of Life* (*Etz HaChaim*, 1910 Jerusalem edition). Rav Chaim Vital wrote (lit. this is his language): "A person should not say, 'I shall go and engage with the Wisdom of Kabbalah before learning the Torah and the *Mishnah* and the *Talmud*,' because our teachers of old have already told us that one should not enter the mystery of Kabbalah (*PARDES*) unless his belly is full of meat and wine. It would be like a soul without a body, which has neither reward nor action nor reckoning until attached to a body that is whole and corrected through the Precepts of the Torah, the 613 precepts."

And the opposite is also true. If someone engages with the wisdom of the *Mishnah* and the Babylonian *Talmud* but does not devote part of

לזכות להמשיך את המאור שבתורה, המביא האמונה בלב האדם,
אלא שעסקו בהסח הדעת מאותו העיקר הנדרש מהתורה, שהוא
המאור המביא לידי האמונה, כאמור.

ואף על פי שכיוונו לו מתחילה, הסיחו דעתם ממנו בעת הלימוד.
ובין כך ובין כך, אין ליפטור את עצמו מן הדין בטענת אונס, אחר
שמחייבים חז"ל בטענה "בראתי יצר הרע בראתי לו תורה תבלין",
כי אם היה בזה איזה יוצא מהכלל, הרי הקושיא של איוב במקומה
עומדת חס ושלום, ודו"ק התבונן ולמד היטב.

בירור בדברי רבי חיים ויטאל שלפעמים יש לעסוק רק בחכמת הקבלה

יט) ובכל המתבאר עד הנה, הסרתי תלונה גדולה ממה שתמהים
על דברי הרב חיים ויטאל ז"ל, בהקדמתו על שער הקדמות מהאר"י
ז"ל, וכן נדפס בתואר הקדמה על ספר העץ חיים (הנדפס בירושלים
שנת תר"ע) וזה לשונו: ואמנם אל יאמר אדם אלכה לי ואעסוק
בחכמת הקבלה מקודם שיעסוק בתורה ובמשנה ובתלמוד, כי כבר
אמרו רבותינו ז"ל, אל יכנס אדם לפרדס אלא אם כן מלא כריסו
בבשר ויין, והרי זה דומה לנשמה בלי גוף, שאין לה שכר ומעשה
וחשבון, עד היותה מתקשרת בתוך הגוף בהיותו שלם מתוקן
במצוות התורה בתרי"ג מצות.

וכן בהפך, בהיותו עוסק בחכמת המשנה ותלמוד בבלי, ולא יתן חלק
גם אל סודות התורה וסתריה, הרי זה דומה לגוף היושב בחושך בלי

his studies to the secrets of the Torah and its mysteries [Kabbalah], this is like a body sitting in the dark without the human soul, which [the soul] is the Creator's flame shining within him. In this way, the body becomes dry, as it does not derive vitality from the Source of life, etc. Thus, the student of the Torah who engages with the Torah For Its Own Sake must first study as much Bible and *Mishnah* and *Talmud* as his mind and intellect can absorb, and only afterwards attempt to know his Maker through the Wisdom of Truth (Kabbalah). And as King David commanded his son Solomon: "Know the Creator of your father, and serve Him." (1 Chronicles 28:9)

And if for such a person studying the *Talmud* would be hard and burdensome, it would be better for him to withdraw from it, after having examined his success (lit. fortune) in that wisdom, and [he should] indulge in the Wisdom of Truth. And this is why it is said that a student who has not seen a sign of success within five years in his studies of the *Mishnah* is unlikely to ever see such a sign (Tractate *Hulin*, 24). And indeed, every person for whom study is easy is enjoined to spend one or two hours every day in studying the *Halachah* and in pondering deeply and giving proper arguments regarding the queries that have to do with the literal interpretation of the *Halachah*. Hereby, his [Rav Chaim Vital's] sacred language is quoted, word for word.

20) And his words are seemingly very bewildering because he says that before a person succeeds with the study of the Revealed he should go and study (lit. engage with) the Wisdom of Truth. This is in contradiction to his own earlier words that the Wisdom of Kabbalah, without the revealed teachings, is like a soul without a body, which has no action nor reckoning nor reward. And the evidence that he presents regarding a student who has not seen a sign of success is even more peculiar. After all, did our sages instruct [this student] to give up his study of the Torah because of this [lack of progress], Heaven forbid? Surely, they are trying to warn him to reflect on his ways and to try with another Rav or in a different tractate, but surely not to leave the Torah, Heaven forbid, not even the Revealed Torah.

נשמת אדם, נר ה', המאיר בתוכו, באופן שהגוף יבש בלתי שואף ממקור חיים וכו'. באופן שהת"ח שהתלמיד חכם העוסק בתורה לשמה צריך שיעסוק מתחילה בחכמת המקרא והמשנה והתלמוד, כפי מה שיוכל שכלו לסבול, ואחר כך יעסוק לדעת את קונו בחכמת האמת. וכמו שצוה דוד המלך עליו השלום את שלמה בנו (דברי הימים א' כח, ט): דע את אלקי אביך ועבדהו.

ואם האיש הזה יהיה כבד וקשה בענין העיון בתלמוד, מוטב לו שיניח את ידו ממנו, אחר שבחן מזלו בחכמה זאת, ויעסוק בחכמת האמת. וז"ש וזה שאמרו, מכאן לתלמיד שלא ראה סימן יפה במשנתו חמש שנים שוב אינו רואה (מסכת חולין דף כ"ד ע"א). ואמנם כל איש שהוא קל לעיון, מחויב לתת חלק שעה או ב' שעות ביום בעיון ההלכה, ולכוין ולתרץ הקושיות הנופלות בפשט ההלכה וכו'. עכ"ל. עד כאן לשונו הקדוש שם מלה במלה.

כ) והנה לכאורה דבריו אלו מתמיהים מאד, כי אומר שבטרם הצליח בלימוד הנגלה ילך ויעסוק בחכמת האמת, שהוא בסתירה לדברי עצמו הקודמים, שחכמת הקבלה בלי תורת הנגלה היא כנשמה בלי גוף, שאין לו מעשה וחשבון ושכר. והראיה שהביא, מתלמיד שלא ראה סימן יפה וכו', היא עוד יותר תמוהה, וכי אמרו חז"ל שיניח משום זה את לימוד התורה חס ושלום, אלא ודאי להזהיר אותו להסתכל על דרכיו, ולנסות אצל רב אחר, או במסכת אחרת, אבל ודאי, לא בשום פנים לעזוב התורה חס ושלום, ואפילו תורת הנגלה.

37

21) **And** an additional difficulty with both the words of Rav Chaim Vital and the words of the *Gemarah* is that their words imply that one must have some special preparation and level of excellence as a prerequisite to merit the wisdom of the Torah. But our sages said (in the *Midrash Rabbah,* regarding the *"Zot HaBrachah"* portion of the week): "The Creator told the people of Israel, 'By your life! The wisdom and the entire Torah is a very easy matter; anyone who has awe towards Me and fulfills the words of the Torah, the entire wisdom and the entire Torah are within his heart,'" end of [Rav Chaim Vital's] quote. Therefore, here, one does not need any prior excellence: The virtue of being in awe of the Creator and of fulfilling the Precepts is in itself sufficient to gain the entire wisdom of the Torah.

The "Light that is in the Torah" in the wisdom of the Concealed [Torah], which is contained fully in the Names of the Creator

22) **Indeed**, if we pay attention to [Rav Chaim Vital's] words, they become [as] clear to us as the clear skies above. When he wrote: "It would be better for him to withdraw from it [the *Talmud*], after having examined his fortune in the wisdom of the Revealed (see here verse 19)," he did not mean the "fortune" of smartness and proficiency, but refers instead to our interpretation above of the commentary on: "I have created the evil inclination, [but] have created the Torah as the antidote." This means that a person may have worked and toiled in the Revealed Torah, yet the evil inclination is still fully there and has not dissolved at all because he [this individual] has not yet been saved from sinful thoughts, as Rashi said in his commentary above on: "I created the Torah as its antidote" (study that place well). Therefore, [Rav Vital] advises [this individual] to let go of [the Revealed Torah] and instead to study the Wisdom of Truth because it is easier to reveal the Light of the Torah by engaging in studying and putting effort into the Wisdom of Truth than by putting effort into the wisdom of the Revealed Torah.

כא) ועוד קשה הן בדברי הרב חיים ויטאל ז"ל והן בדברי הגמרא, דמשמע מדבריהם שצריך האדם לאיזו הכנה והצטיינות מיוחדת כדי לזכות בחכמת התורה, והלא אמרו חז"ל (במדרש רבה פרשת וזאת הברכה) אמר הקדוש ברוך הוא לישראל, כל החכמה וכל התורה דבר קל הוא, כל מי שמתיירא אותי ועושה דברי תורה, כל החכמה וכל התורה בלבו, עכ"ל עד כאן לשונו. הרי שאין צריכים כאן לשום הצטיינות מוקדמת, אלא רק בסגולת יראת השם וקיום המצוות בלבד זוכים לכל חכמת התורה.

ה"מאור שבתורה" בחכמת הנסתר שהיא כולה בשמותיו של הקב"ה

כב) אכן, אם נשים לב לדבריו ז"ל, המה מתבהרים לפנינו כעצם השמים לטוהר, כי מה שכתב, "מוטב לו שיניח את ידו הימנו אחר שבחן מזלו בחכמת הנגלה" (ראה כאן סעיף יט), אין הכוונה על מזל של חריפות ובקיאות, אלא כמו שביארנו לעיל, בפירוש בראתי יצר רע בראתי תורה תבלין, כלומר, שעמל ויגע בתורה הנגלה ועדיין היצר הרע בתוקפו עומד ולא נמוח כלל, כי עדיין לא ניצל מהרהורי עבירה, כמ"ש כמו שכתב רש"י לעיל בביאור בראתי לו תורה תבלין. עש"ה עיין שם היטב. ולפיכך, מיעץ לו, שיניח את ידו הימנו ויעסוק בחכמת האמת, משום שקל יותר להמשיך המאור שבתורה בעסק ויגיעה בחכמת האמת, מביגיעה בתורת הנגלה.

And the reason is very simple: It is because the wisdom of the Revealed Torah is covered with external and material Garments, namely, stealing, plundering, injuries, etc. For this reason, it is very hard and heavy for everyone to attune himself to the Creator during his study in order to reveal the Light of the Torah, [and it is] even more [difficult] then for a person who is slow and finds it hard to study the *Talmud* itself. So how can this person, in addition, remember the Creator during his time of study? As the studying itself deals with material subjects, they cannot, Heaven forbid, be combined in his [mind] at the same time, together with the intention for the Creator [only]. Therefore, [Rav Vital] advises [such a student] to engage with the Wisdom of Kabbalah because this wisdom is entirely vested in the Names of the Creator, so [the student] would be able to focus his mind and his heart on the Creator during his study without any effort, even if he finds it extremely hard to study, because the study of the subjects of the Wisdom [of Truth] and the [study] of the Creator are one and the same, and this is very simple.

A commentary on an essay from our sages about a student who did not see a positive sign in his studies

23) And therefore, [to prove his case, Rav Chaim Vital] brings fitting evidence from the words of the *Gemarah* (see here, verse 19): "From this, we learn that a student who has not seen a positive sign in his studies within five years shall not hence see one anymore." Why has that student not seen a positive sign in his *Mishnah* studies? Surely the reason could only be [that the student] lacks the intention of the heart and not because of a lack of talent for [learning it]. [Studying] the wisdom of the Torah does not need any talent, but as is said in the above *Midrash* (see here, verse 21): "The Creator said to Israel, 'By your life! The entire Wisdom and the entire Torah is an easy matter; anyone who has awe towards Me and fulfills the words of the Torah, the entire Wisdom and the entire Torah are in his heart.'"

והטעם הוא פשוט מאד, כי חכמת תורת הנגלה לבושה בלבושים חיצונים גשמיים, דהיינו גניבה גזילה ונזיקין וכדומה, אשר משום זה קשה וכבד מאד לכל אדם, לכוין דעתו ולבו להשם יתברך בעת העסק, כדי להמשיך המאור שבתורה, ומכל שכן לאיש כזה, שהוא כבד וקשה בעיון התלמוד עצמו, ואיך יוכל לזכור עוד בשעת הלימוד בהשם יתברך, כי להיות העיון הוא בנושאים גשמיים הם חס ושלום אינם יכולים לבא אצלו עם הכוונה להשם יתברך בבת אחת, ולכן מיעצו לעסוק בחכמת הקבלה, אשר חכמה זו לבושה כולה בשמותיו של הקדוש ברוך הוא, ואז כמובן יוכל לכוין דעתו ולבו להשם יתברך בשעת לימוד בלי טורח, ואפילו הוא קשה העיון ביותר, כי העיון בנושאים של החכמה והשם יתברך, הם אחד, וזה פשוט מאד.

ביאור מאמר רבותינו ז"ל על תלמיד שלא ראה סימן יפה במשנתו

כג) ולפיכך מביא ראיה יפה מדברי הגמרא "מכאן לתלמיד שלא ראה סימן יפה במשנתו חמש שנים, שוב אינו רואה" (ראה כאן, סעיף יט') כי למה לא ראה סימן יפה במשנתו, ודאי אין זה אלא משום חסרון כוונת הלב בלבד, ולא משום חסרון כשרון אליה, כי חכמת התורה אינה צריכה לשום כשרון, אלא כמ"ש כמו שכתוב במדרש הנ"ל, (עיין כאן, סעיף כא') "אמר הקדוש ברוך הוא לישראל חייכם, כל החכמה וכל התורה דבר קל הוא, כל מי שמתיירא אותי ועושה ד"ת דברי תורה, כל החכמה וכל התורה בלבו".

Of course, one needs time to adapt to the Light of the Torah and the Precepts, although I don't know how much [time]. One can still be expecting a sign throughout his seventy years [of life], which is why the *Braita* (Tractate *Hulin*, 24) warns us that one should not wait for more than five years, and Rav Yossi says (see Tractate *Hulin*, 24) that three years are more than sufficient to gain the wisdom of the Torah. So, should a person not see a positive sign within this time, he should not fool himself with false hopes and deceitful excuses, but rather he should know that he will never see a positive sign. Therefore, he should immediately find for himself a clever scheme, one that would enable him to achieve [the level of] For Its Own Sake and merit the wisdom of the Torah.

The *Braita* did not specify what this scheme should be, but just gave a warning that one should not remain in the same [unfulfilling] situation and wait any longer. This is what the Rav [Chaim Vital] says, that the best and safest scheme would be to engage in the study of the Wisdom of Kabbalah and to completely withdraw from studying the Revealed Torah, because after all he has already tested his "luck" with it [the Revealed] and not succeeded. And [the student should] give his full time to the Wisdom of Kabbalah, which guarantees his success, for the reasons that we have mentioned earlier. Study that well.

It is essential to study the application of the rules

24) And this is very simple. We are not talking here about the study of the Revealed Torah with regard to whatever one needs to know [to be able] to practice [the Precepts] in the approved manner (according to the *Halachah*). Because an ignoramus cannot be a *Chassid* (pious person), an unintentional mistake in Torah study is equivalent to a malicious deed (Tractate *Avot*), and one sinner causes much goodness to be lost (Ecclesiastes 9:18). Consequently, it is imperative upon [the student] to go over them [the practical rules] as often as is necessary for him, so that he will not fail when it comes to practice.

What is being discussed here refers only to studying the wisdom of the Revealed Torah in order to understand and solve difficulties

אמנם ודאי שצריך זמן, להרגיל את עצמו במאור שבתורה ומצוות, ואיני יודע כמה. ויכול אדם לצפות כן בכל שבעים שנותיו, לפיכך מזהירה אותנו הברייתא (חולין כ"ד) שאין לצפות יותר מחמש שנים, ורבי יוסי אומר רק ג' שנים (עיין שם בחולין דף כ"ד), אשר די ומספיק לגמרי לזכות בחכמת התורה, ואם לא ראה סימן יפה בשיעור זמן כזה, לא ישטה עוד את עצמו בתקות שוא ומפוחי כזב, אלא ידע, שלא יראה עוד סימן יפה לעולם. ולכן יראה תיכף, למצוא לעצמו איזו תחבולה יפה, שיצליח על ידה לבא לשמה ולזכות בחכמת התורה.

והברייתא לא פירשה את התחבולה, אלא שמזהירה, שלא ישב באותו המצב ויחכה עוד. וזהו שאומר הרב, שהתחבולה המוצלחת יותר ובטוחה לו, הוא העסק בחכמת הקבלה, ויניח ידו מעסק חכמת תורת הנגלה לגמרי, שהרי כבר בחן מזלו בה ולא הצליח, ויתן כל זמנו לחכמת הקבלה הבטוחה להצלחתו, מטעם המבואר לעיל, עיין שם היטב.

הכרח לימוד הלכה למעשה

כד) וזה פשוט מאד, שאין כאן שום מדובר מלימוד התורה הנגלית בכל מה שמוכרח לידע הלכה למעשה, כי לא עם הארץ חסיד, ושגגת תלמוד עולה זדון (פרקי אבות), וחוטא אחד יאביד טובה הרבה (קהלת ט, יח), על כן מחוייב בהכרח לחזור עליהם, עד כמה שיספיק לו שלא יכשל למעשה.

אלא כל המדובר כאן הוא רק, בעיון בחכמת התורה הנגלית לכוין ולתרץ הקושיות הנופלות בפשטי ההלכות, כמו שמסיק שם הרב

43

that appear in the simple understanding of the *Halachah*, as Rav Chaim Vital himself has concluded (see here, verse 19), namely, the part of the study of the Torah that does not reach the stage of application and not the *Halachah* that is applied in practice. Indeed, this [kind of study] can be taken less severely and be learned from the short version and not from the sources.

And even this merits thorough contemplation because he who knows the *Halachah* from the source cannot be compared to him who learns from cursory study (lit. a single glance) or from an abbreviated version. And in order not to make an error, Rav Chaim Vital started (lit. immediately in the beginning of his words) by stating that the soul cannot connect with the body unless it [the body] is completed with the 613 Precepts and perfected by them.

Whether it is possible to study and practice the Torah without the study of the Kabbalah

25) Now you will see how all the queries we raised at the beginning of the introduction are total nonsense (lit. Vanity of Vanities), that is, they are the fishing nets that the evil inclination puts out to catch innocent souls to make them depart this world without passion. Look at the first query in which people imagine themselves being able to practice the entire Torah without knowing anything about the Wisdom of Kabbalah. But I hereby tell them: Certainly, if you can actually study the Torah and practice the Precepts according to the *Halachah* For Its Own Sake, that is, only to bring pleasure to the Creator, then you really do not need [to pursue] the study of Kabbalah, because of such people it is said: "The soul of the person shall teach him." In such a case, all the secrets of the Torah shall be revealed to you as an ever-flowing fountain, as Rav Meir said (in the above *Mishnah* from Tractate *Avot*, see here verse 6), [and] without you needing any help from the books.

But if you still remain in the category of engaging [with the Torah] Not For Its Own Sake in the hope that through this, you will

חיים ויטאל בעצמו (ראה כאן, סעיף יט'), דהיינו חלק הלימוד שבתורה שאינה באה לכלל מעשה, ולא כלל בהלכות למעשה, אכן אפשר להקל בזה ללמוד מהקיצורים ולא מהמקורות.

וגם זה צע"ג צריך עיון גדול, כי אינו דומה יודע ההלכה מהמקור, ליודע אותה מסקירה אחת ובאיזה קיצור. וכדי שלא לטעות בזה, הביא הרב חיים ויטאל ז"ל תיכף בתחילת דבריו, שאין הנשמה מתקשרת בגוף אלא בהיותו שלם מתוקן במצות התורה בתרי"ג מצות.

אם יכולים לקיים התורה בלי לימוד הקבלה

כה) עתה תראה, איך כל הקושיות שהבאנו בתחילת ההקדמה המה הבלי הבלים אלא המה הם המכמורים שפורש היצר הרע, לצוד נפשות תמימות, כדי לטורדן מהעולם בלי חמדה. ונראה את הקושיא הא', שמדמים את עצמם שיכולים לקיים כל התורה כולה גם בלי ידיעת חכמת הקבלה, הנה אני אומר להם, אדרבא, אם תוכלו לקיים לימוד התורה וקיום המצוות כהלכתן לשמה, דהיינו כדי לעשות נחת רוח ליוצר ברוך הוא בלבד, אז אינכם צריכים באמת ללימוד הקבלה, כי אז נאמר עליכם: נשמת אדם תלמדנו, כי אז מתגלים לכם כל רזי תורה כמעיין המתגבר, כדברי רבי מאיר (במשנה אבות הנ"ל ועיין כאן בסעיף ו'), בלי שתצטרכו סיוע מהספרים.

אלא אם עדיין אתם עומדים בבחינת העסק שלא לשמה, אלא שתקוותכם לזכות על ידיה לשמה, אם כן יש לי לשאול אתכם, כמה

[eventually] merit reaching For Its Own Sake, then I would have to ask you how many years have you been doing this? If you are still within the five years according to *Tana Kama* (the first Tana) or within three years (according to Rav Yossi), then you should still wait and hope. But if you have been engaged with the Torah Not For Its Own Sake for more than three years according to Rav Yossi or more than five years according to *Tana Kama* (the first Tana), then the *Braita* warns you that you may not achieve (lit. see) any success in this path that you are walking on.

Why then should you delude yourself in false hopes when you have a very easy (lit. close) and sure scheme such as the study of the Wisdom of Kabbalah, as I have proven above? After all, the study of the various topics in this wisdom [of Kabbalah] is one and the same as the Creator Himself. Study that well. (see here verse 19)

26) Let us examine (lit. touch) the second query that asks whether one should first be very well versed in (lit. fill their bellies with) the *Mishnah* and the *Halachah* [before studying Kabbalah]. This is for sure [a true] case, because everyone says so. Yet it refers to the [question] whether a person has already achieved (lit. merits) learning the Torah For Its Own Sake or even Not For Its Own Sake if he has studied for (lit. is within the) three years [according to Rav Yossi] or five years [according to the *Tana Kama*], but no longer (lit. not so after that time). The *Braita* warns that after that period [of either three or five years], you will never be successful, as was explained above. And if this is the case, you must try and see if you are able to succeed in the study of Kabbalah.

שנים אתם עוסקים כן. אם עדיין אתם נמצאים בתוך חמש השנים לדברי תנא קמא התנא הראשון, או תוך שלש השנים לדברי רבי יוסי, אז יש לכם עוד לחכות ולקוות, אבל אם עבר עליכם העסק בתורה שלא לשמה יותר משלוש שנים לדר"י לדברי רבי יוסי וה' שנים לת"ק וחמש שנים לדברי התנא קמא, הרי הברייתא המשנה מזהירה אתכם, שלא תראו סימן יפה עוד בדרך הזה שאתם דורכים.

ולמה לכם להשלות נפשכם בתקות שוא, בשעה שיש לכם תחבולה כל כך קרובה ובטוחה, כמו הלימוד של חכמת הקבלה, כמו שהוכחתי הטעם לעיל, להיות העיון בנושאי החכמה דבר אחד עם השם יתברך עצמו, עיין היטב לעיל (סעיף יט').

כו) וכן נמשש את הקושיא השניה במ"ש במה שכתוב, שצריכים תחילה למלאות כריסם בש"ס בששה סדרי [משנה] ופוסקים. הנה בודאי הוא, שכן הוא לדברי הכל, אמנם ודאי שכל זה אמור, אם כבר זכיתם ללימוד לשמה, או אפילו שלא לשמה אם אתם עומדים בתוך ג' שנים או ה' שנים, מה שאין כן אחר הזמן ההוא, הרי הברייתא מזהירה אתכם, שלא תראו עוד סימן יפה לעולם, וכמו שנתבאר לעיל, ואם כך מוכרחים אתם לנסות הצלחתכם בלימוד הקבלה.

Chapter Three
Now You See It; Now You Don't

Two parts of the Wisdom of Truth: the Secrets of the Torah and the Meanings (lit. Tastes) of the Torah

27) Furthermore, you should know that there are two parts to the Wisdom of Truth. Part one is that which is called the "Secrets of the Torah," which cannot be revealed except by way of a hint from a kabbalist sage to a receipient who comprehends it on his own; also the "study of the Supernal Chariot" and the "Process of Creation" belong to this part. The sages of the *Zohar* call this part "Upper (lit. First) Three *Sefirot*": *Keter* (Crown), *Chochmah* (Wisdom), *Binah* (Intelligence). It is also called the "Head of the *Partzuf*" (a complete spiritual structure). The second part [of the Wisdom of Truth] is called the "Meanings (lit. Tastes) of the Torah," which are allowed to be revealed—in fact, it is considered an act of great importance to reveal it. In the *Zohar*, this is called "Lower Seven *Sefirot* of the *Partzuf*," which is also called the "Body of the *Partzuf*."

The Ten *Sefirot* can be found in each and every *Partzuf* (spiritual structure) of Holiness, and are called: *Keter* (Crown), *Chochmah* (Wisdom), *Binah* (Intelligence), *Chesed* (Mercy), *Gevurah* (Judgment), *Tiferet* (Splendor), *Netzach* (Victory, Eternity), *Hod* (Glory), *Yesod* (Foundation), and *Malchut* (Kingdom). The Upper Three of these *Sefirot* are called the Head of the *Partzuf* (spiritual structure), and the Seven Lower *Sefirot* are called the Body of the *Partzuf*. Even in the soul of the earthly (lit. lower) human being, there are aspects of these Ten *Sefirot* according to their above-mentioned names. And it is [divided] so with every phase, both in the Higher Worlds and the Lower Worlds. With the Creator's help, these matters, along with their significance, will be clarified in this book.

And the reason why the Lower Seven *Sefirot*, which are the Body of the *Partzuf* (spiritual structure), are called *Ta'amei Torah* (the Meanings or Tastes of the Torah) lies in the secret of the scriptural

48

פרק שלישי
לרגע זה מופיע... ושוב זה נעלם

ב' חלקים בחכמת האמת: סתרי תורה וטעמי תורה

כז) עוד צריכים לדעת, שישנם ב' חלקים בחכמת האמת: חלק א',
הוא הנקרא סתרי תורה, שאסור לגלותם זולת ברמיזה, מפי חכם
מקובל, למקבל מבין מדעתו. ומעשה מרכבה ומעשה בראשית
שייכים גם כן לחלק הזה. וחכמי הזוהר מכנים החלק הזה, בשם
ג' ספירות ראשונות: כתר, חכמה, בינה, ומכונה גם כן בשם ראש
הפרצוף. וחלק שני, הוא הנקרא טעמי תורה, שמותר לגלותם, וגם
מצוה גדולה לגלותם. ונקרא בזוהר, בשם ז' ספירות תחתוניות של
הפרצוף, ומכונה גם כן בשם גוף של הפרצוף.

כי בכל פרצוף ופרצוף דקדושה, יש בו עשר ספירות, הנקראות:
כתר, חכמה, בינה, חסד, גבורה, תפארת, נצח, הוד, יסוד, מלכות.
שג' ספירות הראשונות מהם, מכונות ראש הפרצוף. וז' ספירות
התחתוניות מכונות בשם גוף הפרצוף. ואפילו בנשמה של האדם
התחתון, ישנן גם כן בחינות עשר הספירות בשמותיהן הנ"ל, וכן
בכל בחינה ובחינה, הן בעליונים, הן בתחתונים. כמו שיתבארו
הדברים בטעמיהם, בפנים הספר בע"ה.

והטעם, שז' ספירות התחתוניות שהן גוף הפרצוף, נקראות בשם
טעמי תורה, הוא סוד הכתוב (איוב, יב', יא'), חיך אוכל יטעם. כי

saying: "The palate tastes food." (Job 12:11) The Lights that are revealed below the Upper Three [*Sefirot*], which are the secret of the Head, are called "meanings" (Heb. *ta'amim,* a word that also means "tastes"), and the Kingdom of the Head is called "palate." For this reason, they are called the *ta'amim* (tastes) of the Torah. This means that they [the tastes or meanings] are discovered through the "Palate of the Head," or the source of all tastes, which is the Kingdom of the Head. From there [Kingdom of the Head] downwards, there is no prohibition on revealing them. On the contrary, the reward to him who reveals them is great beyond limitation (lit. end) and beyond measure.

Indeed, these Upper Three *Sefirot* and these Lower Seven *Sefirot* that are mentioned here are interpreted as follows: either in the complete general form or in the most particular form that can possibly be divided to, meaning that even the Upper Three *Sefirot*, of *Malchut* (Kingdom) at the end of the World of *Asiyah* (Action), belong to the part of the "Secrets of the Torah" that is not to be revealed, [while] the Lower Seven *Sefirot* in the *Keter* (Crown) at the Head of the World of *Atzilut* (Emanation), belong to the "Meanings (*Ta'amim*) of the Torah" that are permitted to be revealed. And these things were published in many books of Kabbalah.

A *Gemarah* source for these two parts of the Wisdom of Truth

28) And you can locate the reference to these things [two parts of the Wisdom of Truth] in the Tractate *P'sachim* (page 119b), where it is said: "Her merchandise and her hire will be dedicated to the Creator; it will not be stored or hoarded, but her merchandise will supply abundant food and fine clothing for those who dwell before the Creator." (Isaiah 23:18) What does "fine clothing" (*mechase atik*— literally, ancient covering) mean? [There are two interpretations, the first] is he who covers (*mechase*) issues that the *Atik Yomin* (Ancient of Days) has concealed. And what are they [the issues]? They are the Secrets of the Torah. And there are those who say [i.e. the second interpretation]: "He who reveals things that were concealed by the *Atik Yomin* (Ancient of Days). What are they? They are the *Ta'amei Torah* 'Meanings or Tastes of the Torah.'"

האורות המתגלים מתחת לג' הראשונות, שהם סוד ראש, מכונים "טעמים", והמלכות דראש מכונה "חיך". ומשום זה נקראים בשם "טעמי" תורה, כלומר המתגלים מחיך הראש, שהוא בחינת מקור כל הטעמים, שהוא מלכות דראש, אשר משם ולמטה אין שום איסור לגלותם, ואדרבא, שכר המגלה אותם גדול לאין קץ ולאין שיעור.

אכן ג' הספירות הראשונות הללו וז' ספירות התחתוניות הללו, האמורות כאן, מתפרשות: או בכלל כולו, או בפרטי פרטיות שאף אפשר לחלק, באופן, שאפילו ג' הספירות הראשונות, מהמלכות שבסוף עולם העשיה, שייכות לחלק סתרי תורה שאסור לגלותן, וז' הספירות התחתוניות שבבכתר דראש האצילות, שייכות לחלק טעמי התורה אשר מותר לגלותן. והדברים האלה מפורסמים בספרי הקבלה.

מקור בגמרא לב' החלקים בחכמת האמת

כח) ומקור הדברים הללו תמצא במסכת פסחים (דף קי"ט ע"ב), דאמרינן שאומרים שם, כתיב (ישעיהו כ"ג יח') והיה סחרה ואתננה קודש לה' לא יאצר ולא יחסן, כי אם ליושבים לפני ה' יהיה סחרה, לאכול לשבעה, ולמכסה עתיק וכו': מאי מה זה למכסה עתיק, זה המכסה דברים שכיסה עתיק יומין, ומאי נינהו ומה הם, סתרי תורה. ואיכא דאמרי ויש אומרים, זה המגלה דברים שכיסה עתיק יומין, מאי נינהו מה הם, טעמי תורה.

And *Rashbam* (Rav Shmuel ben Meir) interpreted it as follows: "*Atik Yomin* (Ancient of Days) is the Creator, as it is written: '*Atik Yomin* (The Ancient of Days) sits (Daniel, 7:9). *Sitrei Torah* (The Secrets of the Torah) refers to the study of the Supernal Chariot, and the Process of Creation, and the Revelation of the secrets Name of the Creator, as it is written (Exodus 3:15): 'This is My Name forever.' And 'He who covers' means that He does not pass them on to any person, but just on to [the person] who has a concerned heart, as it is said [in the chapter] 'They should not be commented upon' (Tractate *Hagigah* 13a): 'He who reveals subjects that were concealed by the Ancient of Days' refers to a person who covers of the Secrets of the Torah that were covered at first, and the Ancient of Days uncovered them and gave permission to reveal them. And whoever reveals them gains what he said in this verse (Isaiah 23:18)." End of quote [of the Rashbam].

29) And here you explicitly have the great difference between *Sitrei Torah* [and *Ta'amei Torah*. On one hand] *Sitrei Torah* (the Secrets of the Torah): whoever understands them receives all of this great reward (explained in the *Gemarah* in the commentary on the text) for concealing them and not revealing them. And on the other hand *Ta'amei Torah*: whoever understands *Ta'amei Torah* (the Meanings or Tastes of the Torah) receives all this great reward for revealing them to others. Now, "those who say" [mentioned here in verse 28] do not contradict the first statement, rather only the meaning of the [words]: "They should not be commented upon" is under dispute.

The first statement relates to the end of the verse: *mechase Atik* ("and he who covers *Atik*"). This is why [the first statement] comments on the achievement of the great reward by whoever *conceals* the Secrets of the Torah. [On the other hand] "those who say" relates to the beginning of the verse, "and to eat until satisfied," which refers to the Meanings or Tastes of the Torah, according to the secret of the scriptural saying, "The palate tastes the food," (Job 12:11) because the Lights of the Meanings or Tastes are called "eating." And this is why they comment about whoever *reveals* the Meanings of the Torah attaining the great reward mentioned in the verse. [The bottom line is that] both sides believe that the Secrets of the Torah must be concealed and the Meanings and Tastes of the Torah must be revealed.

ופירש רשב"ם רבי שמואל בן מאיר ז"ל, וז"ל וזה לשונו: "עתיק יומין" זה
הקדוש ברוך הוא, דכתיב (דניאל ז', ט'): "ועתיק יומין יתיב יושב, "סתרי
תורה": הוא מעשה מרכבה, ומעשה בראשית, ופירושו של שם,
כדכתיב (שמות ג', טו') זה שמי לעלם, "והמכסה": היינו שאינו מוסר
אותם לכל אדם, אלא למי שלבו דואג, כמ"ש כמו שכתוב בפרק אין
דורשין (חגיגה יג', ע"א): "זה המגלה דברים שכיסה עתיק יומין": והכי
משמע וזה פירושו, למכסה סתרי תורה, שהיו מכוסין מתחילה, ועתיק
יומין גילה אותן, ונתן רשות לגלותם, ומי שמגלה אותם זוכה למה
שאמר בפסוק זה (ישעיהו כג', יח'), עד כאן לשונו [של הרשב"ם].

כט) הרי לך במפורש, ההפרש הגדול בין סתרי תורה אשר המשיגם
נוטל כל השכר הגדול הזה (המפורש שם בגמרא בפירוש הכתוב)
בשביל שמכסה אותם, ואינו מגלה אותם. והיפוכם טעמי התורה,
אשר המשיגם נוטל כל השכר הגדול הזה, בשביל שמגלה אותם
לאחרים. והאיכא דאמרי וה"יש אומרים" [המוזכר כאן בסעיף כח'] לא פליגי
אלישנא קמא לא חולקים על הלשון הראשונה, אלא רק [לגבי] משמעות [המילה]
'דורשין' איכא בינייהו יש ביניהם [מחלוקת].

אשר הלישנא קמא אשר הלשון הראשונה דורשין סיפא דקרא דורשים
את סוף הפסוק "ולמכסה עתיק" ועל כן מפרשין השג השכר הגדול
על מכסה את סתרי התורה, והאיכא דאמרי וה"יש אומרים" דורשין
רישא דקרא דורשים ראש הפסוק "ולאכול לשבעה" שמשמעותו "טעמי
תורה", בסוד הכתוב וחיך אוכל יטעם (איוב יב', יא'), כי אורות הטעמים
מכונים אכילה, ועל כן מפרשים השג השכר הגדול הנאמר בכתוב,
על המגלה את טעמי התורה. אבל אידי ואידי אלה ואלה סוברים, שאת
סתרי התורה חייבים לכסות ואת טעמי התורה חייבים לגלות.

The reason that the holy and the greatest among the *tzadikim* (righteous) revealed the Secrets of the Torah

30) Hereby you have a clear answer to the fourth and fifth queries that were raised at the beginning of this introduction, regarding what you find in the [following] words of our sages, as well as in the Holy Writings: that [this wisdom] should be passed on only to whomever has an concerned heart, etc (see here verse 28). This [wisdom] refers to the part that is called *Sitrei Torah* (the Secrets of the Torah), which is the aspect of the Upper (lit. First) Three *Sefirot*, or the aspect of the Head. This wisdom is not to be passed on, except to the modest [kabbalists] and under known conditions. And in all the books of the Kabbalah, both the handwritten as well as those in print, you shall not find even the slightest mention of them [*Sitrei Torah*] because these are the things covered by the *Atik Yomin* (Ancient One), as mentioned above in the *Gemarah* (see here verse 27).

And furthermore, decide (lit. say) for yourself whether it is possible to imagine or even remotely consider that all these great saints and famous righteous people, who are the greatest members of our nation and the best of the best—such as the authors of *Sefer Yetzirah* (*Book of Formation*) and of the *Zohar*, and Rav Yishmael, author of the *Braita*, and Rav Hai Gaon, and Rav Hamai Gaon, and Rav Eliezer from Worms, and the rest of the Firsts Ravs all the way to Rav Moshe ben Nachman (Nachmanides), and [Rav Yaakov ben Asher], author of *Arba'a Turim*, and [Rav Yosef Karo], author of *Shulchan Aruch*, all the way to the Vilna Gaon (Rav Eliyahu from Vilnius), and the Gaon from Liadi, and the rest of the righteous people of blessed memory from whom we have received the entirety of the Revealed Torah and by whose words (lit. from whose mouths) we live to know what deed we should do to find favor in the eyes of the Creator.

Indeed, all these [righteous people] have written and have published books about the Wisdom of Kabbalah. After all, there is no greater exposure than that of writing a book, where the person writing it has no idea who might be studying his book. It is possible, Heaven forbid, that some evil people might open (lit. be looking into) it. If so, there is no greater revelation of the Secrets of the Torah than this

בטעם שהקדושים וגדולי הצדיקים גילו רזי תורה

ל) הרי לך תשובה ברורה על הקושיות: הרביעית, והחמישית, שבתחילת ההקדמה. שמה שתמצא בדברי חז"ל וגם בספרים הקדושים שאין מוסרים אותה אלא למי שלבו דואג בקרבו וכו' (ראה כאן סעיף כח), היינו את אותו החלק שנקרא סתרי תורה, שהוא בחינת ג' ספירות ראשונות ובחינת ראש, שאין מוסרין אותה אלא לצנועים, ובתנאים ידועים, שבכל ספרי הקבלה שבכתב ושבדפוס, לא תמצא אפילו זכר מהם, כי הם הדברים שכיסה עתיק יומין, כנ"ל בגמרא (ראה כאן סעיף כז).

ואדרבא אמור אתה, אם אפשר להרהר ואפילו להעלות על הדעת, שכל אלו הקדושים והצדיקים המפורסמים, שהם גדולי האומה משופרי דשופרי הטובים שבטובים, כגון ספר יצירה, וספר הזוהר, וברייתא דרבי ישמעאל, ורב האי גאון, ור' חמאי גאון, והר"א והרבי אליעזר מגרמיזא, ויתר הראשונים עד לרמב"ן רבי משה בן נחמן , ובעל הטורים, ובעל השו"ע השולחן ערוך, עד לגאון מוילנא, והגאון מלאדי, ויתר הצדיקים, זכר כולם לברכה, שמהם יצאה לנו כל התורה הנגלית ומפיהם אנו חיים, לידע המעשה אשר נעשה למצוא חן בעיני השם יתברך.

והרי, כל אלו כתבו והדפיסו ספרים בחכמת הקבלה, כי אין לך גילוי גדול מכתיבת ספר, אשר הכותב אותו, אינו יודע מי הם המעיינים בספרו, שיכול להיות שחס ושלום רשעים גמורים יסתכלו בו, ואם כן אין לך גילוי רזי תורה יותר מזה, וחס ושלום

and, Heaven forbid, that we would doubt these saintly, pure people after their death, and suspect that they would have transgressed even one iota from what is written and explained in the *Mishnah* and *Gemarah* (in Tractate *Hagigah*) regarding [the chapter] "They should not be commented upon."

So definitely, all the written and printed books are the aspect of the *Ta'amei Torah* (Meanings of the Torah), which the *Atik Yomin* (Ancient of Days) concealed at first and then revealed, according to the secret of "the palate tastes food," as was mentioned earlier (here, verse 27). One is not prohibited from revealing these secrets, but in fact, it is also a great duty to reveal them, as is mentioned above (Tractate *P'sachim*, 119). And whoever knows how to reveal them and indeed does so, his reward is tremendously great because the coming of *Goel Tzedek* (the Righteous Redeemer)—depends unequivocally on revealing these Lights to the masses. May it happen soon in our times, Amen.

The words of the *Tikkunei HaZohar* about the Wisdom of Kabbalah being connected to the *Ruach* (Spirit) of the Messiah

31) And it is crucial to explain once [and for all] why the coming of the *Goel Tzedek* (the Righteous Redeemer) depends on the dissemination of the teachings of Kabbalah to the masses, which is so often mentioned in the *Zohar* and in all the books of the Kabbalah. But the masses have connected all sorts of nonsense to it—unbearably so. The interpretation of this matter is explained in the *Tikkunei HaZohar* (*Tikkun* 30, starting with the words: *Nativ Tanina* [Second Path]), which goes as follows:

> "Second Path (*Netiv Tanina*), 'And the *Ruach* (Spirit) of the Creator is hovering above the face of the waters.' (Genesis 1:2) What do the words 'and the *Ruach* (Spirit)' mean? Surely, when the *Shechinah* (Divine Presence) is in exile, then this *Ruach* (Spirit) hovers above those who study the Torah, as the *Shechinah* dwells among them, etc. [why should I call]: 'all the flesh is dry straw,' [means] they are like the beasts in the field that eat hay and straw. 'And all his grace is like the

56

להרהר אחר מיטתם של קדושים וטהורים הללו, שיעברו אפילו כקוצו של יוד על מה שכתוב ומפורש במשניות ובגמרא, שאסור לגלות אותם, כמ"ש כמו שכתוב [בפרק] אין דורשין (במסכת חגיגה).

אלא בהכרח, שכל הספרים הנכתבים והנדפסים, המה בבחינת טעמי תורה, שעתיק יומין כיסה אותם מתחילה, ואחר כך גילה אותם בסוד חיך אוכל יטעם כנ"ל (כאן, סעיף כז'), שסודות אלו, לא רק שאין איסור לגלותם, אלא אדרבא, מצוה גדולה לגלותם (כנ"ל בפסחים קי"ט), ומי שיודע לגלות ומגלה אותם, שכרו הרבה מאד, כי בגילוי האורות הללו לרבים, ולרבים דוקא, תלוי דבר ביאת גואל צדק בב"א במהרה בימנו אמן.

לשון התיקוני זוהר בענין חכמת הקבלה שקשורה עם רוחו של משיח

לא) וצריכים מאד להסביר פעם, למה תלויה ביאת גואל צדק בהתפשטות לימוד הקבלה לרבים, המפורסם כל כך בזוהר ובכל ספרי הקבלה. וההמונים תלו בזה בוקי סריקי דברי סרק, עד לבלי סבול. וביאור ענין זה, מפורש בתיקוני זוהר (תיקון ל' ד"ה דבור המתחיל [במילים] נתיב תנינא) וז"ל וזה לשונו:

"נתיב תנינא נתיב שני, 'ורוח אלקים מרחפת על פני המים' (בראשית א', ב'), מאי ורוח מהו "ורוח", אלא בודאי בזימנא דשכינתא נחתת בגלותא בזמן שהשכינה יורדת בגלות, האי רוח נשיב על אינון דמתעסקי באוריתא הרוח הזה נושב על אלו שמתעסקים בתורה, בגין שכינתא דאשתכחא ביניהו בגלל שהשכינה נמצאת בינהם וכו'. [מה אקרא], כל הבשר חציר', כלא אינון כבעירן דאכלין חציר כלם הם כבהמות אוכלי

sprouts of the field' (Isaiah 40:6) [means] all the kindness they show is for their own sake, etc.

"And even [in the case of] all those who are exerting themselves in [following] the Torah, all the kindness they show is only for their own benefit. And at that time 'He is due to remember that they are but flesh, a wind (*Ruach*) [*Ruach* in Hebrew means both 'wind' and also 'spirit.'] that goes by, never to return, (Psalms 78:39) and this is the *Ruach* (Spirit) of the Messiah. Woe to those who cause it to leave the world and not return forever, for they are the ones who make the Torah dry since they do not want to be involved in the study of the Wisdom of Kabbalah. And they cause the Fountain of Wisdom—the letter *Yud*—to depart from it, etc. And this *Ruach* (Spirit) that departs is the Spirit of the Messiah; it is the 'Divine Spirit (lit. of Holiness); the Spirit of wisdom and understanding; the Spirit of counsel and might; the Spirit of knowledge and fear of the Creator.' (Isaiah 11:2)

"Second Precept: 'And the Creator said, Let there be Light, and there was Light.' (Genesis 1:3) This is love, which is the love for kindness, as it is written: 'I have loved you with an everlasting love; hence, I have extended kindness to you.' (Jeremiah 31:3) And in reference to this, it is said: 'Do not arouse or awaken love until it so desires..' (Song of Songs 2:7) Showing kindness and love, this is the main issue, whether for good or for bad, and because of this it is called fear and love, for the sake of receiving a reward. And because of this the Creator said, 'I charge you, daughters of Jerusalem, by the gazelles and by the deer of the fields; stir up not nor awaken the love until it is desired,' [Song of Songs 2:7] referring to showing kindness without [thought of] reward, [and] not for the sake of receiving a reward because fear and love for the sake of receiving a reward belongs to the *Shifcha* (maid-servant). 'And under three things the Earth trembles with anger, etc.' (Proverbs 30:21): under 'a slave, when he rules' and 'a maid-servant, when she succeeds her mistress' (Proverbs 30:22-23)." [End of the *Zohar* quote].

58

עשב וחציר. וכל חסדו כציץ השדה (ישעיהו מ', ו'), כל חסד דעבדין לגרמייהו עבדין כל החסדים שעושים לעצמם הם עושים. וכו'.

ואפילו כל אינון דמשתדלין באורייתא ואפילו כל אלו שמתאמצים להתעסק בתורה כל חסד דעבדין לגרמייהו עבדין [לא עשו זה] אלא לתועלת גופם עצמם. בההוא זימנא בזמן ההוא, 'ויזכור כי בשר המה רוח הולך ולא ישוב לעלמא' לעולם [הזה] (תהלים ע"ח, לט), ודא איהו רוחא דמשיח וזה הוא רוח של המשיח. וי לון מאן דגרמין, אוי להם לאלו האנשים שגורמים דיזיל מן עלמא [שרוחו של משיח] ילך מן העולם, ולא יתוב לעלמא ולא ישוב לעולם, דאלין אינון דעבדי לאורייתא יבשה שהמה הם העושים את התורה ליבשה, ולא בעאן לאשתדלא בחכמה דקבלה ולא רוצים להשתדל [ללמוד] את חכמת הקבלה, דגרמין דאסתלק נביעו דחכמה שגורמים שיסתלק מעיין החוכמה, דאיהו י' מינה שהוא [האות] י' ממנה וכו'. והאי רוח דאסתלק איהו רוח דמשיח ואיהו רוח הקודש והרוח הזה שהסתלק הוא רוחו של משיח ורוח הקודש, ואיהו רוח חכמה ובינה, רוח עצה וגבורה, רוח דעת ויראת ה' (ישעיהו יא', ב').

פקודא תנינא מצווה שנייה, 'ויאמר אלקים יהי אור ויהי אור' (בראשית א', ג'), דא אהבה, דאיהי שהיא אהבת חסד, הה"ד וזה מה שכתוב 'ואהבת עולם אהבתיך על כן משכתיך חסד' (ירמיהו לא', ב'). ועלה אתמר ועליו נאמר, 'אם תעירו ואם תעוררו את האהבה עד שתחפץ' וכו' (שיר השירים ב', ז'), רחימו ודחילו אהבה ויראה, עיקרא דיליה שהם העיקר, בין טב ובין ביש בין טוב ובין רע, ובגין דא אתקריאת האי ומשום זה זה היא נקראת יראה ואהבה, על מנת לקבל פרס. ובגין דא ומשום כך, אמר קדוש ברוך הוא, 'השבעתי אתכם בנות ירושלים בצבאות או באילות השדה אם תעירו ואם תעוררו את האהבה עד שתחפץ', דאיהו רחימו בלאו פרס שהיא אהבה בלא פרס, ולא על מנת לקבל פרס, דיראה ואהבה על מנת לקבל פרס, איהי היא של שפחה, (משלי ל', כא'-כג') 'ותחת שלש רגזה הארץ וגו' תחת עבד כי ימלוך, ושפחה כי תירש גברתה" [סוף ציטוט מהזוהר] .

59

Those who engage with the Torah Not For Its Own Sake is the secret of: "A maid-servant succeeding her mistress"

32) And we will start interpreting the *Tikkunei HaZohar* [backwards] from the end to the beginning. It is said with regard to the fear and the love that one has for engaging with the Torah and the Precepts in order to receive a reward—meaning his hope that he will gain some benefit from engaging with the Torah and with [spiritual] work—that [this love] is like a *Shifcha* (maid-servant), of whom it is written: "when a maid-servant succeeds her mistress." [This concept] is seemingly difficult [confusing] because it has been established that one should always engage with the Torah and the Precepts, even if Not For Its Own Sake (see here, verse 11), so why does the Earth tremble with anger? Also, we have to understand the relationship between Not For Its Own Sake and the phrase "*Shifcha*" (maid-servant), as well as the expression "succeeding her mistress." What sort of succession is [meant] here?

33) And you should understand, in light of all that has become clear in this introduction, that the matter of Not For Its Own Sake was only allowed because of "out of [engagement with the Torah] Not For Its Own Sake, the person will reach [the level of] For Its Own Sake, since the Light within [the Torah] redirects a person to the right path." And therefore, engagement Not For Its Own Sake is considered to be the *Shifcha* (maid-servant), who assists and does the lower chores for her mistress, who is the Holy *Shechinah*. This is because eventually, one is bound to get to For Its Own Sake and will gain the Divine Inspiration of the *Shechinah*. Then the maid-servant who stands for engaging with the Torah Not For Its Own Sake will become the *Shifcha* (maid-servant) of Holiness because she is the one who assists the Holiness and prepares it, although she is called the aspect of the World of Action of the Holiness.

Obviously if, Heaven forbid, [a person's] trust is not complete and if he does engage in the Torah and in acts of [spiritual] work but solely because he was commanded by the Creator to study, then, as it has already been made clear, in the case of such Torah [study] and acts of spiritual work, the Torah's Light would not be revealed at all

העוסקים בתורה שלא לשמה, בסוד: שפחה כי תירש גבירתה

לב) ונתחיל לבאר את תיקוני הזוהר מסיפא לרישא מהסוף להתחלה, כי
אומר, שהיראה והאהבה, שיש לאדם בעסק התורה והמצוות על מנת
לקבל פרס, דהיינו שמקוה שתצמח לו איזו טובה מחמת התורה
והעבודה, הרי זו בחינת שפחה, שעליה כתיב, 'ושפחה כי תירש גברתה',
שלכאורה קשה, הרי קיימא לן ברור לנו 'לעולם יעסוק אדם בתורה
ובמצוות אף על פי שלא לשמה' (כאן, סעיף יא'), ולמה רגזה הארץ. ועוד
יש להבין, דבר היחס של העסק שלא לשמה, לבחינת שפחה דוקא, גם
המליצה "שיורשת את גבירתה" איזו ירושה ישנה כאן.

לג) והענין תבין, עם כל המתבאר לעיל בהקדמה זאת, כי לא התירו
את העסק של לא לשמה, אלא משום, 'שמתוך שלא לשמה בא
לשמה' בהיות המאור שבה מחזירו למוטב', ולפיכך, יחשב העסק
שלא לשמה, לבחינת שפחה המסייעת, ועובדת את העבודות
הנמוכות, בעד גבירתה, שהיא השכינה הקדושה, שהרי סופו לבא
לבחינת לשמה, ויזכה להשראת השכינה. ואז נחשבת גם השפחה,
שהיא בחינת העסק שלא לשמה, לבחינת שפחה דקדושה, שהרי
היא המסייעת ומכינה את הקדושה, אך נקראת בבחינת עולם
עשיה של הקדושה.

אמנם, אם אין אמונתו שלימה חס ושלום, ואינו עוסק בתורה
ובעבודה אלא רק מטעם שהשם יתברך צוה אותו ללמוד, כבר
נתבאר לעיל, שבתורה ועבודה כאלה, לא יתגלה כלל המאור שבה,

[to him]. This is because his eyes are defective, causing the Light to turn into darkness, similar to [the eyes of] a bat, as we have said earlier (see here vers 11).

And such an aspect of study has already left the domain of the *Shifcha* (maid-servant) of Holiness because in this case he shall not, Heaven forbid, merit by it [his flawed study] to come and engage with the Torah For Its Own Sake. And this is why it moves into the domain of the *Shifcha* (maid-servant) of the *klipot* (shells), who inherits that Torah and spiritual work and usurps it for her own self. And this is why the Earth trembles with anger— *eretz* (earth) being a commonly known name for the Holy *Shechinah* (Divine Presence)—because the Torah and spiritual work were supposed to reach and be in the possession of the Holy *Shechinah*, but the lowly maid usurps them and degrades them so that they become the possession of the *klipot* (shells). And so it is in this manner that the *Shifcha* (maid-servant) succeeds her mistress, Heaven forbid.

כי עיניו פגומות, ומהפכות האור לחושך, בדומה לעטלף כנ"ל (עיין
כאן בסעיף יא').

ובחינת עסק כזה, כבר יצאה מרשות שפחה דקדושה, כי לא יזכה
חס ושלום על ידיה לבוא לשמה, ועל כן באה לרשות השפחה
דקליפה, שהיא יורשת את התורה והעבודה האלו, ועושקתן
לעצמה. לפיכך רגזה הארץ, דהיינו השכינה הק' הקדושה שנקראת
ארץ, כנודע, כי אותן התורה והעבודה שהיו צריכות לבא אליה,
לרכושה של השכינה הקדושה, עושקת אותן השפחה בישא הרעה,
ומורידה אותן לרכושן של הקליפות. ונמצאת השפחה, יורשת חס
ושלום את הגבירה.

Chapter Four
A Life of True Freedom

By engaging in the Torah For Its Own Sake one brings about the Redemption

34) And the *Tikkunei HaZohar* explained the secret of the oath [in reference to the passage]: "Do not arouse or awaken love until it so desires." The particular emphasis is that the Israelites will draw the Supernal Light, which is called the Love of Kindness, because that is what is desired. And [this Supernal Light] is drawn in particular [to a person] through his engagement with the Torah and the Precepts with no intention of receiving any reward. And the reason for this is that by this Light of Kindness, the Israelites receive the Light of the Supernal Wisdom, which is revealed and envelops itself with this Light of Kindness that the Israelites have drawn.

And this Light of Wisdom is the hidden meaning of the passage: "And the *Ruach* (Spirit) of the Creator shall rest upon him, the Spirit of wisdom and understanding, the Spirit of counsel and might, the Spirit of knowledge, and the fear of the Creator." (Isaiah 11:2) This is said about the King Messiah. And as it is said further on: "He [the Messiah] will raise an ensign for the nations, and will assemble the outcasts of Israel, and gather the dispersed of Judah from the four corners of the Earth." (Isaiah 11:12)

After the Israelites draw the Light of Wisdom by the Light of Kindness—[that is,] by the secret of "the Spirit of wisdom and understanding, etc."—then the Messiah is revealed and he "assembles the dispersed of Israel, etc." (Isaiah 56:8) After all, everything depends on engagement with the Torah and the worship For Its Own Sake, which has the ability to draw the great Light of Mercy, into which the Light of Wisdom is drawn as it envelops itself with it. This is the secret of the oath to "Do not arouse or awaken love, etc."

פרק רביעי
חיים על וחפץ אמיתי

על ידי העסק לשמה ממשיך הגאולה

לד) ופירשו תיקוני הזוהר סוד השבועה, 'דאם תעירו ואם תעוררו את האהבה עד שתחפץ' שההקפדה היא, שישראל ימשיכו אור החסד העליון, שנקרא אהבת חסד, כי זהו הנחפץ, שהוא נמשך דוקא, על ידי העסק בתורה ובמצוות שלא על מנת לקבל פרס, והטעם כי על ידי אור החסד הזה, נמשך לישראל אור החכמה העליונה, המתגלה ומתלבש, באור החסד הזה שהמשיכו ישראל.

ואור החכמה הזה, הוא סוד הכתוב, 'ונחה עליו רוח ה', רוח חכמה ובינה, רוח עצה וגבורה, רוח דעת ויראת ה' (ישעיה י"א), הנאמר על מלך המשיח, כמו שנאמר שם להלן (פסוק יב'), 'ונשא נס לגוים, ואסף נדחי ישראל, ונפוצות יהודה יקבץ מארבע כנפות הארץ'.

כי אחר שישראל ממשיכין על ידי אור החסד, את אור החכמה, בסוד 'רוח חכמה ובינה' וכו', אז מתגלה המשיח, ו'מקבץ נדחי ישראל' וכו' (ישעיהו נו', ח'). הרי, שהכל תלוי בעסק התורה והעבודה לשמה, המסוגל להמשיך אור החסד הגדול, שבו מתלבש ונמשך אור החכמה. שזה סוד השבועה, 'אם תעירו ואם תעוררו' וכו', כי

This is because the complete redemption and the return from Exile (lit. gathering of the Exiles) cannot happen without it, since the channels of Holiness are arranged thus.

Whether the Spirit of the Creator hovers over those who engage with the Torah Not For Its Own Sake

35) And there are further interpretations [of the phrase]: "And the *Ruach* (Spirit) of the Creator is hovering above the face of the waters." What is [the meaning of] the Spirit of the Creator? Certainly when the *Shechinah* (Divine Presence) is in exile, then this *Ruach* (Spirit) hovers above those who study the Torah, as the *Shechinah* dwells among them." This means that during the Exile, as long as (lit. while) the Israelites still engage with the Torah and the Precepts Not For Its Own Sake—if they are indeed in the stage of "from Not For Its Own Sake they shall come to For Its Own Sake"—then the *Shechinah* is among them, albeit from the aspect of exile because they have not yet reached [the stage of] For Its Own Sake, as is mentioned above in the secret of "the maid-servant of Holiness."

This is what is meant by "because the *Shechinah* dwells among them," but in concealment. Yet in the end, they are bound to merit the revelation of the *Shechinah*. And then the Spirit of the King Messiah hovers above those who thus engage and awakens them to come to engagement For Its Own Sake. This is the hidden meaning behind "the Torah's Light puts them back on the right path": It [the Spirit of Messiah] helps and prepares the emanation of the *Shechinah*, which is "Her Mistress." At the same time, if, Heaven forbid, this matter of engagement Not For Its Own Sake is not fit to bring them to engagement For Its Own Sake for the reasons we mentioned earlier, then the *Shechinah* is distressed and says, "All flesh is like dry straw," [meaning] they are all like beasts who feed on hay and straw.

This means that the elevating human spirit cannot be found among the people who engage with the Torah, but instead they are satisfied with the animal spirit that moves downward. And they explain the

הגאולה השלימה וקיבוץ הגלויות אי אפשר זולתה, היות סדרי צינורות הקדושה מסודרים כן.

אם רוח אלקים מרחפת על העוסקים שלא לשמה

לה) וזה שפירשו עוד: ורוח אלקים מרחפת על פני המים, מאי מהו ורוח אלקים, אלא בודאי, בזמנא דשכינתא נחתת בגלותא בזמן שהשכינה יורדת בגלות, האי רוח הרוח הזה, נשיב על אינון דמתעסקי באורייתא נושב על אלו שמתעסקים בתורה, בגין שכינתא דאשתכחת בינייהו בגלל השכינה שנמצאת בינהם (ראה כאן סעיף לא'). פירוש הדברים, שבזמן גלות, בעת שישראל עדיין עוסקים בתורה ומצוות שלא לשמה, אמנם אם הם בבחינה זו, ש׳מתוך שלא לשמה בא לשמה׳, הרי השכינה ביניהם, אלא בבחינת גלות, מטעם שעדיין לא בא לשמה, וכנ״ל, בסוד השפחה דקדושה.

וז״ש וזה שכתוב בגין שכינתא דאשתכחת בינייהו בגלל השכינה שנמצאת בינהם, כלומר בהסתר, אבל סופם לזכות לגילוי שכינה. ואז הרוח דמלך המשיח מרחפת על העוסקים, ומעוררת אותם לבא לשמה, בסוד המאור שבה מחזירם למוטב, שמסייעת ומכינה להשראת השכינה שהיא גבירתה. אמנם, אם חס ושלום אין העסק הזה דשלא לשמה ראוי להביאם לשמה, מטעמים הנ״ל, אז מצטערת השכינה ואומרת, ׳כל הבשר חציר, כלא אינון כבעירין דאכלין חציר כלם הם כבהמות אוכלי עשב וחציר.

פירוש, שלא נמצא בעוסקים בתורה, אותו רוח האדם העולה למעלה, אלא שמסתפקין ברוח הבהמה היורד למטה. ומפרשים שם

reason: because "all his kindness is like the sprouts of the field," all the kindness they show—even all those who are engaged in the Torah—is only for their own benefit. This means that all their engagement with the Torah and the Precepts is for their own benefit and their personal pleasure, and thus, their engagement with the Torah [Not For Its Own Sake] cannot bring them, Heaven forbid, to [engagement] For Its Own Sake.

And these are the words that are written there: "And in that time, 'He is due to remember that they are but flesh,' a gust of wind (Heb. also *Ruach*) that goes by and shall never return," and this is the *Ruach* (Spirit) of the Messiah. It means that the Spirit of the Messiah does not hover above them, but goes away from them and does not come back because the impure maid-servant exploits their Torah and succeeds the mistress, as we mentioned earlier. [And this occurs] because they are not on the path of moving from [engaging with the Torah] Not For Its Own Sake to [engaging with it] For Its Own Sake, as discussed above (see here, verses 11, 17).

The Spirit of the Creator hovers over those studying Kabbalah

Therefore, the conclusion there is that these [people] are the ones who make the Torah dry, as they do not want to study the Wisdom of Kabbalah. This means that even though they do not succeed through studying the Revealed Torah because it has no Light [for them] and it becomes dry due to their small-mindedness (as was mentioned above, letter 15, starting with the words of the Rav "And so…"), still, they can succeed through engaging with the study of Kabbalah because the Light in [the Wisdom of Kabbalah] is vested with the Garments of the Creator meaning the Holy Names and the *Sefirot*.

And through [studying Kabbalah,] they could very easily come under the category of [engaging] Not For Its Own Sake, which leads to [engaging] For Its Own Sake. And in this case, the *Ruach* (Spirit) of the Creator would hover over them, which is the secret of "the Light of the Torah bringing [people] back to the right path." But they do not want to study Kabbalah in any way. And this is

הטעם, משום דכל חסדו כציץ השדה, ואפילו כל אינון דמשתדלין באורייתא ואפילו כל אלו שמשתדלים בתורה, כל חסד דעבדין לגרמייהו הוא דעבדין כל חסד שעושים - לשם עצמם הם עושים, כלומר, שכל עסקם בתורה ומצות הוא לתועלתם ולהנאתם עצמם, ואין העסק בתורה מסוגל להביאם לשמה חס ושלום.

וז"ש וזה שכתוב שם בההוא זמנא בזמן ההוא, ויזכור כי בשר המה, רוח הולך ולא ישוב לעלמא ולא ישוב לעולם, ודא איהו רוחא דמשיח וזה הוא רוח של המשיח. פירוש, שעליהם אין רוחא דמשיח מרחפת, אלא, הולכת מהם ולא תשוב, כי השפחה הטמאה עושקת תורתם ויורשת את הגבירה כנ"ל, משום שאינם בדרך לבא מתוך שלא לשמה לבחינת לשמה, כנ"ל (ראה כאן סעיפים י"א, ט"ז').

רוח אלקים מרחפת בלומדי הקבלה

ועל כן מסיק שם, דאלין אינון דעבדין לאורייתא יבשה, ולא בעאן לאשתדלא בחכמת הקבלה אלו הם שעושים התורה יבשה ולא רוצים להשתדל בחכמת הקבלה. פירוש הדברים: כי אף על פי שאינם מצליחים על ידי העסק בתורה הנגלית משום שאין בה מאור, והוי יבשה, מסיבת קטנות דעתם (כנ"ל אות ט"ו ד"ה דבר הכתוב והנה), מ"מ מכל מקום הרי יכולים להצליח על ידי העסק בלימוד הקבלה, משום שהמאור שבה מלובש בלבושין דהקדוש ברוך הוא, דהיינו השמות הקדושים והספירות.

אשר בנקל היו יכולים לבא [באמצעות לימוד הקבלה] באותה הבחינה של שלא לשמה המביאתם לשמה, שאז היתה רוח אלקים מרחפת עליהם, בסוד המאור שבה המחזירם למוטב, אמנם בשום אופן אינם חפצים בלימוד הקבלה, וז"ש וזה שכתוב וי לון דגרמין עניותא וחרבא וביזה והרג ואבדן בעלמא אוי להם שגורמים עניות וחרב וביזה והרג

why it is said: "Woe to them, since they bring misery, destruction, plunder, bloodshed, and dismay to the world, and the *Ruach* (Spirit) that departs is the *Ruach* of the Messiah, as it is said: 'This is the *Ruach* (Spirit) of the Holiness, which is the Spirit of Wisdom and Understanding, etc.'"

The reason for the length of the Exile and the pain, as well as its correction through the study of Kabbalah

36) **What has become clear** from the writings of the *Tikkunei HaZohar* is that there is an oath that the Light of mercy and love should not be awakened in the world until the actions of the Israelites to follow the Torah and the Precepts would be with the intention only to give pleasure to the Creator and not for the sake of receiving any reward. This is the hidden meaning of the oath: "I charge you, daughters of Jerusalem," [Song of Songs 2:7] which means that the length of the Exile and the pain that we suffer are pending and are awaiting us until we merit engaging with the Torah and the Precepts For Its Own Sake. But if we merit this, then immediately this Light of love and mercy shall be awakened. This Light has the ability to draw upon us the hidden meaning of the passage: "And the Spirit of the Creator shall rest upon him, the Spirit of wisdom and understanding, the Spirit of counsel and might etc." [Isaiah 11:2] And then we will merit the complete redemption.

And it was also made clear that it is impossible for the entirety of the Israelites to come to this great purity except through the study of Kabbalah, which is the easiest way and is good enough even for people of little understanding. This is in opposition to the path of engagement solely with the revealed aspects of the Torah. [The Divine Understanding] cannot be achieved except by a very few privileged and selected individuals, and [only] through extensive effort. [However, this engagement with the Revealed Torah] is not suitable for most of the population, for reasons explained above (see here verse 22). And this has very clearly demonstrated the insignificance of the fourth and fifth queries at the beginning of this introduction.

ואובדן בעולם, והאי רוח דאסתלק ורוח ההיא מסתלקת, איהו רוח דמשיח, כמא דאתמר דאיהו כמו שנאמר שהיא רוח הקדש, ואיהו רוח חכמה ובינה וכו'.

בטעם אריכות הגלות והיסורים, ותיקונו בלימוד הקבלה

לו) המתבאר מדברי תיקוני הזוהר הוא שישנה שבועה, שלא יתעורר אור החסד והאהבה בעולם, עד שמעשיהם של ישראל בתורה ומצוות, יהיו על הכונה שלא לקבל פרס, אלא רק להשפיע נחת רוח ליוצר ב"ה (ברוך הוא), שזה סוד השבועה: השבעתי אתכם בנות ירושלים וכו' (שיר השירים ב', ז'). באופן, שכל אריכות הגלות והיסורים שאנו סובלים, תלויים ומחכים לנו, עד שנזכה לעסק התורה ומצוות לשמה, ואם רק נזכה לזה, תיכף יתעורר אור האהבה והחסד הזה, שסגולתו להמשיך סוד הכתוב ונחה עליו רוח חכמה ובינה וכו' (ישעיהו יא, ב'), ואז נזכה לגאולה השלימה.

גם נתבאר, שאי אפשר שכל כלל ישראל יבואו לטהרה הגדולה הזו, זולת על ידי לימוד הקבלה, שהיא הדרך הקלה ביותר, המספיקה גם לקטני הדעת, מה שאין כן בדרך העסק בתורת הנגלה בלבד, אי אפשר לזכות על ידה, זולת ליחידי סגולה, ועל ידי יגיעה רבה, אבל לא למרבית העם, מטעם המבואר לעיל (אות כ"ב ד"ה דבור מתחיל [במילה] אכן). ובזה נתבארה היטב האפסיות שבקושיא הרביעית והחמישית שבתחילת ההקדמה.

The reason why some of those studying Kabbalah have gone astray

37) And [as for] the third query, which [pertains to] the fear of going astray, here there [should be] no fear at all because the deviation from the path of the Creator, Heaven forbid, which once used to happen, occurred for two reasons: Either people transgressed the instructions of the sages regarding issues that should not be revealed, or they grasped the words of Kabbalah in their external meaning, that is, in physical indications and [by that] transgressed the commandment of "You shall not make for yourself a graven image or any likeness..." (Exodus 20:3).

For this reason, there has rightfully been a barrier (lit. solid wall) surrounding this wisdom [of Kabbalah] to this very day. Indeed, many have tried and started the study of this wisdom and were not able to follow through with it because of their lack of understanding and because of the [language and] names [using] physical mundane terminology. This is why I have put much effort into the creation of a commentary [named] "Illuminated Face and Welcoming Face" in order to interpret the great book *The Tree of Life*, [penned] by the Ari. My purpose was to undress [clarify] the physical forms [terminology] and to place them according to their spiritual laws beyond space and time, in a way that every beginner would be able to understand things along with their meaning and their reasoning, with very clear arguments and with great simplicity, so that [this book] will be just as comprehensible as the *Gemarah* as augmented by Rashi's commentary.

Engaging with the Torah For Its Own Sake: for the sake of the Torah

38) And we will continue to expound upon the necessity of engaging with the Torah and the Precepts For Its Own Sake, which I started talking about [earlier]. We should hereby understand this term: "Torah *Lishma*," that is, "[Torah] For Its Own Sake (lit. Her Name)."

הטעם על שכמה מלומדי הקבלה החמיצו

לז) והקושיא השלישית, שהיא הפחד שלא יחמיץ, הנה אין כאן
פחד ולא כלום, כי ענין הנטיה מדרך ה' חס ושלום שקרתה פעם,
היתה מב' סיבות: או שעברו על דברי חז"ל בדברים האסורים
לגלות, או משום שתפסו דברי הקבלה במשמעותם החיצונית,
דהיינו בהוראות גשמיות, ועברו על לא תעשה לך פסל וכל תמונה
(שמות כ', ג').

ועל כן באמת היתה חומה בצורה מסביב החכמה הזו עד היום,
אשר רבים נסו והתחילו בלימוד ולא יכלו להמשיך בו מחסרון
הבנה, ומחמת הכינויים הגשמיים, אשר על כן טרחתי בביאור פנים
מאירות ופנים מסבירות לפרש את הספר הגדול עץ החיים מהאר"י
ז"ל ולהפשיט הצורות הגשמיות ולהעמידן בחוקי הרוחניים, למעלה
ממקום ומזמן, באופן שיוכל כל מתחיל להבין הדברים בטעמם
ונימוקם, בשכל בהיר ובפשטות גדולה, לא פחות כמו שמבינים
גמרא על ידי פירוש רש"י ז"ל.

עסק התורה לשמה: לשם התורה

לח) ונמשיך להרחיב את החיוב של העסק בתורה ומצוות לשמה
שהתחלתי לדבר בו. הנה יש להבין את השם הזה של "תורה לשמה",
למה מוגדרת העבודה השלימה הרצויה בשם הזה "לשמה",

73

Why is the complete and desired form of [spiritual] work referred to as For Her Own Name (Sake), while the undesired form of [spiritual] work is referred to as Not For Her Own Name (Sake)? After all, if we go by the very simple meaning—that a person engaging with the Torah and the Precepts has the duty to focus his heart on giving pleasure to his Maker rather than for his own good—then [this work] should have been called and referred to as "Torah for His Sake (lit. Name)" and "Torah Not For His Sake (lit. Name)," that is, for the sake of the Creator (lit. Heaven). So why is it referred to as For Its Own Sake and Not For Its Own Sake, which means for the sake of the Torah [as opposed to for the sake of the Creator]?

Surely there is some deeper understanding than the one we have just discussed because the use of the language here proves that [studying] Torah for His sake—that is, for giving pleasure to his Maker—is not sufficient; rather, [studying Torah] needs to be for its [own] sake (lit. for Her Name), which means for the Sake (or Name) of the Torah. This needs an explanation.

Life for those who engage [with the Torah] For Its [Own] Sake; and the opposite of life to those who engage with the Torah Not For Its [Own] Sake

39) And the issue of the matter is, that it is known that the name of the Torah is: *Torat Chayim* (Torah of Life), as it is said: "For it [the Torah] is life to those who find it" (Proverbs 4:22). And the Scriptures also say: "It is no trifle for you, but it is your life, etc." (Deuteronomy 32:47). And this being the case, then the meaning of Torah For Its Own Sake (Her Name) is that engaging with the Torah and the Precepts provides [a person] with life and long years, and [in doing so,] then the Torah is really [the same] as its name [Torah of Life]. It happens, Heaven forbid, for whoever does not focus his heart and mind on this, that [his] engagement with the Torah and the Precepts brings him the opposite of life and long years, that is, completely Not For Its Name [*Lo Lishma*], since its name is "Torah of Life." Understand this.

והעבודה שאינה רצויה בשם של "לא לשמה", כי לפי המובן הפשוט, שהעוסק בתורה ומצוות מחוייב לכוון לבו לעשות נחת רוח ליוצרו, ולא לשם טובת עצמו, היה צריך לכנות זה ולהגדירו, בשם "תורה לשמו" ו"תורה שלא לשמו", שפירושו לשם שמים, ולמה מגדירים זה בשם "לשמה" ו"שלא לשמה", שפירושו לשם התורה.

אלא ודאי, שיש כאן הבנה יתירה מהאמור, שהרי הלשון מוכיחה, שתורה לשמו, שפירושו לעשות נחת רוח ליוצרו, אינו מספיק עדיין, אלא שצריך עוד שיהיה העסק לשמה, שפירושו לשם התורה, וזה צריך ביאור.

חיים לעוסקים לשמה, והיפך החיים לעוסקים שלא לשמה

לט) והענין הוא, כי נודע, ששם התורה הוא "תורת חיים", כאמור כי "חיים" הם למוצאיהם וגו' (משלי ד' כ"ב). וכן הוא אומר, כי לא דבר ריק הוא מכם, כי הוא חייכם וגו' (דברים ל"ב מ"ז), וכיון שכן, הרי פירושה של תורה לשמה, אשר העסק בתורה ומצוות מביא לו חיים ואריכות ימים, כי אז, התורה היא כשמה. ומי שאינו מכוון את לבו ודעתו לנאמר, נמצא שהעסק בתורה ומצוות, מביא לו את ההיפך מהחיים ואריכות הימים חס ושלום, דהיינו לגמרי ש"לא לשמה", שהרי שמה הוא "תורת חיים", והבן.

75

These issues appear explicitly in the words of the sages (Tractate *Ta'anit* 7a): "Whoever is engaged with the Torah Not For Its Own Sake, his Torah becomes for him a potion of death (here, verse 17); but whoever engages in the Torah For Its Own Sake, his Torah becomes for him a potion of life." Indeed, their words require clarification [in order for us] to understand how and by what the Holy Torah becomes a "potion of death" for [someone]! At the very least, this person's effort would be in vain and without purpose, and he would not gain any benefit from his effort and toil, Heaven forbid. But adding even further that the very "Torah and [spiritual] work" inverts itself and becomes a "potion of death"—this point is very astonishing.

Interpreting the language of the sages: "I have toiled and I have found, you should believe!"

40) And we should first understand the words of our sages who said: "I have toiled and I have found, you should believe; I have not toiled and I have found, you should not believe." (Tractate *Megilah* 6b) We should raise questions about this terminology: "I have toiled and I have found," [two concepts] that seem to contradict each other. After all, "toiling" is a matter of labor and inconvenience, which is given for a price in exchange for any desired object. Also, to acquire an important object, more effort is required, whereas to purchase an object of lesser value, less effort is required.

And this is exactly the opposite of "finding," which normally happens to (lit. reaches) a person completely without anticipation and without the prerequisites of toil, exertion, or a price. If so, why do we say here, "I have toiled and I have found?" If toiling is what is being spoken of here, then we should have said, "I have toiled and I have acquired" or "I have toiled and I have gained," or something of that nature, rather than "I have toiled and I have found."

ודברים אלו, באים מפורשים בדברי חז"ל (תענית ז' ע"א), כל
העוסק בתורה שלא לשמה, תורתו נעשית לו סם המות (כאן, סעיף
טז'). וכל העוסק בתורה לשמה, תורתו נעשית לו סם חיים. אמנם
דבריהם אלו צריכים ביאור, להבין, איך, ובמה, נעשית לו התורה
הקדושה לסם המות. המעט הוא, שמתיגע לריק ולבטלה, ואין
לו שום תועלת מטרחתו ויגיעתו, חס ושלום, אלא עוד, שהתורה
והעבודה עצמה, נהפכת לו לסם המות, שדבר זה מתמיה מאד.

ביאור לשון חז"ל: יגעתי ומצאתי תאמין

מ) ונבין מתחילה את דברי חז"ל (מגילה ו' ע"ב), שאמרו, יגעתי
ומצאתי תאמן, לא יגעתי ומצאתי אל תאמן. ויש להקשות על
הלשון יגעתי ומצאתי, שנראים כתרתי דסתרי אהדדי שנראים כשניים
הסותרים אחד את השני, שהרי "יגיעה" היא ענין עבודה וטורח, שנותנים
במחיר כל קנין רצוי, שבעד קנין חשוב נותנים יגיעה מרובה, ובעד
קנין פחות נותנים יגיעה מועטת.

והיפוכה היא "מציאה", אשר דרכה לבא אל האדם בהסח הדעת
לגמרי, בלי שום הכנה של טורח ויגיעה ומחיר. ואם כך איך תאמר
יגעתי ומצאתי, ואם יגיעה יש כאן היה צריך לומר יגעתי וקניתי או
יגעתי וזכיתי, וכדומה, ולא "יגעתי ומצאתי".

The subject of looking for the Creator Who hides Himself in the Holy Torah

41) And we have learned in the *Zohar*, regarding the passage: "… those who seek Me diligently find Me" (Proverbs 8:17) that it was asked: Where does one find the Creator? And they answered that the only place one can find Him is in the Torah. And they commented similarly on the passage: "Truly, you are a Creator Who hides Himself," (Isaiah 45:15) that the Creator hides Himself in His Holy Torah. And the words of the sages should be properly understood, because seemingly the Creator is hidden only in material things and ways and in all the vanities of the world that are outside the Torah. So how can one say the opposite: that He hides Himself only in the Torah?

Also, regarding the general idea that the Creator hides Himself in a way that He has to be sought after, why does He need this concealment [of Himself]? And regarding [the idea] "that all those who seek Him shall find Him," the meaning of the words [of Proverbs]: "those who seek Me diligently shall find Me," this should be understood well. What is this "seeking" and "finding" all about? What are they [seeking and finding], and what is their purpose?

The reason for all the pain and the failures is our minimal understanding with regards to His Providence

42) You should know that the reason for all this distance—why we are so far away from the Creator and why we are so prone to violate His Will—is all due to one cause, which has become the source of all the pain and agony that we suffer from, and of all the intentional and unintentional wrongdoings by which we fail, Heaven forbid, as we come across them. At the same time, it is obvious that by removing this cause, we immediately get rid of every sorrow and every pain, and are immediately awarded with cleaving to Him with all of our heart, soul, and might. And let me tell you that the original cause is none other than this: [We are distant from the Creator because of] our minimal understanding of His Providence over His created beings, for we do not understand Him properly.

ענין הביקוש את השי"ת המסתיר עצמו בתורה הקדושה

מא) והנה איתא מובא בזוהר, על הכתוב ומשחרי ימצאונני (משלי ח', יז'), שאלו ע"ז על זה היכן מוצאים את השם יתברך, ואמרו שאין מוצאים אותו יתברך, אלא בתורה. וכן אמרו על הכתוב (ישעיהו מ"ה, טו'), אכן אתה אל מסתתר, אשר הקדוש ברוך הוא מסתיר את עצמו בתורה הקדושה. ויש להבין דבריהם ז"ל כראוי, כי לכאורה הקדוש ברוך הוא מוסתר רק בדברים ודרכים הגשמיים, ובכל הבלי העולם הזה שהם מחוץ לתורה, ואיך תאמר את ההיפך אשר רק בתורה הוא מסתיר את עצמו.

גם המובן הכללי, שהקדוש ברוך הוא מסתיר את עצמו באופן שצריכים לבקשו, הסתר זה למה לו. וכן "שכל מבקשי אותו ימצאוהו", המובן בכתוב, ומשחרי ימצאונני, צריך להבין היטב, דבר הביקוש הזה, ודבר המציאה הזו, מה הם, ולמה הם.

סיבת כל המכאובים והכשלונות היא מיעוט הבנתינו בהשגחתו יתברך

מב) וצריך שתדע אמנם, אשר סיבת כל הריחוק הזה, שאנו רחוקים כל כך מהשם יתברך, ומה שאנו עלולים כל כך לעבור על רצונו יתברך, אין כל זה, אלא משום סיבה אחת, שנעשתה למקור, לכל המכאובים והיסורים שאנו סובלים, ולכל הזדונות והשגגות שאנו נכשלים ובאים בהם חס ושלום. שיחד עם זה מובן, שבהסרת הסיבה ההיא, נפטרים תיכף, מכל צער ומכל מכאוב, וזוכים תיכף להדבק בו יתברך בכל לב, נפש ומאד. ואומר לך, שהסיבה המקורית ההיא אינה אינה אחרת, אלא "מיעוט ההבנה שלנו בהשגחתו יתברך על בריותיו", שאין אנו מבינים אותו יתברך כראוי.

43) Let us assume that the Creator would interact with His created beings through clear and visible Providence. For example, everyone who eats something forbidden [non-kosher] would immediately choke, and everyone who fulfills a precept would immediately find in it a wondrous pleasure, similar to the most wondrous pleasures of this material world. In this case, who would be foolish enough to even consider tasting anything that is forbidden knowing that his life would be immediately lost as a result, just as [for the same reason] the person would not consider jumping into a fire? And who would be foolish enough to leave any Precept without fulfilling it with the greatest speed, just as he would not leave or delay any material delight that came his way and rather accept it with all possible swiftness. This means that where we have a Revealed Providence all people of the world would be complete *tzadikim* (righteous people).

44) This is clear evidence that we miss nothing in our world except for a visible Providence, because had we had visible Providence, all the people of the world would have been complete *tzadikim* (righteous people). And they would have completely cleaved to Him with utter love because it would have been a great honor for each and every person to befriend and love Him with all their heart and soul, and to cleave to Him always, without ever missing one minute. But this is not the case: Instead, the reward for fulfilling a precept is not in this world. Furthermore, not only are those who transgress His Will not being punished at all in front of our eyes, but the Creator is very patient with them.

Moreover, sometimes the opposite seems to us to be true, Heaven forbid. As it is said: "Behold, these are the wicked; always at ease, they increase in riches..." (Psalms 73:12) Therefore, it is not that everyone who wants to take the Name can just come and get it; rather, we are tackled at each and every step, Heaven forbid. As the sages said (*Vayikra Raba,* 2) regarding the passage: "One man among a thousand have I found," (Ecclesiastes 7:28) a thousand people enter the Torah study (lit. room) and [only] one of them comes out to be a teacher. Therefore, the understanding of His Providence is the

מג) ונניח למשל, אם היה הקדוש ברוך הוא נוהג עם בריותיו
בהשגחה גלויה באופן, אשר למשל, כל האוכל דבר איסור, יחנק
תיכף על מקומו, וכל העושה מצוה, ימצא בה התענוג הנפלא בדומה
לתענוגות המצוינים ביותר שבעולם הזה, הגשמי, כי אז, מי פתי היה
מהרהר אפילו לטעום דבר איסור, בשעה שהיה יודע שתיכף יאבד
מחמתו את חייו, כמו שאינו מהרהר לקפוץ לתוך הדליקה. וכן מי
פתי היה עוזב איזו מצוה מבלי לקיימה תיכף בכל הזריזות, כמו
שאינו יכול לפרוש, או להתמהמה על תענוג גדול גשמי הבא לידו,
מבלי לקבלו מיד בכל הזריזות שביכלתו. הרי, שאם היתה לפנינו
השגחה גלויה, היו כל באי העולם צדיקים גמורים.

מד) הרי לעיניך, שבעולמנו לא חסר לנו, אלא השגחה גלויה. כי אם
היתה לנו השגחה גלויה היו כל באי עולם צדיקים גמורים. וגם היו
דבקים בו ית' בתכלית האהבה, כי ודאי לכבוד גדול היה זה לכל
אחד ממנו, להתידד ולהתאהב בו יתברך בכל לב ונפש, ולהדבק בו
תמיד, בלי אפילו הפסד רגע. אלא מתוך שאינו כן, אלא שכר מצוה
בהאי עלמא ליכא שכר מצוה אינו בעולם הזה, גם אין עוברי רצונו נענשים
כלל לעינינו, אלא השם יתברך מאריך אפים להם.

ולא עוד אלא שלפעמים נדמה לנו ההיפך חס ושלום, כמ"ש כמו
שכתוב (תהלים ע"ג, י"ב) הנה אלה רשעים ושלוי עולם השגו חיל
וגו', ולפיכך לא כל הרוצה ליטול את השם יבא ויטול, אלא שאנו
נתקלים בכל פסיעה ופסיעה חס ושלום, עד כמ"ש כמו שכתוב חז"ל
(וי"ר פ"ב ויקרא רבה, פרק ב') על הכתוב אדם אחד מאלף מצאתי (קהלת
ז', כ"ח), אשר אלף נכנסים לחדר ואחד יוצא להוראה. הרי שהבנת

reason for all good, and the misunderstanding of it is the reason for all bad. And it turns out that this is the polarity that all human beings fluctuate between: for good or for bad.

Four types of understanding of His Providence

45) When we look closely at [the process] of understanding Providence as it is experienced (lit. being felt) by humans, we find four kinds [of people], where each kind receives the Divine Providence in a special manner. Thus, there are four aspects to comprehending Providence, although, in fact, there are only two, which are: Concealment of Face and Revelation of Face. [These two aspects] are divided further into four because there are two aspects of Providence in the context of Concealment of the Face, namely, One [single] Concealment and Concealment within Concealment. And [likewise,] there are two aspects of Providence in the context of Revelation of the Face: Providence of reward and punishment, and Providence of eternity, as shall be explained further on with the Creator's help.

השגחתו יתברך, היא הסיבה לכל טוב, ואי ההבנה, היא הסיבה לכל רע, ונמצא, שהיא הקוטב אשר כל באי עולם מתגלגלים עליו, אם לשבט ואם לחסד.

ארבע סוגים בהבנת השגחתו יתברך

מה) וכשנתבונן היטב בהשגת השגחה, הבאה להרגשת בני אדם, אנו מוצאים בהם ד' סוגים, שכל סוג וסוג מקבל השגחת השם יתברך עליו במיוחד, באופן, שיש כאן ד' בחינות של השגת ההשגחה, ובאמת הן רק שתים, דהיינו: הסתר פנים וגילוי פנים. אלא שנחלקים לארבע, כי יש ב' בחינות בהשגחה של הסתר פנים, שהם: הסתר אחד, והסתר בתוך הסתר. וב' בחינות בהשגחה של גילוי פנים, שהן: השגחה של שכר ועונש, והשגחת הנצחיות. כמו שיתבארו לפנינו בעזרת השם.

Chapter Five
The Creator's Providence – Revealed and Concealed

And I will hide and conceal My Face [Haster Astir]: Double Concealment

46) And here the Scriptures say: "Then My anger will be kindled against them on that day, and I will forsake them and 'hide My Face' from them, and they will be devoured; and many evils and troubles will come upon them; and they will say on that day, 'Have not these evils come upon me because my Creator is not within me?' And I will 'hide and conceal' My Face in that day on account of all the evil that they have done because they have turned to other Gods." (Deuteronomy 31:17-18)

And if you look closely, you will see that at first it says: "My anger will be kindled, etc." … "and I will hide My Face" [*vehistarti Panay*], namely, One [single] Concealment; and then it says: "…and many evils and troubles will come upon them etc." … "And I will hide and conceal My face" [*Haster Astir*], which means a Double Concealment. We must understand what this Double Concealment means.

Aspects of Front (lit. Face) and Back of the Creator

47) At first, we must understand what the Face of the Creator means when the Scriptures say: "I will hide My Face." You have to understand that this is similar to [a situation where] a person sees the face of his friend and immediately recognizes him. However, this is not the case when he sees [his friend] from the back because then he is not sure regarding the identification and may have doubts, thinking it could be someone other than his friend.

This is also the case with what is in front of us here. Because everyone knows and feels that the Creator is good and that it is the nature of good to bestow goodness, therefore when the Creator keeps bestowing goodness on His created beings, whom He has

84

פרק חמישי
השגחת הבורא – גלויה ונסתרת

ואנכי הסתר אסתיר: הסתר כפול

מו) והנה הכתוב אומר (דברים ל"א י"ז), וחרה אפי בו ביום ההוא ועזבתים "והסתרתי פני" מהם והיה לאכל ומצאהו רעות רבות וצרות, ואמר ביום ההוא, הלא על כי אין אלקי בקרבי, מצאוני הרעות האלה. ואנכי הסתר אסתיר פני ביום ההוא, על כל הרעה אשר עשה, כי פנה אל אלהים אחרים.

וכשתסתכל בדברים תמצא, שמתחילה כתוב וחרה אפי וגו' והסתרתי פני וגו', דהיינו הסתר אחד, ואחר כך כתוב, ומצאוהו רעות רבות וצרות וגו' ואנכי הסתר אסתיר פני וגו', דהיינו הסתר כפול, וצריכים להבין הסתר כפול זה מהו.

בחינות פנים ואחור אצל השם יתברך

מז) ומתחילה נבין, מה הפירוש של הפנים של השם יתברך, שהכתוב אומר עליו והסתרתי פני. ותבין זה, בדומה לאדם, בשעה שרואה הפנים של חברו מכירו תיכף, מה שאין כן בראוהו דרך אחוריו, כי אז אינו בטוח בהכרתו, ועלול להיות בספק אולי אחר הוא, ואינו חברו.

וכן הדבר שלפנינו, כי הכל יודעים ומרגישים את השם יתברך כי טוב הוא, ומדרך הטוב להיטיב, ולפיכך בשעה שהשם יתברך הולך ומטיב עם בריותיו אשר ברא כמתנת ידו הרחבה, נבחן זה, שפניו

created out of generosity, it is considered as if His Face is exposed to His created beings. And then everyone knows Him and is familiar with Him, inasmuch as He behaves in a way that is appropriate to His Name and stature, as was made clear above regarding the visible Providence. (Study that well, verses 54-55; 97-98)

48) Indeed when He behaves with His created beings in an opposite way to the one mentioned above—when [His beings] receive pain and suffering in His world—it is equivalent to the Back of the Creator because His Face, that is, the degree of his complete goodness, is completely hidden from them because this type of behavior does not fit His Name. This is similar to seeing one's friend from behind and having doubts regarding his identity; thinking he may be someone else.

And this is the meaning of the passage: "Then My anger will be kindled against them... and I will hide My Face from them." (Deuteronomy 31:17) When the Creator is angry (lit. During the anger) and people are afflicted with troubles and pains, it turns out that the Creator conceals His Face, His utter benevolence, and only His Back is apparent. In this state, great strengthening in our trust in Him is required in order that we beware of [any] thoughts of transgression since it is hard to know Him from behind. And this [Concealment of the Face] is called One [single] Concealment.

Interpretation of Concealment of the Face alone, and the Concealment of both the Face and the Back together

49) Indeed, when trouble and pain are increased to an exceptional degree, Heaven forbid, this causes a double concealment, which is called in the [kabbalistic] books, Concealment within Concealment, which means that even His Back can no longer be seen, Heaven forbid. This means that people do not believe that the Creator is angry with them and is punishing them, but, Heaven forbid, they blame everything on chance and on nature, and through this [thinking, they] arrive at heretical denial of His Providence of reward and punishment. And this is what is meant by "and I will

יתברך מגולות לבריותיו, כי אז הכל יודעים ומכירים אותו בהיותו מתנהג כראוי לשמו יתברך, כמו שנתבאר לעיל בדבר ההשגחה הגלויה, (עש"ה עיין שם היטב סעיפים נד-נה; צז-צח) .

מח) אמנם בשעה שמתנהג עם בריותיו להיפך מהאמור, דהיינו בעת שמקבלים יסורים ומכאובים בעולמו יתברך, הרי נבחן זה לאחורים של השם יתברך, כי הפנים שלו, דהיינו מידת טובו השלמה, נסתרה מהם לגמרי, שאין מנהג זה מתאים לשמו יתברך. ודומה, לרואה את רעהו מאחוריו, שהוא עלול להטיל ספק ולחשוב אולי אחר הוא.

וזש"ה וזה שאומר הכתוב, וחרה אפי וגו' והסתרתי פני מהם וגו', כי בעת חרון האף, שהבריות מקבלים צרות ומכאובים, נמצא שהקדוש ברוך הוא מסתיר פניו יתברך, שהם מידת טובו השלמה, ורק אחוריו מגולים. ואז, צריכים להתחזקות גדולה באמונתו יתברך כדי להזהר מהרהורי עבירה חס ושלום, משום שקשה להכיר מאחוריו, כמבואר. וזהו הנקרא הסתר אחד.

ביאור הסתר הפנים בלבד, והסתר הפנים ואחור יחד

מט) אמנם ברבות חס ושלום הצרות והמכאובים במידה מרובה ביותר, הנה גורם זה להסתר כפול, שנקרא בספרים, הסתר תוך הסתר, שפירושו שאפילו אחוריו יתברך אינם נראים חס ושלום, כלומר, שאינם מאמינים שהשם יתברך כועס עליהם ומענישם, אלא תולים חס ושלום זאת במקרה ובטבע ובאים לידי כפירה בהשגחתו יתברך בשכר ועונש. וזש"ה וזה שאומר הכתוב ואנכי הסתר אסתיר פני

hide and conceal My Face [*Haster Astir*]...because one has turned to other Gods." In other words, one has come to heresy and, Heaven forbid, turned to idolatry.

50) This was not the case beforehand, where the Scriptures talk about only one concealment and end by saying: "Is it not that because my Creator is not within me that these evils have befallen me?" (Deuteronomy 31:17) This means that [here] people still believe in the Providence of reward and punishment, and they say that they deserve the trouble and pain because they do not cleave to the Creator, as it is said: "It is because my Creator is not within me that these evil troubles have befallen me." Here it is considered that they still see the Creator, but only from His Back. This is why it is called One Concealment: that is, the Concealment of the Face alone.

An evil man who is not totally evil; and an evil man who is totally evil

51) This explains the two aspects of the Concealed Providence that created beings perceive: that is, the One [single] Concealment and the Concealment within Concealment. One Concealment means only the Concealment of the Face, but the Back is still seen. This means that they believe that the Creator has caused them to suffer as a punishment, and even though they are led into transgression because it is more difficult to always recognize the Creator from His Back, as we have explained above they are referred to as an "evil [man] who is not completely [evil]." This means that their transgressions are similar to unintentional wrongdoings because they transgressed (lit. made them) because of their large degree of suffering. But in general, [such people] still believe in reward and punishment, as we have discussed.

52) And Concealment within Concealment means that even the Back of the Creator is concealed from [the people] because they do not believe in reward and punishment, as is mentioned above. In this case, their transgressions are considered to be intentional actions,

וגו', כי פנה אל אלהים אחרים, דהיינו שבאים לידי כפירה, ופונים לעבודה זרה חס ושלום.

נ) מה שאין כן לפני זה, שהכתוב מדבר רק מבחינת הסתר אחד, מסיים הכתוב, "ואמר ביום ההוא, הלא על כי אין אלקי בקרבי מצאוני הרעות האלה" (דברים ל"א, י"ז). כלומר, שמאמינים עוד בהשגחת שכר ועונש, ואומרים שהצרות והיסורים מגיעים להם מחמת שאינם דבוקים בהשם יתברך, ככתוב, על כי אין אלקי בקרבי מצאוני הרעות האלה, שזה נבחן שרואים עוד את השם יתברך, אבל רק דרך אחוריו. ועל כן נקרא הסתר אחד, דהיינו הסתר הפנים בלבד.

דרגות: רשע שאינו גמור ורשע גמור

נא) והנה נתבארו ב' הבחינות של תפיסת ההשגחה הנסתרת המורגשות לברויות, דהיינו הסתר א', והסתר תוך הסתר. ההסתר הא' פירושו, הסתר פנים בלבד, והאחוריים מגולים להם, כלומר שמאמינים, שהשם יתברך סיבב להם היסורים מחמת עונש, ואף על פי שקשה להם להכיר את השם יתברך תמיד דרך אחוריו, כמבואר לעיל, שבאים מחמת זה לידי עבירה עם כל זה, אפילו אז, נקראים בבחינת רשע שאינו גמור, כלומר, שהעבירות הללו דומות לשגגות, כי הגיעו להם מחמת ריבוי היסורים, שהרי בכללות המה מאמינים בשכר ועונש כאמור.

נב) והסתר תוך הסתר, שפירושו שאפילו אחוריו של הקדוש ברוך הוא נסתרו מהם, כי אינם מאמינים בשכר ועונש כנזכר לעיל, הנה העבירות שבידיהם נבחנות לזדונות, ונקראים רשעים גמורים,

and they are called "completely evil" because they are heretics who say that the Creator does not supervise over His created beings. And so they turn to idolatry, as it is written: "…he turned to other Gods," Heaven forbid.

Once one has finished making an effort, the Creator then helps him

53) We should know that when it comes to the [spiritual] work that one puts in to perform the Torah and the Precepts through free will that it is through the two aspects of Concealed Providence, as explained earlier. And about such a time, Ben Ha-Ha says, "The reward is [always] according to the effort." (Tractate *Avot* 5:22) This is because His Providence is not a Revealed one and it is impossible to see Him except through the Concealment of the Face, that is, only from the Back. This is similar to a person who sees his friend from the back and might doubt and think that [the friend] is someone else.

So in this manner, the free will [to decide] whether to fulfill the Creator's Will or, Heaven forbid, to transgress It is always in the hands of the individual because the trouble and the pain that he experiences cause him to doubt the reality of the Creator's supervision over His created beings, as explained above. Whether this [transgression] takes the first form, which is unintentional wrongdoings, or, Heaven forbid, the second form, which is intentional.

Whether it is one or the other, he is in great sorrow and goes through much toil and effort. And about such a time, the Scriptures say: "Whatever is in your ability to do, do it with your might, etc." (Ecclesiastes 9:10) This is because a person will not merit the revelation of [the Creator's] Face, which means the full measure of His goodness, before he makes an effort and does anything and everything that is within his power to do, and [he will gain] the reward according to the effort.

54) And indeed, after the Creator sees that this person has completed his labor and has finished all that he needed to do with

משום שהם פוקרים ואומרים שהשם יתברך אינו משגיח כלל על בריותיו, ופונים לעבודה זרה, כמ"ש כמו שאומר הכתוב, כי פנה אל אלהים אחרים, חס ושלום.

אחרי שהאדם משלים יגיעתו אז עוזר לו השי"ת

נג) וצריכים לדעת, שכל ענין העבודה, הנוהגת בקיום התורה והמצוות בדרך הבחירה, נוהגת בעיקר בב' הבחינות של ההשגחה המוסתרת האמורות. ועל הזמן ההוא, אומר בן הא הא, לפום צערא אגרא לפי המאמץ - השכר (פרקי אבות ה', כב'). שהיות שהשגחתו יתברך אינה גלויה, ואי אפשר לראותו יתברך אלא בהסתר פנים, דהיינו רק דרך אחוריו, בדומה לאדם הרואה רעהו מאחוריו שעלול להטיל ספק ולחשוב אולי אחר הוא.

הנה בדרך זאת, נמצאת תמיד הבחירה בידי האדם, אם לקיים רצונו יתברך או חס ושלום לעבור על רצונו, כי הצרות והמכאובים שמקבל, מביאים לו את הספק במציאות השגחתו יתברך על בריותיו, כנ"ל, אם כבחינה א', שהמה שגגות, אם חס ושלום כבחינה ב' שהמה זדונות, עש"ה.

ובין כך ובין כך, הוא נמצא בצער רב ויגיעה מרובה, ועל הזמן ההוא אומר הכתוב, כל אשר תמצא ידך לעשות בכחך עשה וגו' (קהלת ט', י'), כי לא יזכה לגילוי הפנים, שפירושו המידה השלימה של טובו יתברך בטרם שישתדל ויעשה, כל מה, שאך בידו ובכחו לעשות, ולפום צערא אגרא ולפי היגיעה - השכר.

נד) אמנם אחר שרואה השם יתברך, שהאדם השלים מידת יגיעתו, וגמר כל מה שהיה עליו לעשות בכח בחירתו והתחזקותו באמונת

the power of his free will and an increasing strength in his trust in the Creator, then the Creator helps him and he merits the attainment of the visible Providence, that is, the Revelation of the Face. And then he gains complete repentance (*teshuvah*), which means that he "returns" (*shav*) and once again cleaves to the Creator with all his heart, soul, and might. It is as if he is drawn from the side of being aware of the visible Providence.

By perceiving Providence the person becomes confident in himself that he shall not sin

55) The aforementioned awareness and repentance come to a person in two stages. The first [stage] is an absolute perception of Providence of reward and punishment. Besides perceiving very clearly what the reward of each precept is for the World to Come, he is also gifted with wonderful delight immediately in this world during the fulfillment of the precept. And furthermore, besides receiving the bitter punishment, which will come about (lit. being drawn) after his death for every transgression [he made during his lifetime], he also gains the ability to feel the bitter taste of every transgression even while he is still alive.

And of course, a person who merits this visible Providence is very sure in himself that he will never again commit any sin, just like a person who surely will not cut his own limbs and cause himself tremendous agony. And he also becomes very sure in himself that he will not leave any precept unfulfilled immediately as it comes his way, just like a person who surely will not neglect [to avail himself of] any pleasure or any great profit that comes his way in this world.

Repentance (*Teshuvah*): Testimony of the Creator and the revelation of the aspect of the Face

56) By this, you will understand what our sages said: "How do we know that repentance (*teshuvah*) [has been done]?"—"When He Who knows all mysteries bears witness that [a sinner] will not return to his foolishness again." (According to Psalms, 85:9) These appear

השם יתברך, אז עוזר לו השם יתברך, וזוכה להשגת ההשגחה הגלויה, דהיינו לגילוי פנים, ואז זוכה לתשובה שלימה, שפירושה ש"שב" ומתדבק בהשם יתברך בכל לב, נפש ומאד, כמו שנמשך מאליו מצד ההשגה של ההשגחה הגלויה.

בהשגת ההשגחה האדם בטוח בעצמו שלא יחטא

נה) והנה השגה זאת ותשובה זו האמורות, באות לו לאדם בב' מדרגות, שהראשונה היא, השגת השגחת שכר ועונש בהחלט, ומלבד שמשיג בהשגה ברורה את שכרה של כל מצוה לעולם הבא, זוכה גם כן להשיג התענוג הנפלא שבעת קיום המצוה, תיכף בעולם הזה. וכן מלבד שמשיג העונש המר, הנמשך מכל עבירה לאחר מיתתו, זוכה גם כן להרגיש את טעמה המר של כל עבירה, גם כן בעוד בחיים חיתו.

ומובן מאליו, שהזוכה להשגחה הגלויה הזאת, בטוח בעצמו שלא יחטא עוד, כמו שאדם בטוח שלא יחתוך באבריו ויגרום לעצמו יסורים נוראים. וכן בטוח בעצמו, שלא יעזוב המצוה מלקיימה תיכף כשבאה לידו, כמו שהאדם בטוח, שלא יעזוב שום תענוג העולם הזה או ריוח גדול הבא לידו.

תשובה: עדות השי"ת וגילוי בחינת פנים

נו) ובזה תבין מ"ש ז"ל מה שאמרו חכמינו זכרונם לברכה, היכי דמי מה היא תשובה, עד שיעיד עליו יודע תעלומות שלא ישוב לכסלו עוד (לפי תהילים, פה, ט'). שלכאורה הדברים מתמיהים, שאם כן, מי יעלה

to be surprising words because if [they are true], who can ascend to Heaven to hear the testimony of the Creator, and before whom does the Creator have to give this testimony? Is it not enough that the Creator Himself knows that this person has truly repented with all his heart and will not sin again?

From what has been explained, it turns out that it [the answer] is very simple. In reality, prior to attaining the awareness of the Providence of reward and punishment that we have commented upon, namely, the Revelation of the Face, as mentioned above, one is never sure that he will not sin anymore. And this Revelation of the Face that comes as salvation from the Creator is called 'testimony,' for it is the salvation from the Creator Himself that has brought about the perceiving of reward and punishment, which guarantees that a person will never sin again, as is explained above.

This is equivalent to the Creator giving testimony on [the sinner's behalf]. And this is what is meant by: "How do we know that repentance has been done?" or stated differently: "How does one become certain that he has achieved complete repentance?" Therefore a very clear sign has been given, namely, "When He Who knows all mysteries bears witness that he will not return to his foolishness again," namely, that he will merit this Revelation of the Face, and then the salvation from the Creator itself will testify "that he will not return to his foolishness again," as we have explained.

Commentary from the Sages that he who does repentance out of fear, his malicious sins are turned into errors

57) This said repentance is called Repentance Out of Fear (lit. awe). Because [a person may] return (lit. repent) to the Creator with all his heart and soul, to the extent that He who knows all mysteries bears witness on his behalf, that he will not return to his foolishness anymore, as explained earlier. At the same time, however, all this certainty that he will not sin again is because of his awareness and apprehension of the terrible punishment and the awful tortures

השמימה לשמוע עדותו של השם יתברך, גם לפני מי צריך השם יתברך להעיד עדותו זאת, וכי לא מספיק שהשם יתברך בעצמו יודע, שהאדם שב בכל לבו ולא יחטא עוד.

ומהמתבאר הדבר פשוט לגמרי, כי באמת אין האדם בטוח לחלוטין שלא יחטא עוד, בטרם שיזכה להשגת ההשגחה של שכר ועונש המבוארת, דהיינו גילוי פנים כנ"ל. וגילוי פנים זה שמצד ישועת השם יתברך, מכונה בשם עדות, שהרי ישועתו יתברך בעצמו, להשגה הזו של שכר ועונש, היא המבטיחה לו שלא יחטא עוד, כמבואר לעיל.

ונבחן על כן, שהשם יתברך מעיד עליו. וז"ש, היכי דמי מההיא תשובה, כלומר, מתי יהיה אדם בטוח שיזכה לתשובה שלמה. ועל כן נתנו לו אות ברור, דהיינו, עד שיעיד עליו יודע תעלומות שלא ישוב לכסלו עוד, כלומר שיזכה לגילוי פנים, שאז ישועתו יתברך עצמו מעידה עליו שלא ישוב לכסלו עוד, כמבואר.

ביאור מאמר חז"ל שהעושה תשובה מיראה זדונות נעשין לו כשגגות

נז) והנה תשובה זו האמורה נקראת בשם תשובה מיראה, כי הגם ששב אל השם יתברך בכל לב ונפש, עד שמעיד עליו יודע תעלומות שלא ישוב לכסלו עוד, כמבואר, עם כל זה הרי כל הבטחון הזה, שלא יחטא עוד, הוא מטעם השגתו והרגשתו, את העונש והיסורים הרעים הנמשכים מהעבירות, אשר על כן בטוח בעצמו שלא יחטא

that are caused (lit. drawn) by his transgressions. This is why he is so confident that he will not sin again, as mentioned earlier, in the same manner that he is sure not to cause himself terrible torture, although ultimately (lit. eventually), this repentance and this confidence are only a result of [him] fearing the punishment caused by the transgressions. This means that his repentance is only because of fear of punishment, and for this reason, it is referred to as Repentance Out of Fear.

58) This explains the words of the sages that [say] "A person who does Repentance Out of Fear merits that his acts of malice (intentional transgressions) are turned into unintentional errors." (Tractate *Yoma* 86b) And we must understand how this is done. What has been said above [will help] you understand it well. It was explained earlier (in verse 52, starting with the words: "And the Concealment..."), that the intentional transgressions that one performs come upon him from the aspect of receiving the Providence of the Double Concealment, which is Concealment within Concealment. This means that [the person] does not believe in the Providence of reward and punishment, Heaven forbid.

But [when a person] is in the aspect of One Concealment, which means that he does believe in the Providence of reward and punishment, but due to the abundance of [his] suffering, sometimes he may be led to sinful thoughts. [This happens] because although he believes that he has received this suffering as a punishment, he is still analogous to someone who sees his friend from behind and may lose confidence and think that maybe [this friend] is someone else (as mentioned above; study that well). So his sins are just unintentional errors because, in general, he believes in reward and punishment.

59) Therefore, after [the person] arrived at this Repentance Out of Fear, that is, at a clear perception of the Providence of reward and punishment to the point that it is certain that [the person] will not sin [again], then the aspect of Concealment within Concealment is completely corrected for him. Because now he sees clearly that there is reward and punishment and it is clear to him that the abundance of suffering he has felt at any time in the past was a punishment

כנ"ל, ע"ד על דרך שבטוח שלא יסבב לעצמו יסורים נוראים, אמנם סוף סוף, נמצאים התשובה והבטחון הזה, שהוא רק מחמת יראת העונשים הנמשכים מהעבירות, ונמצא שתשובתו היא רק מיראת העונש, ונקראת משום זה תשובה מיראה.

נח) ועם זה מובנים דברי חז"ל, שהעושה תשובה מיראה, זוכה שהזדונות נעשין לו כשגגות (מסכת יומא פו', ע"ב), ויש להבין, איך נעשה זה ועם הנ"ל תבין היטב, כי נתבאר לעיל (אות נ"ב ד"ה והסתר), שהזדונות שהאדם עושה המה נמשכים לו, מבחינת קבלת ההשגחה של ההסתר הכפול, שהוא הסתר בתוך הסתר, שפירושו, שאינו מאמין בהשגחת שכר ועונש חס ושלום.

אמנם מבחינת הסתר אחד, שפירושו שמאמין בהשגחת שכר ועונש, אלא שמתוך ריבוי היסורים בא לפעמים לידי הרהורי עבירה, כי אף על פי שמאמין שהיסורים הגיעו לו מחמת עונש, עם כל זה דומה לרואה את רעהו מאחוריו, שעלול להטיל ספק ולחשוב אולי אחר הוא, כנ"ל עש"ה עיין שם היטב, שהחטאים האלה המה רק שגגות, שמתוך שמאמין בכלל בהשגחת שכר ועונש, ע"ש.

נט) ולפיכך, אחר שזכה לתשובה מיראה הנ"ל, שפירושה בהשגה ברורה של השגחת שכר ועונש, עד שבטוח שלא יחטא, הנה נתקנת לו לגמרי, בחינת ההסתר בתוך הסתר, שהרי עתה רואה הוא בעליל, שיש השגחת שכר ועונש, וברור לו שכל ריבוי היסורים שהרגיש

that came directly from the Providence of the Creator for sins he had committed. So in retrospect, it is clear to him that he made a bitter mistake then.

Therefore, he uproots all those deeds that he performed intentionally out of malice, although not completely, for [now] they are considered (lit. become) unintentional errors. In other words, this is similar to the transgressions that he committed that were in the One Concealment category; when he faltered due to the confusion that befell him because of (lit. caused by) the abundance of his suffering, [as such suffering can] confuse the mind of a person. And these are considered unintentional errors, as is mentioned above.

60) However, the first Concealment of the Face, which was his frame [of mind] before, was not correct by this repentance; this [correction] is only from this point onwards—after he has merited the Revelation of the Face, as mentioned above. But in terms of the past, before he gained repentance the Concealment of the Face and all his unintentional [transgressions] remain as they were without any correction or change at all because even at that time he believed that the trouble and suffering came to him because of punishment, as is said (see here, verse 46): "Have not these evils come upon me because my Creator is not within me?" as mentioned above. Study that well.

The level of an incomplete righteous person, [that is,] a middling

61) However, [this person] is not yet called "completely righteous." Only he who merits the Revelation of the Face, namely, the complete amount of the Creator's goodness as befits Him (as mentioned above, verse 55, starting with the words: "The aforementioned …") is called *tzadik* (righteous or just) because [this person] justifies [the Creator's] Providence as it really is: that is, He treats His created beings with utter goodness and utter perfection, in such a manner that He does good both for the good and for the wicked. [A person who] has gained the Revelation of the Face from this point on is deserving of being called *tzadik* (righteous or just).

מעודו, היו לו לעונש מהשגחתו יתברך על החטאים שעשה, ואגלאי
מלתא למפרע והתברר הדבר מלכתחילה, שהיתה לו אז טעות מרה.

ולפיכך עוקר הזדונות האלה משרשם, אמנם לא לגמרי, אלא
שנעשים לו לשגגות, כלומר בדומה לעבירות שעשה מבחינת הסתר
אחד, שנכשל, מחמת בלבול הדעת שהגיע לו מתוך ריבוי היסורים,
שמעבירים את האדם מדעתו, שהמה נחשבים רק לשגגות כנ"ל.

ס) אמנם את הסתר הפנים הא', שהיה לו לפני זה, לא תיקן כלל
בתשובתו זאת, רק מכאן ולהבא, אחר שזכה לגילוי פנים, כנ"ל.
אבל לשעבר, בטרם שזכה לתשובה, הרי נשארו לו הסתר הפנים
וכל השגגות כמו שהיו, מבלי שום תיקון ושינוי כלל, שהרי גם אז
האמין, שהצרות והיסורים באו לו מחמת עונש, כמש"ה כמו שאומר
הכתוב: (ראה סעיף מו'), ואמר ביום ההוא על כי אין אלקי בקרבי מצאוני
הרעות האלה, כנ"ל עש"ה עיין שם היטב.

דרגת צדיק שאינו גמור ובינוני

סא) ולכן עדיין לא נקרא צדיק גמור, כי הזוכה לגילוי פנים,
שפירושו מידת טובו השלימה כראוי לשמו יתברך, (כנ"ל, אות סעיף
נ"ה ד"ה דבור המתחיל [במילה] והנה) הוא הנקרא בשם צדיק, להיותו
מצדיק את השגחתו יתברך כמות שהיא באמת, דהיינו שנוהג עם
בריותיו בתכלית הטוב ובתכלית השלימות, באופן, שמטיב לרעים
ולטובים. ועל כן, כיון שזכה לגילוי פנים מכאן ואילך, ראוי להקרא
בשם "צדיק".

Yet still, because he corrected only the aspect of Concealment within Concealment, the One Concealment is not corrected yet except from this point on. As it turns out, that at that time, before he gained repentance, he is not yet worthy to be called "righteous" because the Concealment of the Face still remains as it was. And because of this, he is called an "incomplete righteous person," meaning that he still has to correct his past.

62) And he is also called a "middling" because after he had anyway gained Repentance Out of Fear, he was then made fit to merit Repentance Out of Love as well by his [subsequent] complete engagement with the Torah and with good deeds. And then he would merit the level of "complete righteous." As a result he is now in the middle between love and fear, which is why he is called a "middling." This was not the case earlier, when he was not even fit to prepare himself for Repentance Out of Love. (Tractate *Yoma*)

63) We have hereby fully (lit. well) explained the first stage of perceiving the Revelation of the Face, that is, [understanding the concept of] grasping and feeling the Providence of Reward and Punishment as the way that He Who knows all mysteries bears witness on [the sinner's] behalf, [guaranteeing] that he will not go back anymore to his foolishness, as mentioned above (verse 56). This is called Repentance Out of Fear, where [the sinner's intentional] malicious actions are considered as [unintentional] errors. And [for this reason,] he is called an "incomplete righteous" and is also called a "middling," as was mentioned earlier.

The perceiving of His Eternal Providence

64) And now we will clarify the second stage of the perception of the Revelation of the Face, which is perception of the complete, true, and Eternal Providence (*Hashgacha*). This means that [the person understands that] the Creator supervises (*mashgiach*) His created beings in the sense of Him being both good as well as the provider of goodness to both the evil and the good. Therefore, [the person] is now called a "complete righteous," and [his] repentance is out of

אמנם מתוך שלא תיקן לגמרי אלא את בחינת הסתר בתוך הסתר, אבל בחינת הסתר א' עדיין לא תיקן, אלא רק מכאן ואילך כנ"ל, ונמצא שהזמן ההוא, דהיינו מטרם שזכה לתשובה, אינו ראוי עדיין להקרא בשם צדיק, שהרי אז נשאר לו הסתר הפנים כמו שהיה, ועל כן נקרא צדיק שאינו גמור, כלומר שעדיין יש לתקן את העבר שלו.

סב) ונקרא גם כן בינוני, משום שאחר שזכה על כל פנים לתשובה מיראה, נעשה מוכשר על ידי העסק השלם בתורה ומעשים טובים, לזכות לתשובה מאהבה גם כן, אשר אז, יזכה לבחינת צדיק גמור, ולפיכך נמצא עתה, שהוא הבינוני בין היראה לאהבה, שעל שם זה נקרא בינוני, מה שאין כן בטרם זה, לא היה מוכשר לגמרי אפילו להכין את עצמו לתשובה מאהבה (מסכת יומא).

סג) והנה נתבארה היטב המדרגה הראשונה של השגת גילוי הפנים, דהיינו, ההשגה והרגשת השגחת שכר ועונש, באופן שיעיד עליו יודע תעלומות שלא ישוב לכסלו עוד כנ"ל (כאן, סעיף נו'), שזה נקרא תשובה מיראה, שהזדונות נעשו לו כשגגות, ונקרא צדיק שאינו גמור, וגם נקרא בינוני, כמבואר.

השגת השגחתו יתברך הנצחית

סד) ועתה נבאר את המדרגה השניה של השגת גילוי הפנים, שהיא השגת ההשגחה השלימה האמיתית הנצחית, שפירושה, שהשם יתברך משגיח על בריותיו בבחינת הטוב והמיטיב לרעים ולטובים, אשר עתה הוא נקרא צדיק גמור, ותשובה מאהבה, אשר זוכה שהזדונות נהפכו לו לזכויות. והנה נתבארו כל ד' הבחינות של הבנת

101

love. So now his malicious actions become virtuous. Thus we have explained all four aspects of understanding the [Creator's] Providence, which are common among created beings. And we have seen that the first three aspects—Double Concealment, One Concealment, and Perception of Providence Over Reward and Punishment—are but preparations through which one gains the fourth aspect, which is the perception of the true and eternal Providence, which shall be clarified further on, with the Creator's help.

65) And we should understand why the third degree [of Providence], which is the Perception of Providence Over Reward and Punishment, is not enough for someone. As we have said, [this degree] is one in which He Who knows all mysteries bears witness on [the sinner's] behalf, [guaranteeing] that he will not sin again, so why is he still called a "middling" or an "incomplete righteous?" Since this name proves that his [spiritual] work is not yet desired in the eyes the Creator, and there still [must be] some lack and some defect in his Torah [engagement] and his [spiritual] work.

Explaining the Precept to love the Creator

66) Let us start to clarify the question that some commentators have raised regarding the Precept of loving the Creator. How could the Holy Torah impose us to perform a commandment that we are completely incapable of fulfilling? It is completely possible for a human being to force himself and commit himself to do anything—but when it comes to love, no coercion and no enforcement in the world can help. And they explain that once a person performs all the 612 Precepts according to the *Halachah* [in an explicit and proper manner], then a love for the Creator is automatically afforded (lit. drawn upon) him, and therefore, it is considered within his reach to fulfill [this Commandment] because he is able to force [himself] and commit himself to performing the 612 Precepts and doing them properly. And thus he gains a love for the Creator as well.

ההשגחה, הנוהגים בבריות. אשר שלש הבחינות הראשונות, שהם: הסתר כפול, והסתר אחד, והשגת השגחת שכר ועונש, אינם אלא הכנות, שעל ידיהם יזכה האדם לבחינת הד', שהיא השגת ההשגחה האמיתית הנצחית, שענינה יתבאר לפנינו בע"ה.

סה) ויש להבין אמנם, למה לא די לו לאדם בבחינה ג', שהיא השגת ההשגחה של שכר ועונש, שאמרנו, אשר כבר זכה שהיודע תעלומות מעיד עליו שלא יחטא עוד, ולמה נקרא עדיין בינוני או צדיק שאינו גמור, ששמו מוכיח עליו שעדיין אין עבודתו רצויה בעיני השם יתברך, ועדיין נמצא חסרון ופגם בבחינת התורה והעבודה שלו.

ביאור תוכן מצוות אהבת ה'

סו) ונקדים לברר מה שהקשו המפרשים על המצוה של אהבת ה', כי איך חייבה אותנו התורה הקדושה במצוה שאין בידינו לקיימה כלל, שהרי על הכל אפשר לו לאדם, שיכוף את עצמו וישעבד את עצמו לקיימו, אבל על אהבה, אינם מועילים שום שעבוד וכפיה שבעולם. ותירצו, שמתוך שהאדם מקיים את כל תרי"ב (612) המצוות כהלכתן, נמשכת לו אהבת השם מאליה, ולפיכך נחשבת לו כמו בידו לקיימה, שהרי יכול לשעבד ולכוף את עצמו בתרי"ב (612) המצוות שיקיימן. כהלכתן, שאז זוכה גם באהבת ה'.

67) Indeed, these words require a more comprehensive explanation because ultimately love for the Creator should have not been put to us (lit. reached us) as a Precept, since it does not constitute any action or commitment on our part at all. Rather, it comes by itself after we fulfill the [other] 612 Precepts. But if this is the case, the commandment to perform the 612 Precepts should have been sufficient for us, so why was the Precept of loving [the Creator] written?

All the attributes that are created in a human being are for [spiritual] work for the Creator

68) In order to understand this, first we need a true understanding of the essence of the love for the Creator. And one should know that all the tendencies and *midot* (attributes) inherent in a human being for the sake of interacting with his friends are the very same natural tendencies and attributes that are necessary for the [spiritual] work for the Creator. In fact, they were created and are inherent in humans to begin with for the reason of their final function, which is the destiny and ultimate purpose of all humans. This is in accord with the secret meaning of the passage: "…[He] Who devises means not to keep His banished one an outcast," (II Samuel 14:14) because He needs all of them [attributes] to become whole in ways of receiving the abundance and fulfilling the desire of the Creator.

And this is what is meant by the passage: "Everyone who is called by My Name, whom I created for My glory, whom I formed and made," (Isaiah 43:7) and also: "The Creator has made everything for His sake." (Proverbs 16:4) So for the time being, a whole world has been prepared for the human being, so that all these natural tendencies and attributes that are in him will evolve and be perfected by his interaction with [other] created beings, in a way that they will be worthy of their ultimate purpose. And this is what our sages said: "One should say, 'The world was created for me,'" because all the created beings of the world are needed for each individual, for they [all] are the ones who [help] develop and prepare the tendencies and attributes of every [other] individual, until they [all] are fit and made ready to become serving tools in the service of His [spiritual] work.

סז) אמנם דבריהם אלו צריכים עוד לביאור רחב, כי סוף סוף לא היתה אהבת ה' צריכה להגיע לנו בבחינת מצוה, מאחר שאין לנו בה שום מעשה ושעבוד כלל מידינו אלא שבאה מאליה אחר שנשלמים בתרי"ב (612) המצוות. ואם כן די לנו ומספיק לגמרי הציווי של תרי"ב (612) המצוות, ולמה נכתבה מצות האהבה.

כל המדות שנבראו באדם הם בשביל עבודת השי"ת

סח) וכדי להבין זאת, צריכים מקודם להבנה אמיתית במהותה של אהבת ה' עצמה. ויש לדעת, שכל הנטיות והמדות הטבעות באדם לשמש עמהן כלפי חבריו, הנה כל אלו הנטיות והמדות הטבעיות כולן נחוצות לעבודת השם יתברך, ומתחילה לא נבראו והוטבעו באדם, אלא רק משום תפקידן הסופי האמור, שהוא תכלית וסוף כל האדם, בסו"ה בסוד הכתוב (שמואל ב, יד', יד'): ולא ידח ממנו נדח, אשר אז צריך להם לכולם, כדי להשתלם עמהם בדרכי קבלת השפע, ולהשלים חפץ ה'.

וז"ש וזה שכתוב: כל הנקרא בשמי ולכבודי בראתיו וגו' (ישעיה מ"ג ז'), וכן כל פעל ה' למענהו וגו' (משלי ט"ז ד'), אלא שבינתים הוכן לו לאדם עולם מלא, כדי שכל אלו הנטיות והמדות הטבעיות שבו, יתפתחו וישתלמו על ידי שיתעסק בהן עם הבריות, באופן, שיהיו ראויים לתכליתם וז"ש וזה שאמרו חז"ל, חייב אדם לומר בשבילי נברא העולם, משום שכל בריות העולם נחוצים ליחיד, שהמה המפתחים ומכשירים את נטיותיו ומדותיו, של כל אדם יחיד, עד שיוכשרו ויעשו לכלי שרת לעבודתו יתברך.

Chapter Six
A Life of Love

Four attributes [levels] of love between a person and his friend

69) This being the case, we must understand [how] the essence of loving the Creator [arises] out of the attributes [levels] of love that one applies to his friend. This is because love for the Creator, of necessity, flows through these attributes as well because they were embedded in humans from the beginning only for the Sake (lit. Name) of the Creator as explained above. And when we look at the attributes of love between one person and his friend, we will find in it four levels of love, one above the other; that is to say, two that are four [two attributes, each divided into two.

70) The first [attribute] is Love that Depends on Something [conditional love], which means that because of an abundance of goodness, pleasure, and benefit that one has received from his friend, his soul clings to [that friend] with a wonderful love. In this [first attribute of love], there are two levels. The first one is that before [these two friends] learned to know and love each other, they had caused some harm to each other, but they do not want to remember that because "love covers up all faults." (Proverbs 10:12) And the second level is that they have always done only good to each other and brought benefit to each other, and no trace of harm or misdoing has ever occurred between them.

72) The second [attribute] is Love that Does Not Depend on Anything [unconditional love], which means that one has recognized that the excellent quality of his friend is superb and goes far beyond anything that can be approximated or imagined, and out of that, his soul cleaves to [this friend] indefinitely and with abundant endless love. And here also there are two levels. One level is [love] before he knows all the habits and activities of his friend [in relation to] other people. [This level] is considered a non-absolute love because his friend may have some interactions

106

פרק שׁישׁי
וּיים עֹל אהבה

ארבע מדות של אהבה שבין אדם לרעהו

סט) וכיון שכן, הרי יש לנו להבין את מהותה של אהבת ה', מתוך מדות האהבה, שהאדם נוהג בהן כלפי חברו, אשר בהכרח גם אהבת ה' מושפעת במדות אלו, כי מתחילה לא הוטבעו באדם אלא לשמו יתברך, כמבואר לעיל. וכשנתבונן במדות האהבה שבין איש לרעהו, נמצא בהן ד' מדות של אהבה, זו למעלה מזו, כלומר, שתים שהן.

ע) הא' היא אהבה התלויה בדבר, שפירושה, אשר מרוב טובה ותענוג ותועלת שקיבל מחברו, דבקה בו נפשו בו באהבה נפלאה. ובזה ב' מדות: מידת א', שבטרם שהכירו ונתאהבו זה בזה, גרמו רעות אחד לחברו, אלא שאינם רוצים לזכור אותן, משום שעל כל פשעים תכסה אהבה (משלי, יב'). ומידה ב' היא, שמעודם עשו טובות ותועלת זה לזה, ושום זכר של נזק ורעה כלשהם איננו ביניהם מעולם.

עב) הב' היא, אהבה שאינה תלויה בדבר, שפירושה, שהכיר מעלת חברו, שהיא מצויינת ועולה בהפלגה גדולה על כל המשוער והמדומה, שמתוך כך דבקה נפשו בו באהבה רבה לאין קץ. וגם כאן, יש ב' מידות: מידה א' היא, בטרם שמכיר כל הליכותיו ועסקיו של חברו עם אחרים שאז נבחנת אהבה זו, לאהבה בלתי מוחלטת, משום שנמצא לחברו אילו עסקים עם אחרים, שבשטחיות נדמה

107

with others, which at first (lit. shallow) sight [give the appearance] that his carelessness causes them harm and wrong in such a manner that if the loving person would see them, then the excellence of his friend would be tarnished [in his eyes], and the love between them would be ruined. But so far, he has not seen these activities and therefore, their love [for each other] is complete, great, and exceedingly wondrous.

73) **The second level** in Love that Does Not Depend on Anything is the fourth level of love in general. It also comes from the recognition of the high quality of his friend, as stated above (see here, verse 72), except that now added to it is the fact that he knows about all of his [friend's] activities and interactions with everyone; none are hidden. And he has investigated and found out that not only do they not have any defect in them, but his goodness surpasses them without end, and goes way beyond all that is approximated or imagined, and now [his love for his friend] is "eternal and absolute love."

The four attributes of the love between man and the Divine Presence

74) **These** four attributes [levels] of love that occur between a person and his friend also occur between a person and the Creator. Not only so, but they have appeared here in stages, in the loving for the Creator, by the way of cause and effect. It is impossible to achieve any of [the higher levels] before one has achieved the first attributeof Love that Depends on Something [conditional love]. Once [the person] has gained this [level] completely, then this first level [of attributes] becomes the springboard (lit. cause) for him gaining the second, and after he has gained the second and reached its end, [the second level] then becomes the springboard (lit. cause) for him gaining the third level, and then the third leads to the fourth, [culminating in] the eternal love.

75) **This raises** a question: How can it be possible (lit. pictured) for a person to merit the first degree of loving the Creator, which is the first attribute of Love that Depends on Something, referring to

כמי שגורם להם רעות ונזק מתוך התרשלות, באופן, שאם היה
האוהב רואה אותם היתה נפגמת כל מעלתו של חברו, והיתה
האהבה מתקלקלת ביניהם. אלא שעדיין לא ראה עסקיו אלה,
ולכן, עדיין **אהבתם** שלימה וגדולה בהפלאה יתירה.

עג) מידה ב" באהבה שאינה תלויה בדבר, היא המידה הד" של
האהבה בכללה, היא באה גם כן מהכרת מעלה שבחברו כנ"ל (בסעיף
הקודם), אלא נוסף על זאת עתה מכיר הוא כל עסקיו והליכותיו
עם כל אדם, אף אחד מהם לא יחסר, ובדק ומצא שלא לבד שאין
בהם שמץ דופי, אלא, טובתו מרובה עליהם לאין קץ, ועולה על כל
המשוער והמדומה, ועתה היא "אהבה נצחית ומוחלטת".

ארבע מידות של אהבה בין אדם למקום

עד) והנה כל אלו ד' המידות של האהבה, הנוהגות בין איש לרעהו,
המה נוהגות גם כן בין האדם למקום. ולא עוד, אלא שהמה נעשו
כאן באהבת ה', בבחינת מדרגות, על דרך סיבה ומסובב, ואי אפשר
לזכות בשום אחת מהן, בטרם שיזכה למידה הא' של האהבה
התלויה בדבר, ואחר שזכה בה על על שלימותה, המידה הא' הזאת
מסבבת לו לזכות במידה הב', ואחר שזכה בה במידה הב' והגיע
לסופה, הרי היא מסבבת לו לזכות במידה הג', וכן המידה הג'
למידה הד', לאהבה הנצחית.

עה) ולפי זה מתעוררת השאלה, איך יצוייר לו לאדם לזכות למדרגה
ראשונה של אהבת ה', שהיא מידה א' של האהבה התלויה בדבר,

[the conditional] love that comes out of the great goodness that he received from his loved one when we know that "the reward is not received in this world?" (see verse 44)

And even more so, [how can this be possible] when according to what has been explained, everyone has to pass through the first two aspects of Providence in the mode of the Concealment of the Face, which means that His Face, that is, His goodness—since it is the nature of the good to bestow goodness—was hidden at that time, as is mentioned above (verse 47 starting from the words: "At first…") study that well. And this is why we receive sorrow and suffering (see there).

Indeed, it has been explained that the entire engagement in the Torah and in the [spiritual] work through free will occurs mainly during the time of the Concealment of the Face (see here, verses 47-48). This being the case, how can we imagine that one can gain the second level of Love that Depends on Something—meaning that from the start up to this very day, the loved person has only done him abundant and marvelous favors, and has not caused him any trace of evil of any kind—to say nothing about gaining the third and fourth degrees?

Interpreting the words of our sages: "You shall see your world in your lifetime, etc."

76) We have indeed dived into very deep waters, and at least we should come out with a precious pearl. Therefore, we will interpret the words of our sages (Tractate *Berachot* 17a). "Our sages were departing from the house of Rav Ami and some [other sages] say of Rav Hanina—they said to him as follows: "Definitely, you shall see your world in your lifetime! And you are destined for the life in the World to Come, etc… and your steps will hasten to listen to the words of the Ancient One." End of quote [from the Talmud].

And this demands a [deeper] understanding: Why did they not say, "You will **receive** your world in your lifetime," but rather, "You will **see**?" And if they came to bless, they should have blessed fully, that

שפירושה, אהבה הבאה מחמת רוב טובה שהשיג מהנאהב בעת שקיימא לן, שכר מצוה בהאי עלמא ליכא שכר מצוה לא קיים בעולם הזה (ראה סעיף מד').

ומכל שכן לפי המתבאר, שכל אדם מוכרח לעבור, דרך ב' הבחינות הראשונות של ההשגחה בדרך הסתר פנים, שפירושה, שהפנים שלו יתברך, דהיינו, מידת טובו יתברך, שמדרך הטוב להיטיב, הן נסתרות באותו זמן, כנ"ל, (אות סעיף מ"ז ד"ה דבור המתחיל [במילה] ומתחילה) עש"ה עיין שם היטב, ולפיכך מקבלים אז צער ויסורים ע"ש.

אמנם נתבאר, שכל העסק בתורה ובעבודה דרך בחירה, נוהגים בעיקר בזמן ההוא של הסתר פנים, ע"ש עיין שם (סעיף מז'-מח'). ואם כן איך יצוייר, שיזכה למידה ב' של האהבה התלויה בדבר, שפירושה, שמעודו עד היום הזה עשה לו הנאהב רק טובות מרובות ונפלאות, ולא גרם לו שום שמץ של רע כל שהוא, ואין צריך לומר, שיזכה למדרגה ג' או ד'.

ביאור מאמר חז"ל : עולמך תראה בחייך כו'

עו) אמנם כן צללנו לתוך מים אדירים ולכל הפחות יש לנו להעלות מכאן מרגלית יקרה. ונבאר על כן מאמר חז"ל (תלמוד, מסכת ברכות י"ז, ע"א), כי הוו מפטרי רבנן מבי רבי אמי כשיצאו החכמים מבית רבי אמי, ואמרי לה מבי רבי חנינא ויש אומרים מבית רבי חנינא, אמרי ליה הכי אמרו לו כך: עולמך תראה בחייך, ואחריתך לחיי העולם הבא וכו' ופעמיך ירוצו לשמוע דברי עתיק יומין, עכ"ל עד כאן לשון [התלמוד].

ויש כאן להבין, למה לא אמרו עולמך תקבל בחייך, אלא, רק "תראה", ואם באו לברך, היה להם לברך בשלימות, דהיינו, שישיג

111

is, that [a person] would attain and receive his world in his lifetime. And we should also understand why a person should see the World to Come while still alive, being satisfied with the [blessing] that he will end up with in the World to Come. And more: Why did they mention this blessing first?

77) **First** of all, one should understand what this "seeing" of the World to Come in one's life actually means, because surely nothing spiritual can be seen through physical eyes. In addition, it is not the habit of the Creator to change the laws [of Creation] that were established in Genesis. [This is] because all the orderly laws established at the beginning of Creation were arranged by the Creator in a specific manner, exactly [in a way that] they [would be] most useful and successful for the purpose desired of them: that through them, man would be able to cleave to Him, as explained earlier, as the Scriptures say: "The Creator has made everything for His sake." (Proverbs 17:4) This being the case, we must understand how a person will see the next world while still alive.

With reference to the saying of the sages that the soul is made to take the oath: "In your eyes, you shall be as 'a wicked'"

78) **Let me** tell you that this "seeing" comes to a person through the "opening of the eyes" to the Sacred Torah, as it is written: "Open my eyes, that I may behold wondrous things out of Your Torah." (Psalms 119:18) And this is why the soul is made to take an oath before it enters your body (Tractate *Niddah*, 30b) that even if the whole world tells you that you are a righteous and virtuous person, you should appear wicked "in your eyes." [The oath] emphasizes "in your eyes" because as long as you have not gained the "opening of the eyes" to the Torah, you should consider yourself wicked. And you should not delude yourself by the great reputation you have obtained for being righteous. So this makes it clear why "you shall see your world with your own eyes" was [set to be] at the beginning of the blessings, because prior to that, one does not even merit the degree of being an "incomplete righteous."

ויקבל עולמו בחייו. ועוד יש להבין בכלל, למה לו לאדם לראות העולם הבא שלו בחייו, המצער הוא אשר אחריתו לחיי העולם הבא. ועוד, למה העמידו ברכה זו בראשונה.

עז) והנה קודם כל צריכים להבין, ראיה זו של העולם הבא שלו בחייו, איך היא. כי ודאי, שבעינים הגשמיות אין רואים שום דבר רוחני, גם אין מדרכו של השם יתברך לשנות סדרי בראשית, כי כל סדרי בראשית מתחילתם, לא סדרם השם יתברך בסדרים הללו, אלא משום, שהמה המוצלחים ביותר לתכלית הנרצית מהם, דהיינו, שיזכה האדם על ידיהם להתדבק בו יתברך כנ"ל, כמ"ש כמו שכתוב (משלי טז', ד'): כל פעל ה' למענהו. וא"כ ואם כן, יש להבין, איך יצוייר לאדם, ראיית עולמו בחייו.

במאמר חז"ל שמשביעים להנשמה "תהיה בעיניך כרשע"

עח) ואומר לך שראיה זו מגיעה לו לאדם על ידי "פקיחת עינים" בתורה הקדושה, עד"ה על דרך הכתוב (תהלים קיט', יח'): "גל עיני" ואביטה נפלאות מתורתך. ועל דבר זה משביעים לה לנשמה, בטרם ביאתה לגוף (מסכת נדה דף ל' ע"ב), אשר אפילו כל העולם יאמרו לך שצדיק אתה, תהיה "בעיניך" כרשע. דהיינו בעיניך דוקא, פירוש כל עוד שלא זכית לפקיחת "עינים" בתורה, תחזיק את עצמך כרשע, ובל תשטה את עצמך מכח הפרסום שיש לך בכל העולם לצדיק, ובזה תבין גם כן, למה העמידו הברכה של עולמך תראה בחייך בראש הברכות, כי לפני זה, אינו זוכה אפילו לבחינת "צדיק שאינו גמור".

79) Indeed, this should be understood properly: If someone truly knows that he has already followed and learned the entire Torah; and if the whole world has, likewise, agreed with him on that, why would all this not be sufficient? Rather, he is being forced (lit. sworn) to continuously consider himself as "a wicked." And because he is missing the wondrous stage of the "opening of the eyes" to the Torah, [thus] enabling him to see his world while still alive, you consider him wicked—this is very peculiar!

The virtue of spiritually working for the Creator out of free will and effort

80) The four ways that people conceive of [the Creator's] Providence have been explained, and these include two from the category of the Concealment of the Face and two from the category of the Revelation of the Face. And it was explained that the purpose (lit. sense) of the Concealment of the Face from the created beings is intended (lit. with great intention) to give people space to toil and engage in His [spiritual] work—through the Torah and the Precepts—out of free will. This is because a great spiritual pleasure is being elevated [all the way] up to the Creator along with their engagement with His Torah and His Precepts, in fact more pleasure [with His created beings] than with His angels on High, "who do not have free will" who are rather obligated to perform their duties (lit. mission), as is known. There are further significant reasons to this, but this is not the place to consider them at length.

81) And despite all the said praise about the category of the Concealment of the Face, [this method of perceiving the Creator's Providence] is not considered perfection, but [is] only a transition. This is because [the aspect of Concealment of the Face] is the place from which the entirety of the perfection that is aspired for is gained. That means that the entire reward that has been prepared for man is not gained only through his effort in studying the Torah and performing good deeds during the time of the Concealment of the Face, that is, his doing these things out of free will. This [period]

עט) אמנם יש להבין, אם באמת יודע בעצמו, שכבר קיים כל התורה כולה, וכן כל העולם כולו הסכימו לו בזה, למה כל זה לא יספיק לו כלל, אלא שמושבע ועומד להחזיק את עצמו לרשע. ומשום, שחסרה לו המדרגה הנפלאה הזאת של פקיחת העינים בתורה, לראות עולמו בחייו, אתה מדמה אותו לרשע, דבר זה מתמיה ביותר.

מעלת עבודת ה' מתוך בחירה ויגיעה

פ) אמנם כבר נתבארו ד' הדרכים של השגתם של בני האדם את השגחתו יתברך עליהם, שהן: שתים מבחינת הסתר הפנים, ושתים מבחינת גילוי הפנים. ונתבאר הטעם של "הסתרת הפנים" מהבריות, שהיא בכונה גדולה, כדי ליתן מקום לבני אדם להתיגע, ולעסוק בעבודתו יתברך בתורה ומצוות מבחינת "בחירה", כי אז עולה נחת הרוח לפני המקום מעובדתם בתורתו ומצוותיו, ביותר מהנחת רוח שלו מהמלאכים של מעלה, "שאין להם בחירה", אלא שמוכרחים בשליחותם, כנודע. גם יש עוד טעמים מובהקים ביותר, שאין כאן המקום להאריך בהם.

פא) ועם כל השבח האמור על בחינת הסתר פנים, איננה נחשבת לשלימות, אלא לבחינת "מעבר" בלבד. כי היא המקום, שמשם זוכים לכל השלימות המקווה, דהיינו, שכל שכר מצוה המוכן לאדם, אינו זוכה בה, אלא מתוך יגיעתו בתורה ומעשים טובים בזמן של הסתר הפנים, כלומר, מזמן שעוסק מכח "בחירה", כי אז יש לו

is when he experiences agony because he is becoming more fixed in his trust in the Creator and in performing His Will. [Thus] the entire reward that he gets is in proportion to the sorrow that he experiences in living in accord with the Torah and the Precepts. In the words of Ben Ha-Ha: "The reward is in direct proportion to the effort [no pain – no gain]."

The secret of "Torah" is in its numerical value: 611

82) And therefore, every person must go through this transition starting with the time of the Concealment of the Face, and when that is done, he then gains the visible Providence, that is, the Revelation of the Face, as was mentioned above. But before gaining the Revelation of the Face, even though one sees the Back [of the Creator], it is impossible not to sin once in a while, as mentioned above (verse 53, starting with the words: "We should…;" study that well).

Not only is the person incapable of fulfilling the 613 Precepts because love does not come through coercion and force, but one is not even complete with regard to the 612 Precepts because one's desire 'out of fear' is not properly set, as was mentioned before. This is the secret of the numerical value (*gematria*) of the word "Torah," which is 611 (every *gematria* is the secret of the Back), so one cannot even fulfill 612 Precepts. And this is the secret of "for he shall not struggle [Heb. יריב] forever" (Psalms 103:9), because in the end, he is bound to receive the Revelation of the Face, as mentioned.

The stages of the Revelation of the Face and the level of the person who is gifted with the "opening of the eyes" in the Torah

83) The first degree of the Revelation of the Face, which is the perception of the Providence of reward and punishment in complete clarity, does not come to a person unless it is through [the Creator's] help (lit. salvation), as he is then gifted with wonderful understanding with the "opening of the eyes" to the Holy Torah. And he becomes

צער מתוך התחזקותו באמונתו יתברך בקיום רצונו, וכל השכר של
האדם אינו נמדד, אלא לפי הצער שסובל מקיום התורה והמצוה,
כדברי בן הא הא, לפום צערא אגרא לפי המאמץ כך השכר (פרקי אבות ה', כב').

סוד "תורה" בגימטריא תרי"א

פב) ולפיכך, מוכרח כל אדם לעבור ה"מעבר" הזה, של הזמן
מהסתר הפנים, וכשמשלים זה, אז זוכה להשגת ההשגחה הגלויה,
דהיינו, לגילוי הפנים כנ"ל. ובטרם שזוכה לגילוי הפנים, ואף על פי
שרואה את האחוריים, אי אפשר לו שלא יבא פעם לידי עבירה,
כנ"ל (כאן, סעיף נג, ד"ה דבור המתחיל [במילה] וצריכים עש"ה עיין שם היטב.

ולא בלבד שאין בידו לקיים כל תרי"ג (613) המצוות, משום, שאין
האהבה באה בדרך הכפיה והאונס, אלא אפילו בתרי"ב (612) מצוות
גם כן אינו שלם, כי אפילו, היראה שלו אינה קבועה כהלכתה, כנ"ל.
זה סוד, אשר "תורה" היא בגימטריא תרי"א 611 (שכל גימטריא
הוא סוד אחוריים) שאפילו תרי"ב 612 אינו יכול לקיים כהלכתן, וזה
סוד לא לנצח יר"יב וכו' (תהילים,קג', ט'), אלא סופו לזכות לגילוי הפנים,
כאמור.

מדריגות גילוי הפנים ודרגת הזוכה לפקיחת עינים בתורה

פג) והנה, מדריגה ראשונה של גילוי הפנים, שהיא השגת השגחת
שכר ועונש בבירור המוחלט, אין זו באה לו לאדם, אלא על ידי
ישועתו יתברך, שזוכה בפקיחת עינים בתורה הקדושה, בהשגה

like an ever-flowing fountain, according to Rav Meir (Tractate *Avot* 6a). And through every Precept of the Holy Torah that he had performed by toil and by his own free will, he merits seeing the due reward that awaits him in the World to Come. Likewise, [he is able to see] the great loss that comes with [every] transgression.

84) And even though the reward has not yet reached him because "the reward of a Precept does not apply to this world," still this very clear perception is enough for him from here onwards to feel the great delight of fulfilling every Precept because "that which is due to be collected can be considered as already received." This is like a merchant who has made a deal that has yielded him a large sum of money. Even though that money is bound to reach him [only] after a long time, nevertheless, if he is sure without any shadow of a doubt that the profit will reach him eventually (lit. on time), he is then as happy as if he had received it right away.

85) Of course, such visible Providence indicates that from now on, one will adhere to the Torah and the Precepts with all his heart, soul, and being, and also that he will renounce and flee from transgressions as he would flee from fire. And even though he is not yet a 'complete righteous,' as mentioned above, because he has not yet merited Repentance Out of Love, still his great cleaving to the Torah and to good deeds helps him to gradually also merit Repentance Out of Love, which is the second degree of the Revelation of the Face. And then he can fulfill all the 613 precepts completely and become a "complete righteous."

More on the saying of the sages about making the soul take an oath

86) And now the question that we asked regarding the oath—that even if the whole world tells you that you are righteous, you should regard yourself as wicked—that the soul has to take before coming to this world has become clear to us. (Tractate *Niddah* 30b, see also here, verse

נפלאה. ונעשה כמעיין המתגבר כדברי רבי מאיר (פרקי אבות ו', א')
ובכל מצוה שבתורה הקדושה, שכבר קיים אותה מתוך היגיעה
מבחירתו, זוכה ורואה בה את שכר המצוה המיועד לו לעוה"ב לעולם
הבא. וכן ההפסד הגדול שבעבירה.

פד) ואף על פי שעדיין לא הגיע השכר לידו, כי שכר מצוה בהאי
עלמא ליכא שכר מצוה לא בעולם הזה, עם כל זה מספיקה לו ההשגה
הברורה הזאת מכאן ואילך, להרגיש התענוג הגדול בעת עשיית כל
מצוה, כי כל העומד לגבות כגבוי דמי כל דבר העומד להגבות נחשב כאילו כבר נגבה.
למשל, כסוחר שעשה עסק והרויח בו סכום גדול, אף על פי שעתיד
הריוח להגיע לידו לאחר זמן רב, מ"מ מכל מקום אם הוא בטוח בלי
שום צל של ספק קל, שהריוח יגיע לידו בזמן, הרי אצלו השמחה
שוה, כמו שהגיע לידו תיכף.

פה) ומובן מאליו, שהשגחה גלויה כזאת מעידה עליו שמכאן
ואילך יתדבק בתורה ומצות בכל לב ונפש ומאד, וכן שיפרוש
ויברח מהעבירות כמו שבורח מפני אש, ואף על פי שאינו עוד צדיק
גמור כנ"ל, משום שלא זכה עדיין לתשובה מאהבה, מ"מ מכל מקום,
הדביקות הגדולה שלו בתורה ומעשים טובים עוזרת לו לאט לאט,
לזכות גם כן, בתשובה מאהבה, דהיינו המדרגה הב' של "גילוי פנים",
ואז יכול לקיים כל תרי"ג (613) המצוות בשלימות, ונעשה צדיק גמור.

עוד במאמר חז"ל על השבעת הנשמה

פו) ועתה מובן לנו היטב, מה שהקשינו בענין השבועה, שמשביעין
את הנשמה טרם ביאתה לעולם הזה, אשר אפילו כל העולם
אומרים לך צדיק, אתה תהיה בעיניך כרשע (מסכת נדה ל', ע"ב וגם סעיף
עח' כאן), שהקשינו, מאחר שהעולם כולו מסכימים עמו שהוא צדיק,

78). We asked why, if the whole world agrees with [someone] that he is righteous, why is he [still] obliged to regard himself as wicked and [the opinion of] the entire world should not be trustworthy? And we should ask even further—regarding the phrase: "even if the whole world says, etc.,"—what the testimony of the whole world has to do with this matter, since a person knows himself much better than the whole world does. So [the Creator] should have made [this person] take an oath that "even if you know in yourself that you are righteous, etc."

And especially hard [to understand] is the explicit *Gemarah* [where] Rabba said: "A person should know about himself if he is completely righteous or not." (Tractate *Berachot* 61b) End of quote. This means that there is an obligation and a practical reality in truly becoming a "complete righteous." Moreover, one is obligated to investigate this truth and to inform himself about it. And if this is the case, how is the soul made to take an oath so that it will always be considered "in its own eyes" as wicked and hence would never know by itself the truth, after our sages made an opposite demand, as explained?

Love and Fear come only after complete Divine Perception

87) Indeed, these are very accurate words. Surely the person himself, as long as he has not yet merited this "opening of the eyes" to the Torah by wondrous perception sufficiently for him to gain the complete perception of understanding reward and punishment, would not be able to fool (lit. cheat) himself in any way by presenting himself (lit. hold of himself) as a righteous man. [This is] because he still of necessity feels that he is missing two of the most inclusive precepts in the Torah, which are Fear and Love.

Even attaining [the level of] fear perfectly—in the sense that He Who knows all mysteries would be able to bear witness on his behalf, [guaranteeing] that he would not return to his foolishness because of his deep fear of the punishment and the loss caused by the transgression, as mentioned earlier—is something totally hard

למה מחויב להחזיק עצמו כרשע, וכל העולם כולו לא יהיה נאמן לו. ויש עוד להוסיף להקשות, על הלשון "ואפילו כל העולם כולו אומרים וכו'", מה ענין העדות של העולם כולו לכאן, והלא האדם יודע בעצמו יותר מכל העולם כולו, והיה לו להשביעו שאפילו אתה יודע בעצמך שצדיק אתה, וכו'.

וביותר קשה, הלא גמרא מפורשת היא (מסכת ברכות סא' ע"ב), אמר רבא, לידע איניש בנפשיה יודע איש בנפשו, אם צדיק גמור הוא אם לאו, עכ"ל עד כאן לשונו. הרי, שיש חיוב ומציאות להיות באמת צדיק גמור, ולא עוד, אלא מחויב לחקור ולידע בעצמו את האמת הזו, ואם כן, איך משביעים את הנשמה, שתמיד תהיה בעיניה כרשע, ושלא תדע לעולם את האמת בעצמה, אחר שחז"ל חייבו את ההיפך, כמבואר.

אהבה ויראה באים רק אחרי השגה שלימה

פז) אמנם, הדברים מדויקים מאד, כי האדם עצמו, כל עוד שלא זכה לפקיחת עינים בתורה בהשגה נפלאה, עד שיספיק לו להשגה ברורה בהשגת שכר ועונש, הנה ודאי, שלא יוכל לרמות את עצמו בשום אופן, להחזיק את עצמו כצדיק, כי מרגיש בהכרח, שחסרים לו ב' המצוות הכוללות ביותר שבתורה, שהן "אהבה ויראה".

שאפילו, לזכות ליראה בשלימות, דהיינו, באופן שיעיד עליו יודע תעלומות שלא ישוב לכסלו עוד, מחמת רוב יראתו, מהעונש וההפסד של העבירה, כנ"ל, הנה, זה לא יצויר לאדם כלל, בטרם

for anyone to imagine before he has reached a complete, clear, and absolute understanding regarding the Providence of reward and punishment. This means gaining the first stage of the Revelation of the Face, which one achieves by the "opening of the eyes" to the Torah, as mentioned above. And needless to say regarding [the level of] love, which is completely beyond [a person's] ability [to understand and achieve] because it depends on the Understanding of the Heart, and no amount of hard work or coercion will help him here.

88) Accordingly, the wording of the oath is "even if the whole world tells you that you are righteous (*tzadik*), etc." This is because these two precepts, Love and Fear, are given to each person himself, and no one from among all human beings, except for that person, can recognize them and know them. For this reason, when people see him as having fulfilled (lit. complete with regard to) the 611 Precepts, they immediately say that most probably he has acquired the precepts of love and fear as well. But because the nature of a human being is to always believe in the majority (lit. the world), he is very likely to make a grievous error, and this is why the soul is made to take an oath, even before coming into this world—and may it be of some benefit to us. Although, as far as the person himself, he is obligated to search and find out within his own soul whether he is completely righteous, as mentioned above (verse 86).

89) We have also clarified the question that was raised above regarding the merit of love. We asked how we could even gain the first degree of love while at the same time, "the reward of a Precept does not apply to this world." (Verses 44, 75, 84; study that well.) And now it is very clear that one does not actually need to receive the reward for having fulfilled the Precept in his own life, which is why [our sages] have clarified this point (lit. made it more precise): You "will see" your world in this life, but you will end up with it in the World to Come (verses 76-77). This indicates that the reward for fulfilling the Precepts does not apply to this world, but rather to the World to Come.

Surely, in order to see, to know, and to feel the reward that a person is destined to have in the future in the World to Come, he has to

שיזכה להשגה שלימה וברורה ומוחלטת, בהשגחת שכר ועונש. דהיינו, הזכיה של מדרגה א' של גילוי פנים, המגיעה לו לאדם על ידי פקיחת עיניים בתורה, כנ"ל. ואין צריך לומר לאהבה, שעניינה לגמרי מחוץ לגדר יכלתו, להיותה תלויה באבנתא דליבא בהבנת הלב, ושום יגיעה וכפיה אינה מועילה לו כאן.

פח) ולפיכך, לשון השבועה היא "ואפילו כל העולם אומרים לך צדיק אתה וכו'". כי ב' המצוות האלו "אהבה ויראה" הן מסורות רק לאדם עצמו, ואין אחד מבני העולם זולתו, יכול להבחין בהן ולדעת אותן. ולפיכך, כיון שרואים אותו שלם בתרי"א (611) מצוות, מיד אומרים, שמן הסתם יש המצוות של אהבה ויראה ג"כ גם כן. ומתוך שטבע האדם מחייב להאמין לעולם, הריהו עלול מאד ליפול לטעות מרה, לפיכך, משביעים את הנשמה על זה, עוד טרם ביאתה לעולם הזה, והלואי שיועיל לנו. אמנם, האדם כשהוא לעצמו מחויב ודאי לחקור ולידע בנפשו אם צדיק גמור הוא, כנ"ל (סעיף פו').

פט) גם מובן היטב מה שהקשינו לעיל בדבר זכיית האהבה. הקשינו, איך אפשר לזכות אפילו למדרגה ראשונה של אהבה, בה בשעה שקיימא לן שכר מצוה בהאי עלמא ליכא שברור לנו ששכר מצוה אינו בעולם הזה, **עש"ה** עיין שם היטב (סעיפים מד', עה', פד') **ועתה מובן היטב,** שהרי, אינו צריך לקבל ממש, את שכר המצוה בחייו, כי על כן דייקו, עולמך "תראה" בחייך, ואחריתך לחיי העולם הבא (סעיף עו'-עז'), דהיינו, להורות ששכר מצוה בהאי עלמא ליכא ששכר מצוה אינו בעולם הזה, אלא, בעוה"ב בעולם הבא.

אמנם, לראות ולידע ולהרגיש שכר המצוה העתיד לבא בעולם הבא, הוא מוכרח באמת לדעת זה בבירור גמור, בעוד בחיים חיתו,

know this truly and with complete clarity while still alive. [This realization is made possible] through his wondrous understanding of the Torah, as mentioned above. It is then that he merits at least the degree of Love that Depends on Something [conditional love], which is the first degree of coming out of 'the Concealment of the Face and coming into [the degree of] the Revelation of the Face. [This progression] is essential for him to properly fulfill the Torah and the Precepts, in such a way that "He Who knows all mysteries will bear witness on his behalf, [guaranteeing] that he will not return to his foolishness," as discussed above (Verse 56 starting with the words: "From what has been explained …"). Study that well.

Degrees of Love and Fear in a "complete righteous" and in an "incomplete righteous"

90) And henceforth, because of his effort to observe the Torah and the Precepts out of Love That Depends on Something, which comes from knowledge of the reward that he can expect in the World to Come from the aspect of "that which is due to be collected can be considered as already received," as mentioned above (verse 84, starting with the words: And even though…), he then goes on and merits the second degree of the Revelation of the Face—the aspect of [the Creator's] Providence in the world that comes out of His Eternity and His Truth. In other words, [the Creator] is good and benevolent to the evil [people] as well as to the good, so the person gains Love that Does Not Depend on Anything [unconditional love], when his malicious actions are transformed into merits (see verses 53-58). And from then on, he is called a "complete righteous" because he can fulfill the Torah and the Precepts with Love and Fear and is thus called "complete" because he has all the 613 Precepts in their completeness.

91) We have thus [dealt with and] settled our earlier question (verses 55-56) regarding the person who merits the third degree of the [Creator's] Providence, meaning the Providence over reward and punishment, because He who knows all mysteries is already

דהיינו, על ידי השגתו הנפלאה בתורה כנ"ל, כי אז זוכה עכ"פ על
כל פנים, לבחינת האהבה התלויה בדבר, שהיא מדרגה ראשונה של
היציאה מהסתר פנים, וביאתו לגילוי פנים, המוכרחת לו לאדם
לקיום תורה ומצוות כהלכתן, באופן שיעיד עליו יודע תעלומות
שלא ישוב לכסלו עוד, כנ"ל (סעיף נו', דבור המתחיל [במילה] ומהמתבאר)
עש"ה עיין שם היטב.

דרגות אהבה ויראה בצדיק גמור וצדיק שאינו גמור

צ) ומעתה, מתוך שמתאמץ בשמירת התורה והמצוות מבחינת
אהבה התלויה בדבר, הבאה לו מידיעת השכר העתיד לו בעולם
הבא, מבחינת כל העומד לגבות כגבוי דמי העומד להגבות נחשב כאילו כבר
נגבה, כנ"ל ראה סעיף פד' (ד"ה דבור המתחיל במילים ואע"פ ואף על פי), אז הולך
וזוכה למדרגה הב' של גילוי הפנים, שהיא בחינת השגחתו יתברך
על העולם מתוך נצחיותו ואמיתיותו, דהיינו, שהוא טוב ומיטב
לרעים ולטובים, וזוכה לאהבה שאינה תלויה בדבר, שאז הזדונות
נעשים לו כזכויות (סעיפים נג-נח), ומשם ואילך, נקרא צדיק גמור, כי
יכול לקיים התורה והמצוות באהבה ויראה, ונקרא גמור, כי יש לו
כל תרי"ג 613 המצוות בשלימות.

צא) ומיושב גם כן מה שהקשינו לעיל (סעיף נה'-נו'), בזוכה בבחינה ג'
של ההשגחה, דהיינו, השגחת שכר ועונש, שכבר יודע תעלומות
מעיד עליו שלא ישוב לכסלו עוד, ועכ"ז ועם כל זה נקרא עדיין רק
צדיק שאינו גמור, ע"ש עיין שם. ועתה מובן היטב, כי סוף סוף עדיין

bearing witness on [this person's] behalf, [guaranteeing] that he will not return to his foolishness anymore, and yet he is only called an "incomplete righteous;" see there. And it is now well understood that he is still missing one final Precept, which is the Precept of love, as was explained. And he is surely not complete because he still, of necessity, needs to complete the number of 613 Precepts, which themselves are the first step over the threshold toward perfection.

92) And in all that has been said the specific questions posed by [our sages] have become very clear to us. For they have inquired: How can the Torah command us to love, while this Precept is not at all in our own hands to engage with in any way, or to even touch in whatever form? Study that well. And now, you will understand and see that this is what our sages warned us against: "I have toiled and did not find, don't believe." (Tractate *Megillah*, 6b) And also: "A person should always engage with Torah and Precepts Not For Its Own Sake because from Not For Its Own Sake he shall come to For Its Own Sake." (Tractate *Pesachim* 50 and also see here verse 17) And it is with reference to this subject that the verse proclaims: "Those who seek Me diligently shall find Me." (Proverbs 8:17 and also here, verse 41)

חסרה לו "מצוה אחת", דהיינו מצות האהבה, כמבואר, והוא אינו גמור ודאי, שהרי צריך לגמור בהכרח מספר תרי"ג 613 המצוות, שהן בהכרח הפסיעה הראשונה על מפתן השלימות.

צב) ובכל האמור, יתבארו לנו היטב הקושיות המפורשות, שהקשו, איך חייבה אותנו התורה במצות האהבה, בשעה שהמצוה הזאת איננה כלל בידינו לעסוק ולנגוע בה אפילו במגע כל שהוא עש"ה עיין שם היטב. ועתה, תבין ותראה, שעל הדבר הזה, הזהירונו חז"ל , יגעתי ולא מצאתי אל תאמן (מגילה, ו' ע"ב), וכן, לעולם יעסוק אדם בתורה ומצוות שלא לשמה, כי מתוך שלא לשמה בא לשמה (פסחים נ' וכן סעיף טז). וכן שעל דבר זה מעיד הכתוב, ומשחרי ימצאונני (משלי ח' וכן סעיף מא').

Chapter Seven
A Life of Unlimited Ability

More about the words of the sages: "I have toiled and I have found, you should believe; I have not toiled and found, you should not believe."

93) And these are the words of the sages (Tractate *Megillah*, 6b): "Rav Yitzhak said: If a person tells you, I have toiled and have not found, you should not believe; I have not toiled but found, you should not believe; I have toiled and found, you should believe. These words refer to engaging in [spiritual work of the] Torah studies, but in [business] negotiations, [toiling and finding] is achieved through the help of the Heavens". And we have wondered (see above, verse 40, starting with the words: And we should first understand…) about what is said—[that is,] "I have toiled and found, you should believe"—for the language seems to contradict itself. After all "toiling" is in [the category of] the act of gaining property, while "finding" is in [the category of] something that one gets unintentionally and without any effort whatsoever. So what should have been said is: "I have toiled and I have gained ownership." See there (verse 40).

Yet, you should know that the term "finding" that is mentioned here refers to the words of the passage: "Those who seek Me diligently shall find Me." (Proverbs 8:17) This refers to the presence of the Face of the Creator, as we have learned in the *Zohar* that one cannot find Him except in the Torah. This means that by toiling in the Torah, one finally merits finding the Revelation of the Face of the Creator. (see verse 41)

Therefore, the sages were very accurate when they said, "I have toiled and I have found, you should believe." Because the "toiling" [refers to engaging] in the Torah, and the "finding" is regarding the Revelation of the Face of the Providence of the Creator (as mentioned above verse 47, starting with the words: At first…). And it was deliberate that they did not say, "I have toiled and I have gained, therefore you should believe," or "I have toiled and I have

פרק שביעי
חיים של יכולת בלתי מוגבלת

עוד במאמר חז"ל: "יגעתי ומצאתי, תאמן; לא יגעתי ומצאתי, אל תאמן".

צג) וזהו לשון חז"ל (מגילה דף ו' ע"ב): "אמר רבי יצחק, אם יאמר לך אדם יגעתי ולא מצאתי, אל תאמן, לא יגעתי ומצאתי, אל תאמן, יגעתי ומצאתי, תאמן. הני מילי בדברי תורה, אבל, במשא ומתן סיעתא דשמיא עזרה מן השמים הוא". והנה, הקשינו (לעיל כאן, סעיף מ' ד"ה דבור המתחיל [במילה] ונבין) על מ"ש מה שכתוב יגעתי ומצאתי תאמן, שהלשון לכאורה סותרת את עצמה, כי יגיעה נופלת על קנין, ומציאה נופלת על דבר שמגיע לו בלי טורח כלל ובהסח הדעת, והיה לו לומר, יגעתי וקניתי, ע"ש עיין שם (סעיף מ').

אמנם תדע, שלשון מציאה זו שמזכירים כאן, הכונה היא על לשון הכתוב "ומשחרי ימצאונני", וסובב על מציאות פניו של השם יתברך, ע"ד שאיתא בזוהר שאינם מוצאים אותו יתברך, אלא רק בתורה, כלומר, שעל ידי יגיעה בתורה, זוכים למצוא גילוי הפנים של השם יתברך (עיין שוב בסעיף מא').

ולפיכך דייקו חז"ל בדבריהם, ואמרו יגעתי ומצאתי תאמן: כי "היגיעה" היא בתורה, ו"המציאה" היא בגילוי הפנים של השגחתו יתברך (כנ"ל סעיף מז' ד"ה דבור המתחיל [במילה] ומתחילה). ובכונה לא

gained ownership," because then it could have been misleading, indicating that the gaining or the acquisition of ownership pertains only to (lit. around the) "gaining ownership" of the Torah. For this reason, they used very precise language, saying, "I have found," meaning that the intention is something over and above "gaining ownership" of the Torah, namely the "finding" of the Revelation of the Face of the Creator, as is explained above.

94) And now what was said is being clarified: "I have not toiled and I have found, you should not believe," because [this idea] seems surprising. Who would be so silly as to consider in his mind the possibility of gaining the Torah without the need to toil for it? But since everything is in the context of "those who seek Me diligently shall find Me," this means that anyone, whether young or old (lit. small and big), who seeks the Creator, shall find Him right away. This is what is indicated by the language "those who seek Me diligently." One would think that [seeking the Creator] does not need so much toiling and that even a lowly person, who is not willing to invest much effort in [study], would also find Him. For this reason, we were warned by the sages that such an explanation should not be believed. Rather, the toiling is very necessary here, hence: "I have not toiled and have found, you should not believe."

The reason the Torah is called by the name "Life"

95) And now you will understand why the Torah is called by the name "Life" (see again verse 3), as it is said: "Behold, I have set before you this day life and good...etc.," (Deuteronomy 30:15) and also: "... and you shall choose life, etc.," (Ibid.19) and also: "For it is life for him who finds it," (Proverbs 4:22) because this [name] extends to [the Torah] from the scriptural passage: "In the Light of the King's Face is Life." (Proverbs 16:15) Since the Creator is the source of all life and all goodness, life is bestowed upon (lit. attracted to) those branches that cling to their Source. This is said regarding those who have toiled and found the Light of His Face in the Torah, which means that they [will] have gained the "opening of the eyes" in the Torah

אמרו, יגעתי וזכיתי תאמן או יגעתי וקניתי, כי אז היה מקום לטעות
בדברים, שהזכיה או הקנין סובבים על קנין התורה בלבד, ולפיכך
דייקו בלשון "מצאתי" להורות, שהכוונה היא על דבר נוסף על קנין
התורה, דהיינו, מציאות גילוי פניו של השגחתו יתברך, כמבואר.

צד) **ובזה** מתיישב גם כן מ"ש מה שכתוב, לא יגעתי ומצאתי אל
תאמן, כי לכאורה תמוה מי פתי יעלה על דעתו, שאפשר לזכות
בתורה בלי שיהיה צריך להתיגע עליה. אלא, מתוך שהדברים
סובבים על הכתוב ומשחרי ימצאונני (משלי ח' י"ז) שהמשמעות
היא כל מי שהוא, כקטן כגדול, המבקש אותו יתברך, תיכף מוצא
אותו, כי כן מורה הלשון "ומשחרי", והיה אפשר לחשוב, שאין
צריך לזה יגיעה כל כך, ואפילו איש פחות, שאינו מוכן ליתן על זה
שום יגיעה, גם הוא ימצא אותו יתברך. לזה הזהירונו חז"ל, שאל
תאמין לפירוש כזה, אלא, היגיעה היא הכרחית כאן, ולא יגעתי
ומצאתי אל תאמן.

בטעם שהתורה נקראת בשם חיים

צה) **ובזה** תבין, למה נקראת התורה בשם חיים (עיין שוב בסעיף ג'),
כמ"ש כמו שכתוב, ראה נתתי לפניך היום את החיים ואת הטוב וגו'
(דברים ל' ט"ו), וכן ובחרת בחיים וגו', וכן כי חיים הם למצאיהם
(משלי ד' כ"ב), כי דבר זה נמשך לה מהכתוב, כי באור פני מלך
חיים (משלי ט"ז). בהיות שהשם יתברך הוא מקור כל החיים
וכל הטוב, ועל כן, החיים נמשכים לאותם הענפים הדבקים
במקורם, שזה אמור באותם שהתייגעו ומצאו אור פניו יתברך

with wondrous perception until they have merited the 'revelation of the Creator's Face', meaning the perception of real Providence, which is worthy of the Creator's Name "the Good" because it is the nature of the Good to bestow goodness, as we have mentioned earlier (see above, verse 8 starting with the words: We have thus...); study that well.

96) **And those** [who are] worthy are no longer able to divorce themselves from fulfilling the Precepts properly, just like someone who cannot divorce himself from a great pleasure that has befallen him. In the same manner, they run away from transgressions as one would run away from a fire (as mentioned above (verse 83), starting with the words: The first ...); study that well. And about these [people], it is said: "But you who are cleaving to the Lord, your Creator, are all alive on this day" (Deuteronomy 4:4) because His love comes to them and is bestowed upon them with natural love through the natural channels that were made ready for each person by the very nature of Creation. This is because now the branch is properly attached to its root and life is constantly being bestowed upon him with great abundance from its Source. And for this reason, the Torah is called "*Chaim*" (Life).

The virtue of toiling in the Torah For Its Own Sake

97) **Therefore,** our sages have warned us in a number of places that there is a necessary precondition for the study of the Torah: that [such study] should be specifically For Its Own Sake means that it will be done in a manner that the person will gain life from [the Torah] because it is a Torah of life. And this is why [the Torah] was given to us, as it is said: "And you shall choose life." Therefore, every person, while engaging with the Torah, must toil in it and give it his mind and his heart, and [must] find in it the Light of the Face of the King of Life. This means, perceiving the visible Providence, which is called the Light of the Face (as was mentioned above (verse 47), starting with the words: At first).

בתורה, דהיינו שזכו לפקיחת עינים בתורה בהשגה הנפלאה, עד שזכו לגילוי הפנים, שפירושו, השגת ההשגחה האמיתית הראויה לשמו יתברך "הטוב", ושמדרך הטוב להיטיב, כנ"ל (סעיף ח' ד"ה דבור המתחיל [במילה] והנה) עש"ה עיין שם היטב.

צו) והזכאים הללו, כבר אינם יכולים לפרוש את עצמם מקיום המצוה כהלכתה, כמו אדם שאינו יכול לפרוש את עצמו מתענוג נפלא שהגיע לידו, וכן בורחים מפני העבירה כבורח מפני הדליקה (כנ"ל סעיף פג' ד"ה דבור המתחיל [במילה] והנה) עש"ה. ועליהם נאמר (דברים ל' ט"ו): ...ואתם הדבקים בה' אלקיכם חיים כלכם היום, להיות אהבתו יתברך מגיעה ומושפעת אליהם באהבה טבעית, בצנורות הטבעיים המוכנים לו לאדם מטבע הבריאה, כי עתה נמצא הענף דבוק בשרשו כראוי, והחיים מושפעים לו בשפע רב ממקורו בלי הפסק, ועל שם זה נקראת התורה בשם חיים.

מעלת היגיעה בתורה לשמה

צז) ולפיכך הזהירונו חז"ל במקומות הרבה, על תנאי המחוייב בעסק התורה, שיהיה "לשמה" דוקא, דהיינו, באופן שיזכה על ידה לחיים, כי תורת חיים היא, ולדבר זה היא ניתנה לנו, כמ"ש, ובחרת בחיים. ולפיכך, מוכרח כל אדם, בשעת העסק בתורה, להתייגע בה וליתן דעתו ולבו, למצוא בה את אור "פני" מלך חיים, השגת ההשגחה הגלויה, שנקראת אור הפנים (כנ"ל סעיף מז' ד"ה דבור המתחיל [במילה] ומתחילה).

And everyone is capable of this, as it is said: "Those who seek Me diligently shall find Me," and as it is [also] said: "I have toiled and have not found, you should not believe." And there is nothing that a person lacks in this regard apart from his toiling, according to the verse: "Anyone who engages with the Torah For Its Own Sake only, his study of the Torah becomes for him a potion of life." (Tractate Ta'anit, 7a). That is, he should only put his mind and his heart to merit life, which is the meaning of For Its Own Sake, as we have explained (verse 17).

The way to reach the Precept of Love

98) Now you shall see that what the commentators inquired regarding the Precept of Love—that is to say, that this precept is not within our ability (lit. hands) to fulfill because love does not come to [a person] through coercion and subjugation—is not [really] a question at all because [fulfilling the Precept of Love] is completely within our reach. After all, it is possible for everyone to put effort in the Torah, until he achieves (lit. finds] the perception of His "visible Providence.". This is what our sages meant when they said: "I have toiled and I have found, [therefore] you should believe." And when [a person] attains the "visible Providence." love has already been extended to him on its own through natural channels, as we have discussed above (see verse 66).

And whoever does not believe that he can attain this level through his effort, whatever the reason may be, does not, of necessity, believe in the words of the sages, Heaven forbid. He imagines to himself that toiling is not enough for each and every person, which is the opposite of the saying [of the sages]: "I have toiled and I have *not* found, you should not believe." And [this person's opinion] is also contrary to the scriptural passage: "Those who seek Me diligently shall find Me," which refers specifically to (lit. says particularly] "*those* who seek Me diligently," whoever "those" may be, young or old, yet effort is surely required of them.

וכל אדם מוכשר לזה, כמ"ש כמו שכתוב: "ומשחרי" ימצאונני,
וכמ"ש וכמו שכתוב יגעתי ולא מצאתי אל תאמן, וכלום חסר לו
לאדם בדבר זה, רק היגיעה בלבדה, וז"ש וזה שכתוב, כל העוסק
בתורה "לשמה" תורתו נעשית לו סם חיים (תענית ז' ע"א),
דהיינו, רק שיתן דעתו ולבו לזכות לחיים, שזהו פירושו של
לשמה, כמבואר (ראה סעיף טז').

הדרך להגיע למצות אהבה

צח) עתה תראה, שמה שהקשו המפרשים על מצות האהבה (ראה
סעיף סו'), לומר, שהמצוה הזאת איננה בידינו, משום שאין האהבה
באה בדרך כפיה ושעבוד, שאין זו קושיא כלל, כי הוא לגמרי בידינו,
שהרי, אפשר לכל אדם להתייגע בתורה, עד שימצא השגת השגחתו
יתברך הגלויה, כמ"ש ז"ל כמו שאמרו [חכמינו] זכרונם לברכה, יגעתי ומצאתי
תאמן, וכשזוכה להשגחה הגלויה, כבר האהבה נמשכת לו מאליה
בצנורות הטבעיים, כמ"ש לעיל (ראה סעיף 66).

ומי שאינו מאמין, שאפשר לו לזכות לזה על ידי יגיעתו, יהיה זה
מטעם שיהיה, נמצא בהכרח שאינו מאמין חס ושלום, בדברי חז"ל,
אלא מדמה לעצמו, שהיגיעה אינה מספקת לכל אדם, שהיא בניגוד
למ"ש יגעתי ולא מצאתי אל תאמן. וכמו כן בניגוד לדברי הכתוב,
שאומר ומשחרי ימצאונני, דהיינו "ומשחרי" דייקא דייק, יהיה מי
שיהיה, כקטן כגדול. אמנם, ליגיעה הוא צריך ודאי.

The manner in which the Creator hides Himself in the Torah

99) From this commentary, you can also understand what our sages said: that whoever engages with the Torah Not For Its Own Sake, then his Torah becomes for him a potion of death. (Tractate *Ta'anit*, 7a and here, verse 17) Also, referring to the passage: "Truly, You are a Creator (*El*) who hides Himself," (Isaiah 54:15) since the Creator hides Himself in the Torah. And we have raised a difficulty (see above (verse 41), starting with the words: And we have...): it would be reasonable to think that the Creator would be hiding, particularly in worldly matters and in the vanities of this world, which are outside the Torah, and not in the Torah itself, because [logically] all revelation occurs there alone. The *Zohar* says (Terumah, 260), that the Creator is hiding Himself so that He will be sought after and found—and we ask further about this hiding: "What do I need all this [hiding] for?"

100) From the commentary above, you will understand well that this concealment—where the Creator hides Himself in order to be sought after—refers to the Concealment of the Face, [and is] His way of dealing with His created beings, with its two aspects: One Concealment and Concealment within Concealment (as mentioned above (see verse 80), starting with the word: The four ways. And the *Zohar* lets us know that no one should even think that the Creator wants to remain, Heaven forbid, in the state of Providence of Concealment of the Face from His created beings.

But just like a person who hides himself on purpose so that his friend [can] look for him and find him, so too, the Creator, when He interacts with His created beings in the mode of the Concealment of the Face, is only doing so because He wants His created beings to search for the Revelation of His Face and find Him. And all this is because there would not be any [other] way or manner for created beings to be deserving of the Light of the Face of the King of Life, had He not first interacted with them through the Concealment of the Face in such a way that this hiding is only a preparation for the Revelation of the Face, (as explained above (see verse 93) starting with the words: And we have wondered ...).

אופן הסתרת הקב"ה את עצמו בתורה

צט) ומהמתבאר תבין גם כן, מ"ש חז"ל מה שאמרו חכמינו זכרונם לברכה, כל העוסק בתורה שלא לשמה תורתו נעשית לו סם המות (תענית ז' ע"א וכן סעיף טז'). גם על מ"ש מה שנאמר על הכתוב, אכן אתה אל מסתתר (ישעיהו מה, טו'), שהקדוש ברוך הוא מסתיר את עצמו בתורה, שהקשינו (לעיל סעיף מא' ד"ה דבור המתחיל [במילה] והנה), שהדעת נותנת שהשם יתברך מוסתר דוקא במלי דעלמא בדברים של העולם ובהבלי העולם הזה, שהמה מחוץ לתורה, ולא בתורה עצמה, שרק שם מקום הגילוי בלבד. ועוד הקשינו, הסתר זה, שהקדוש ברוך הוא מסתיר עצמו כדי שיחפשוהו וימצאו אותו כמ"ש בזוהר (תרומה, סעיף רס), כל זה למה לי.

ק) ומהמתבאר תבין היטב, שהסתר זה שהקדוש ברוך הוא מסתיר את עצמו כדי שיבקשוהו, פירושו, דבר הסתר הפנים, שנוהג עם בריותיו, בב' הבחינות: הסתר אחד, והסתר בתוך הסתר (כנ"ל כנזכר לעיל, סעיף פ' ד"ה דבור המתחיל [במילה] אמנם). ומשמיענו הזוהר, שאל יעלה על הדעת, שהשם יתברך רוצה להשאר חס ושלום, בבחינת השגחה של הסתר פנים מבריותיו.

אלא בדומה לאדם שמסתיר את עצמו בכונה, כדי שחברו יחפש אחריו וימצאהו, כן השם יתברך, בשעה שנוהג עם בריותיו בהסתר פנים, זה רק משום שרוצה, שהבריות יבקשו את גילוי פניו, וימצאו אותו. כלומר, משום שאין שום דרך ומבוא לבריות, שיוכלו לזכות באור פני מלך חיים, אם לא היה נוהג עמהם מתחילה בהסתר פנים, באופן, שכל ההסתר הוא רק הכנה בעלמא אל גילוי הפנים, כמבואר לעיל (סעיף צג' ד"ה דבור המתחיל [במילה] והנה).

How can the Torah bring about the Concealment of the Face?

101) The verse says (see verse 41) that the Creator hides Himself in the Torah. This means [that] the suffering and the sorrow that one experiences during the period of the Concealment of the Face is not the same for someone who has many transgressions and who has engaged [very] little with the Torah and the Precepts, compared with someone who has engaged extensively with the Torah and the Precepts. This is because the former is bound to judge his Maker favorably (lit. side of merit)—that is to say, to believe that his suffering was well deserved by him because of his sins and the minute amount of his [engagement with the] Torah.

Not so for the other: It is very difficult for him to pass favorable judgment on his Maker because according to him, he does not deserve such harsh punishments. This is even more so when he sees that his friends, who are much worse than him, are not suffering as much [as he is], as was said in the Scriptures (Psalms 73:12-13): "Behold, these are the wicked; always at ease, they increase in riches; and so all in vain have I kept my heart in sorrow." (See also verse 44)

From here, you can see that as long as a person does not gain the Providence of the Revelation of the Face he finds that the Torah and Precepts he has abundantly engaged with greatly burden him with the Concealment of the Face. This is why it is said that the Creator hides Himself in the Torah—and you should contemplate on this point deeply. In fact, all this great heaviness that [a person] deeply feels because of the Torah is only a forewarning (lit. because it is a message) of sorts. It is a means for the Holy Torah itself to call upon him to urge him to hurry up and quickly devote (lit. give] the amount of toiling that is required of him so that he can attain the Revelation of the Face without delay, as the Creator wishes; you should understand this [point] well.

102) And this is why it is said that: "Anyone who learns [the Torah] Not For Its Own Sake, the Torah becomes like a potion of death for him." Not only does he not come out of the aspect of the Concealment of the Face into the Revelation of the Face,

איך התורה יכולה לגרום להסתר פנים

קא) וז״ש וזה שנאמר בסעיף מא', שהקדוש ברוך הוא מסתיר את עצמו
בתורה. כי ענין היסורים והצער, שהאדם משיג בשעת הסתר הפנים,
אינו דומה, באדם שיש בידו עבירות ומיעט בתורה ומצוות, לאדם
שהרבה בתורה ומעשים טובים, כי הראשון מוכשר ביותר לדון את
קונו לכף זכות, דהיינו, לחשוב שהיסורים הגיעו לו, מחמת העבירות
ומיעוט התורה שבידו.

מה שאין כן השני, קשה לו ביותר לדון את קונו לכף זכות, שהרי
לפי דעתו, אינו ראוי לעונשים קשים כל כך, ולא עוד, אלא שרואה
שחבריו הגרועים ממנו, אינם סובלים כל כך, עד״ה על דרך הכתוב
(תהילים עג, יב'): רשעים ושלוי עולם השגו חיל, וכן לשוא הכיתי לבבי
ועיין גם בסעיף מד.

ומכאן תראה, אשר כל עוד שהאדם אינו זוכה להשגחה של גילוי
פנים, נמצא, שהתורה והמצוות שהרבה, מכבידים לו הסתר הפנים
במידה מרובה. וז״ש וזה שכתוב, אשר הקדוש ברוך הוא מסתיר עצמו
בתורה, ודו״ק ודייק כאן. ובאמת, כל הכובד הזה שהוא מרגיש ביותר
על ידי התורה, אינו אלא, כבחינת כרוזים, אשר התורה הקדושה
בעצמה, קוראת אליו על ידי זה, ומעוררתו להזדרז ביותר, ולמהר
ליתן את סכום היגיעה הנדרש ממנו, בכדי לזכותו תיכף לגילוי
הפנים, כחפץ ה', והבן מאד.

קב) וז״ש שכל הלומד שלא לשמה, תורתו נעשית לו סם המות,
כי מלבד שאינו יוצא מבחינת הסתר פנים לגילוי פנים, שהרי לא

because he did not intend to toil to deserve it, but over and above that, the more he engages with the Torah, the more he increases the Concealment of the Face by a large degree until, Heaven forbid, he falls into the [aspect of] Concealment within Concealment. And this amounts to death—[in effect,] being completely disconnected from his root [which is the Creator]—and in this way, his Torah becomes a potion of death for him.

The order to the understanding of the Torah: the Concealed [Torah] and the Revealed [Torah]

103) And here the two names that are used for the Torah—the Revealed and the Concealed—are explained, for one should understand the questions (lit. matter) of "why should I [engage with] the Concealed Torah" and "why the whole Torah is not Revealed?" Indeed, there is a profound meaning (lit. deep intention) here because the "Concealed" Torah is a hint for us that the Creator "hides in the Torah," as explained above (see verse 41), which is why it is called the Concealed Torah. And the name "Revealed" is there because the Creator is "revealed by the Torah," as mentioned above.

Therefore, the kabbalists have told us—and we have also learned this in the *siddur* (prayer book) of Rav Eliyahu from Vilnius, (the Vilna Gaon)—that the order to the understanding of the Torah starts from the *sod* (secret, also referred to as the "concealed") and ends with the *p'shat* (simple, the literal, also referred to as the "Revealed"). This means, as we have explained, that through the appropriate effort that one puts into studying the Concealed Torah from the start, he [thereby] attains the Revealed Torah, which is the *p'shat* (literal), as was well explained above. So one starts with the Concealed, which is the *sod,* secret [Torah], and once he merits [it], he finishes with the *p'shat* (literal) Revealed [Torah].

כיוון דעתו להתייגע ולזכות לו, הנה עוד התורה שמרבה, מוסיפה לו הסתר פנים במידה מרובה, עד שנופל חס ושלום להסתר, תוך הסתר. שהוא בחינת מות, להיות מנותק לגמרי משורשו, ונמצא שתורתו נעשית לו סם המות.

סדר השגת התורה: נסתר ונגלה

קג) ובזה מתבארים ב' השמות הנוהגים בתורה, שהם: נגלה, ונסתר, שיש להבין ענין תורת הנסתר למה לי, ולמה אין כל התורה מגולה. אמנם יש כאן כונה עמוקה, כי תורת "הנסתר" מרמזת, אשר השם יתברך "מסתתר בתורה", כמבואר לעיל (סעיף מא'), ועל שם זה נקראת תורת הנסתר. ו"נגלה" נקראת, משום, שהשם יתברך מתגלה על ידי התורה, כנ"ל.

ולפיכך, אמרו המקובלים, וכן איתא מובא בסידור הגר"א הגאון רבי אליהו [מווילנא], אשר סדר השגת התורה, מתחילה בסוד ומסיימת בפשט, דהיינו כאמור, שעל ידי היגיעה הרצויה שהאדם מתייגע מתחילתו בתורת הנסתר, זוכה על ידיה לתורת הנגלה שהיא הפשט, כמבואר לעיל היטב, הרי שמתחיל בנסתר שנקרא סוד, וכשזוכה מסיים בפשט.

The ways of love through abundance of goodness and love through suffering

104) What we have asked about earlier (verse 75, starting with the words: This raises a question…) has been explained well. That is, how to gain the first degree of love, which is Love That Depends on Something. We have come to learn that although the reward for fulfilling a Precept does not apply to this world, perceiving the reward from [fulfilling] the Precept is, in any case, achievable in this world, and [this perception] comes to a person by the "opening of the eyes" in the Torah, etc.

And as has been mentioned above, this clear perception is considered (lit. similar) to him completely as if he had received the reward from fulfilling the Precept on the spot, (as mentioned above [verse 84] starting with the words: And even though…); study that well. So because of this, he feels [the Creator's] great beneficence contained in the [Divine] Thought of Creation, which is to bring fulfillment to His created beings in accord with His full, good, and abundant will (lit. hand). And out of the great goodness that [the person] gains, a great love between him and the [Creator's] Providence is revealed. [This love] is bestowed upon him endlessly, in the same ways and channels that natural love gets revealed, etc., as mentioned above (see verse 47).

105) Indeed, all this happens to him from the moment of attaining this awareness onwards. As far as all the sufferings caused by the Providence of the Concealment of the Face, which [the person] endured before he attained the above mentioned Revelation of the Face—even though he does not want to remember [the sufferings] because "love covers up for all crimes," (Proverbs 10:12), they are still considered to be a great defect, even from the point of view of love between people (as mentioned above (see verse 70), starting with the words: The first…). Not to mention with regard to the integrity of His Providence, [that is,] that He is good and benevolent to the evil [people] as well as to the good.

דרכי האהבה ע"י השפעת הטובה וע"י יסורים

קד) ונתבאר היטב מה שהקשינו לעיל (סעיף עה', ד"ה ולפי"ז דבור המתחיל [במילה] ולפי זה...) איך אפשר לזכות למדרגה ראשונה של אהבה, שהיא בחינת האהבה התלויה בדבר, כי נודענו, שאף על פי ששכר מצוה בהאי עלמא ליכא *ששכר מצוה לא נמצא העולם הזה,* מ"מ השגת שכר המצוה, ישנה גם בהאי עלמא *בעולם הזה,* הבאה לו לאדם על ידי פקיחת עינים בתורה וכו', וכנ"ל.

אשר ההשגה הברורה הזאת, דומה לו לגמרי, כמו שמקבל שכר המצוה תיכף על המקום, כנ"ל (כנזכר לעיל בסעיף פד' ד"ה דבור המתחיל [במילה] ואע"פ *ואף על פי*) עש"ה *עיין שם היטב,* שמשום זה, מרגיש הטבתו הנפלאה הכלולה במחשבת הבריאה, שהיא כדי להנות לנבראיו כידו המלאה הטובה והרחבה יתברך, שמתוך רוב הטובה שמשיג, מתגלה בינו לבין המקום יתברך אהבה נפלאה, המושפעת אליו בלי הפסק, באותם הדרכים והצנורות שבהם מתגלה האהבה הטבעית וכו', כנ"ל (ראה שוב סעיף מז').

קה) אמנם כל זה מגיע לו מעת השגתו ואילך, אבל כל כל בחינת היסורים, מחמת השגחת הסתר הפנים שסבל בטרם שזכה לגילוי פנים האמור, אע"פ *אף על פי* שאינו רוצה לזכור אותם, כי על כל פשעים תכסה אהבה (משלי י, יב'), אמנם נחשבים ודאי לפגם גדול, אפילו מבחינת אהבה שבין הבריות (כנ"ל סעיף ע' ד"ה דבור המתחיל [במילה] הא') ואין צ"ל כלפי אמיתיות השגחתו יתברך, להיותו טוב ומיטיב לרעים ולטובים.

143

Therefore, one must understand how it is possible to merit the Creator's love in such a way that he would feel and know that the Creator has always done great wondrous favors for him from the moment of his birth onward, and has never ever caused him even a speck of harm, and never will. And this is the second virtue of love (as mentioned above (see verse 70), starting from the words: The first...)

Explaining the transformation of malicious actions into merits through Repentance Out of Love

106) In order to understand this, we need the words of our sages, who said of a person who has Repented Out of Love, that his malicious (intentional) actions are turned into merits (see verse 64). This means that not only does the Creator forgive his malicious actions, but also that the Creator turns every wicked action and every transgression that he [has ever] committed into the merit of having fulfilled a Precept.

107) And therefore, after a person has gained the Illumination of the Face to such a degree that every transgression he [has ever] committed—even those that he performed with evil intent— is transformed and turned into a [meritorious performance] of a Precept, then as a result, this person becomes happy and glad about all his prior experiences (lit. feelings) of bitter sufferings and pain as well as the many troubles that he has ever undergone, from the time he was under the influence of the two aspects [that is, the One Concealment and the Concealment within Concealment] of the above-mentioned Concealment of the Face. This is because it was [these two aspects] that caused all these malicious actions, which have now been turned into [meritorious] Precepts. And this is due to the Illumination of the Face of the Creator, the Wondrous Maker of Wonders, as is mentioned above.

And each and every sorrow and trouble, which caused [the person] to lose his self-control and to fail [either] by committing various errors, as in [the aspect of] the One Concealment, or by

ולפיכך יש להבין, איך אפשר לו לאדם לזכות לאהבתו יתברך בבחינה כזו, אשר ירגיש וידע, שהשם יתברך עשה לו טובות נפלאות תמיד, מעת הולדו ואילך, ולא עשה לו שום גרם של רע כל שהוא, מעודו ולתמיד, שהיא בחינה ב' של אהבה (כנ"ל סעיף ע' ד"ה דבור המתחיל [במילה] הא').

ביאור הפיכת הזדונות לזכיות בתשובה מאהבה

קו) וכדי להבין זאת, לדברי חז"ל אנו צריכים, שאמרו, שהעושה תשובה מאהבה נעשו לו הזדונות כזכויות (ראה שוב סעיף סד'). פירוש, שהשם יתברך, לא בלבד, שמוחל לו הזדונות, אלא כל זדון ועבירה שעשה, מהפך השם יתברך למצוה.

קז) ולפיכך, אחר שזכה האדם להארת פנים במידה כזו, שכל עבירה שעשה, אפילו אותן שעבר במזיד, היא נהפכת ונעשית לו למצוה, הנה נמצא מחמת זה, ששש ושמח, על כל רגשי היסורים והמכאובים המרים, והטרדות המרובות, שעברו עליו מעודו, מעת היותו נתון בב' הבחינות של הסתר הפנים הנ"ל, כי המה, הם שגרמו והביאו לו את כל הזדונות הללו, שנהפכו לו עתה למצוות, מסיבת הארת פניו יתברך המפליא פלאות כנ"ל.

וכל צער וטרדה, שהעבירו אותו על דעתו, ונכשל בשגגות, כבהסתר הא', או שנכשל בזדונות, כבהסתר הכפול (כנ"ל סעיף נב' ד"ה דבור

committing intentional malicious actions, as in [the aspect of] the Double Concealment (as mentioned above (see verse 52), starting with the words: And Concealment …)—all these are now transformed and become a platform for him and a preparation for fulfilling a Precept, to receive a great and wonderful reward for all eternity for this [action]. And therefore, every [former] agony [now] becomes for him a great joy, and every [former] evil [is transformed] into a wonderful benefit.

108) This is analogous to a story that is told by many concerning an Israelite who was a trusted worker for a certain master and whom the master loved as himself. And it happened one time that the master was travelling and appointed a surrogate to handle his business. This surrogate was an anti-Semite. What did he do? He took the Israelite and struck him five times in public for all to see, to deeply humiliate him.

And when the master returned, the Israelite went to him and told him all that had happened. And [his master] became very angry, and he called his surrogate and commanded him to immediately hand out one thousand coins to the Israelite for each time that he had struck him. The Israelite took the coins and returned home. His wife found him weeping, so she said to him with great concern, "What happened to you with the master?" He told her. So she asked, "If so, why are you weeping?" He said, "I am crying because he only struck me five times. I wish he would have struck me at least ten times because then I would have gained ten thousand coins."

109) And here you have learned that after a person has gained forgiveness for his sins in such a way that his malicious actions become like merits for him, then he also merits to approach the Creator in the aspect of love related to the second degree, where the one who is loved has never caused any evil to the one who loves him. [Indeed, he has caused] not even a shadow of evil, but rather, he keeps on doing him many wondrous favors for the entire time of his life, (as mentioned above (see verse 70), starting with the words: The first…), in such a way, that Repentance out of Love and the transformation of malicious actions into merits comes as one, as mentioned by the sayings of the sages above (see verse 64).

המתחיל [במילה] והסתר), נהפך ונעשה לו עתה, לבחינת גרם והכנה רגילה, לקיום מצוה, ולקבל עליה שכר גדול ונפלא לנצח. ונהפך לו על כן, כל צער לשמחה גדולה, וכל רעה לטובה נפלאה.

קח) וזה דומה, למעשה שמספר העולם, על יהודי נאמן בית אצל אדון אחד, שהיה האדון אוהבו כנפשו, וקרה פעם, שהאדון נסע לדרכו, והניח עסקיו ביד ממלא מקומו, והאיש הזה היה שונא ישראל, מה עשה, נטל ליהודי והלקה אותו חמש מכות, בפרהסיא לעיני כולם, כדי להשפילו היטב.

וכאשר חזר האדון, הלך אליו היהודי, וסיפר לו כל שקרה לו. ויחר אפו מאד, ויקרא לממלא המקום, ויצוהו ליתן ליהודי תיכף על יד, אלף אדומים בעד כל מכה שהלקהו. נטלם היהודי ושב לביתו, מצאה אותו אשתו בוכה, אמרה לו בחרדה רבה, מה קרה לך עם האדון. סיפר לה, אמרה לו, אם כך למה אתה בוכה. אמר לה, אני בוכה משום שלא הלקה לי אלא חמש מכות, והלואי היה נותן לי לכל הפחות עשר מכות, כי עתה היו לי עשרת אלפים אדומים.

קט) והנה הראית לדעת, אשר אחר שזכה האדם למחילת עוונות, בדרך שהזדונות נעשו לו כזכיות, הנה אז זוכה גם כן לבא עם השם יתברך, בבחינת אהבה במדרגה הב', אשר הנאהב לא גרם לאוהבו מעודו שום רע, ואפילו צל של רע, אלא הולך ועושה לו טובות מרובות ונפלאות מעודו ולתמיד(כנ"ל סעיף ע' ד"ה דבור המתחיל [במילה] הא'). באופן, שתשובה מאהבה, והתהפכות הזדונות לזכיות, באים כאחד, כדברי חז"ל הנ"ל (סעיף סד').

Aspects of Love that do not depend on something

110) So far, we have explained only the aspect of Love That Depends on Something [that is, conditional love] in its two aspects. But we must still understand how a person merits approaching his Maker in the two aspects of Love that Does Not Depend on Something [that is, unconditional love. And in this regard, we must understand well the words of the sages (Tractate *Kidushin*, 40b): "Our sages said the following: A person must always look at himself as if his one half is guilty and the other half is innocent. Having fulfilled one Precept, he is fortunate to have tipped [the scales of justice] for himself towards the side (lit. pan) of innocence; [but] having committed one transgression, woe to him for having tipped towards the side of guilt, as it is said: "One sinner loses much goodness." (Ecclesiastes 9:18)

Rav Elazar, son of Rav Shimon, says, 'Since the world is judged by the majority [of its people] and the individual is judged by his majority [his actions], having fulfilled one Precept, he is fortunate to have tipped towards the side of merit for himself and for the world; [but] having performed one transgression, woe to him for having tipped [the scales of justice] for himself and for the world towards the side (lit. pan) of guilt, as it is said: "One sinner loses much goodness." And because of this one sin that he has committed, he and the whole world have lost much goodness." (End of quote from Tractate *Kiddushin*)

בחינות אהבה שאינה תלויה בדבר

קי) ועד כאן לא ביארנו, אלא בחינת האהבה התלויה בדבר, בב'
דרגותיה, אבל עדיין צריך להבין, איך זוכה האדם לבא עם קונו
יתברך, בב' הבחינות של האהבה שאינה תלויה בדבר. ובדבר הזה,
צריכים להבין היטב דברי חז"ל, במ"ש (קידושין דף מ' ע"ב), ת"ר תנו רבנן,
לעולם יראה אדם את עצמו, כאלו חציו חייב וחציו זכאי, עשה מצוה
אחת, אשריו שהכריע עצמו לכף זכות, עשה עבירה אחת, אוי לו
שהכריע את עצמו לכף חובה, שנאמר וחוטא אחד וגו'.

רבי אלעזר ברבי שמעון אומר, לפי שהעולם נידון אחר רובו,
והיחיד נידון אחר רובו, עשה מצוה אחת, אשריו שהכריע את עצמו
ואת כל העולם לכף זכות, עבר עבירה אחת, אוי לו שהכריע את
עצמו ואת כל העולם לכף חובה, שנאמר וחוטא אחד וגו'. בשביל
חטא יחידי שעשה זה, אבדה ממנו ומכל העולם טובה הרבה (עד
כאן מסכת קידושין).

Chapter Eight
Saving the World From Chaos

Clarification of the [above] topic from the *Talmud*

111) These points appear to be difficult to understand from their beginning to their end because [Rav Elazar] says that whoever performs one Precept immediately tips [the scale] towards the side of merit, since he is judged according to the majority [of his actions]. Indeed, this refers to those people who are half guilty and half innocent, something that Rav Elazar, son of Rav Shimon, does not speak about at all, and the main part is missing from the book [the *Talmud*].

And Rashi commented on [Rav Elazar's] words, which have to do with the words of the *Tana Kama*, who says, "A person should always see himself as if one half of him is guilty and the other half is innocent." And Rav Elazar adds that he should also see the whole world as if half is guilty and half is innocent; study that well. But indeed, the main part is missing from the book. And furthermore, why did he change his words (lit. language)? Why doesn't he speak with the same language as the *Tana Kama*, if the meaning is one and the same?

112) The main idea [here], that the person should see himself as if he is only half guilty is particularly difficult:. [The following] is a wonder: If the person is aware of (lit. knows) his many transgressions, would he lie to himself by saying that he is half and half? The Torah commands us: "Keep afar from lying." (Exodus 23:7) Furthermore, he is relating to the phrase: "One sinner loses much goodness," meaning that because of one transgression, [a sinner] tips himself *and* the whole world towards the side (lit. pan) of guilt. Therefore, we are speaking about a true reality and not just some false invention (lit. imagination) that a person imagines for himself and for the world.

פרק שמיני:
מצילים את העולם מכאוס

ביאור סוגיית התלמוד שבמצוה אחת מכריע לכף זכות כו'

קיא) ולכאורה הדברים הללו מוקשים, מתחילתם עד סופם, כי אומר שהעושה מצוה אחת, תיכף מכריע לכף זכות, בשביל שנידון אחר רובו. הלא זה אמור, רק באותם שחציים חייב וחציים זכאי, שמזה אין ר"א בר"ש רבי אלעזר בן רבי שמעון מדבר כלל, והעיקר חסר מהספר.

ורש"י ז"ל פירש דבריו, שסובבים על דברי תנא קמא התנא הראשון, שאומר, לעולם יראה אדם את עצמו כאילו חציו חייב וחציו זכאי, ור"א ורבי אלעזר מוסיף, שיראה כן גם את העולם כולו, כאלו הם חציים חייבים וחציים זכאים עש"ה עיין שם היטב, אמנם העיקר חסר מהספר. ועוד, למה שינה לשונו, ולמה אינו מדבר כמו הלשון של תנא קמא התנא הראשון, אם המשמעות היא אחת.

קיב) וביותר קשה על הדבר גופו, שהאדם יראה את עצמו כאלו הוא רק מחצה חייב, שזה פלא, אם האדם יודע את עונותיו המרובים, ישקר בעצמו לומר, שהוא מחצה על מחצה, והתורה אמרה מדבר שקר תרחק. ועוד, הרי קרא קדריש פסוק הוא דורש, וחוטא אחד יאבד טובה הרבה, דהיינו, משום עבירה אחת מכריע את עצמו ואת העולם כולו לכף חובה, הרי, שהמדובר הוא ממציאות אמיתית, ולא באיזה דמיון כוזב, שהאדם צריך לדמות את עצמו ולעולם.

151

The "One Precept" is the Precept of Love

113) And [something else] is also peculiar: Could it be that there aren't many people who fulfill one Precept in each and every generation, and still the world is not tipped towards the side of innocence? [If so], this might mean that the situation does not change at all; rather, the world behaves according to its all-time habit. Rather, we need [to explore this matter in] greater depth because on the surface, these things do not make sense at all.

Surely the *Braita* does not speak at all about a person who knows in himself that his sins are many, [thereby] allowing (lit. teaching) him to lie [to himself] that he is half and half, so as to induce him [to believe] that he lacks only one Precept [yet to be fulfilled]. This is completely not the way of the wise. Rather, the *Braita* speaks about a person who feels and imagines that he is totally a complete righteous and considers himself to be the embodiment of perfection. This is because he has already gained the first degree of love by the "opening of the eyes" in the Torah, as mentioned above, so much so that 'He Who knows all mysteries' testifies on his behalf that he will never return to his foolishness anymore, as mentioned above (starting from the words see verse 56: And from what has been explained….)

And it is to him that the *Tana* speaks and sorts out his ways and proves to him that he is not yet a righteous, but a middling, meaning half-guilty and half-innocent. And this is because he is still missing "one Precept" out of 613 Torah's Precepts. It is the Precept of Love, as mentioned above ((see verse 71) starting from the words: We have thus settled) study that well. The testimony of He Who knows all mysteries that [such a person] will no longer sin anymore is only because of the clarity of his understanding of the great loss [arising from] any transgression, as mentioned above, and consequently, is considered as fear of punishment, and for this reason, it is called Repentance out of Fear, as we have explained at length above (see verse 109 starting from the words: And here….)

"מצוה אחת" היא מצות האהבה

קיג) וכן תמוה, היתכן שאין בכל דור ודור אנשים הרבה, שעושים מצוה אחת, ואין העולם מוכרע לכף זכות. כלומר, שאין המצב משתנה כלל, אלא, עולם כמנהגו נוהג. אלא, שצריכים כאן לעמקות יתירה, כי הדברים על פי שטחיותם אין להם שום הבנה.

אמנם הברייתא אינה מדברת כלל, על אדם שיודע בעצמו שעוונותיו מרובים, ללמד אותו לשון שקר שהוא מחצה על מחצה, וכן לפתותו, שאינה חסרה לו אלא מצוה אחת, שאין זה מדרך חכמים כלל. אלא, הברייתא מדברת, על אדם שמרגיש ומדמה עצמו שצדיק גמור הוא לגמרי, ומוצא את עצמו בתכלית השלימות, שהוא, משום שכבר זכה למדרגה ראשונה של אהבה, על ידי פקיחת עינים בתורה, כנ"ל, אשר כבר היודע תעלומות מעיד עליו שלא ישוב לכסלו עוד, כנ"ל (סעיף נו', ד"ה דבור המתחיל [במילה] ומהמתבאר).

ואליו מדבר התנא ומברר לו את דרכיו, ומוכיח לו, שעדיין אינו צדיק, אלא שהוא בינוני, שפירושו, מחצה חייב ומחצה זכאי. והוא, משום שעדיין חסרה לו "מצוה אחת", ממספר תרי"ג המצוות שבתורה, שהיא מצות האהבה כנ"ל סעיף צא', (ד"ה דבור המתחיל [במילה] ומיושב) עש"ה. כי כל עדותו של היודע תעלומות שלא יחטא עוד, הנה הוא רק מחמת הבהירות שבהשגתו, בהפסד הרב של העבירה כנ"ל, שזה נבחן ליראת העונש, ומכונה משום זה, תשובה מיראה, כמו שהארכנו בזה לעיל (סעיף קט', ד"ה דבור המתחיל [במילה] והנה).

The meaning of half-guilty and half-innocent

114) It was also explained above that this stage of Repentance out of Fear does not correct the person [totally], rather [it corrects him] only from the moment of repentance onward. All the agony and painfulness that he suffered before he merited the Revelation of the Face remain as they were without any correction. In addition, the transgressions that he performed [prior to repenting] are not completely repaired, but rather they are there in the form of errors, as we have explained at length earlier (see verse 58 starting from the words: This explains...), study that well.

115) And therefore, the *Tana Kama* says that a person who still misses "one Precept" should see himself as if half of him is guilty and half is innocent. That is, one should imagine in himself that the point where he cleansed himself [to achieve] repentance is the middle of his years. In this way, he is half guilty. This means that in the particular half of his years that he has lived before doing repentance, he is surely guilty because Repentance out of Fear does not correct [those transgressions] as was mentioned earlier (see verse 59). And it also turns out that he is half innocent, namely, in the half of his years since the time he gained repentance and onward. For at this time, he is surely innocent because he is certain that he will no longer sin, as was mentioned above. Thus, in the first half of his years, he is guilty, and in the last half of his years, he is innocent.

Accuracy of the language: tipping towards the side (lit. pan) of merit

116) And the *Tana* tells him to consider that if he [now] fulfills the "one Precept," that is, the Precept that he has missed from the 613 (as mentioned above (see verse 91), starting with the words: We have thus...), then he would be fortunate for having tipped himself towards the side (lit. pan) of innocence, because the malicious actions of whoever gains the Precept of Love—that is, through Repentance

פירוש חציו חייב וחציו זכאי

קיד) גם נתבאר לעיל, שמדרגה זאת של תשובה מיראה, עדיין אינה מתקנת את האדם, אלא מעת התשובה ואילך, אמנם כל הצער והיסורים שסבל בטרם שזכה לגילוי הפנים, נשארים כמות שהיו בלי שום תיקון. גם העבירות שעשה, לא נתקנו לו לגמרי, אלא, שנשארים בבחינת שגגות. כמו שהארכנו בזה לעיל (סעיף נח', ד"ה דבור המתחיל [במילה] ועם זה) עש"ה עיין שם היטב.

קטו) ולפיכך אומר התנא קמא התנא הראשון, שאדם כזה שעדיין חסרה לו "מצוה אחת", יראה את עצמו, כאילו הוא חציו חייב וחציו זכאי. כלומר, שידמה לעצמו, שאותה העת שזכה לתשובה, הרי היא נמצאת באמצע שנותיו, שבאופן זה, נמצא "חציו חייב", דהיינו, באותה מחצית שנותיו שעברה עליו בטרם שעשה תשובה, שהוא מאז בודאי חייב, כי התשובה מיראה אינה מתקנת אותם, כנ"ל (סעיף נט'). ונמצא גם כן, שהוא "חציו זכאי", דהיינו במחצית שנותיו, מעת שזכה לתשובה ואילך, שאז הוא זכאי ודאי, להיותו בטוח שלא יחטא עוד, כנ"ל. הרי שבחצי שנותיו הראשונים הוא חייב, ובחצי שנותיו האחרונים הוא זכאי.

דיוק לשון: הכרעה לכף זכות

קטז) ואומר לו התנא, שיחשוב בעצמו, שאם עשה "מצוה אחת", דהיינו, אותה המצוה שחסרה לו מממספר תרי"ג (כנ"ל סעיף צא', ד"ה דבור המתחיל [במילה] ומיושב), אשריו שהכריע עצמו לכף זכות,

out of Love, as mentioned above— are turned into merits. And then all the sorrow and sadness that he has ever suffered prior to cleansing himself [to achieve] repentance are turned into wondrous delights without end, to the point where he is sorry that he did not suffer twice as much (as mentioned above about the master and his loving Israelite servant; (see verse 108), starting from the words: This is...). This is what is meant by "tipping the [pans of the scale] towards the side of innocence (*z'chut*)" because all his feelings concerning the mistakes and the malicious actions have been transformed into merit (*z'chut*). And this is the tipping towards the side of innocence (*z'chut*) because the entire pan full of guilt has been transformed into a pan full of merit (*z'chut*). And in the language of the sages, this transformation is called, "tipping (lit. ruling)."

With one sin he loses much goodness

117) And the *Tana* speaks further and warns [this person] that as long as he is a middling and has not yet gained that "one Precept" that is missing from the 613 [Precepts], he should not trust himself until the day of his death. And he should not even trust the testimony of "He Who knows all mysteries" that he would not return to his foolishness, but rather [trust that] he might still commit a sin. Therefore, he must think in his mind that woe unto him if he commits [even] one transgression, because he has ruled himself towards the side of guilt. And then he immediately loses all his wondrous perceptions in the Torah and the entire Revelation of the Face that he has gained, and he returns to the [aspect of the] Concealment of the Face. And thus he tips himself towards the side of guilt because the merits and goodness will be lost even from the second half of his life. And on this, the *Tanna* provides him with evidence from the text: "And one sinner loses much goodness." (Ecclesiastes 9:18)

כי הזוכה למצות האהבה, דהיינו, על ידי התשובה מאהבה כנ"ל, שזוכה על ידיה שהזדונות נהפכו לו לזכויות, שאז גם כל צער ועצב שסבל מעודו, מטרם שזכה לתשובה, נהפכים לו לתענוגות נפלאים לאין קץ, עד שמצטער בעצמו, על מה שלא סבל מהם כפלי כפליים, כמשל הנ"ל מהאדון ואוהבו היהודי (ראה סעיף קח', ד"ה דבור המתחיל [במילה] וזה), הנה זהו שנקרא "הכרעה לכף זכות", שהרי, כל רגשותיו עם השגגות והזדונות, נהפכו לו ל"זכויות". והיינו הכרעה ל"כף זכות", שכל הכף המלאה חובות, נהפכה ונעשתה לכף מלאה זכויות, והתהפכות זו, מכונה בלשון חכמים "הכרעה".

בחטא אחד יאבד טובה הרבה

קיז) ועוד אומר התנא, ומזהיר אותו, שכל עוד שהוא בינוני, ולא זכה ל"מצוה אחת" החסרה לו מהמספר תרי"ג, אל יאמין בעצמו עד יום מותו, ולא יסמוך עצמו, גם על העדות של היודע תעלומות שלא ישוב לכסלו עוד, אלא שהוא עלול עוד לבא לידי עבירה, ולפיכך יחשוב בעצמו, אם עבר עבירה אחת, אוי לו שהכריע את עצמו לכף חובה, כי אז יאבדו תיכף, כל השגתו הנפלאה בתורה וכל גילוי הפנים שזכה, וחוזר לבחינת הסתר פנים, ונמצא מכריע את עצמו לכף חובה, כי יאבדו כל הזכויות והטוב אפילו מחצי שנותיו האחרונים. ועל זה מביא לו התנא ראיה מהכתוב (קהלת ט, יח'), וחוטא אחד יאבד טובה הרבה.

The degree of eternal love

118) Now You will understand the addition that Rav Elazar, son of Rav Shimon, makes to the words of the *Tana Kama*, as well as the reason he does not use (lit. bring) the language of being 'half-guilty and half-innocent, as the *Tana Kama* does. This is because the *Tana Kama* speaks about the second and third degrees of love, as explained above (see verse 70 starting with the words: The first attribute..., and then: The second attribute. And Rav Elazar, son of Rav Shimon, speaks regarding the fourth degree of love, as mentioned earlier (see verse 73 starting with the words: The second level...), which is the eternal love: that is, the Revelation of the Face as it truly is, in the sense of "He Who is good and does good [both] to those who are good and to those who are bad."

119) And it has been explained there that there is no way of gaining the fourth degree [of love] except when one is conversant, knowledgeable, and proficient with all the ways (lit. occupations) of the Loved One and how He behaves with all others, without missing anyone. Therefore, the great privilege that a person gains to tip [the scale] for himself towards the side of innocence is still not enough for him to gain the full love, namely, the fourth degree, because as yet, he still does not perceive the Creator's greatness from the aspect of "He Who is good and does good [both] to bad [people] and to the good." But rather, he perceives [the Creator's greatness] only through His Providence towards him personally, similar to what was mentioned above (see verse 107 starting with the words: And therefore...). Yet [this person] still does not know about [the Creator's] Providence in this superb and wonderful way, towards the rest of the people of the world.

And it has been explained above that as long as he does not know about all the dealings of the Loved One with others to the point that not even one of them is missing, then the love is not yet eternal, (as was mentioned above (see verse 73) starting with the words: The second level...); study that well. Therefore, he is urged to rule the whole world towards the side of innocence, for only then will the eternal love be revealed to him.

דרגת אהבה הנצחית

קיח) עתה תבין את ההוספה שר"א בר"ש שרבי אלעזר בן רבי שמעון מוסיף על דברי התנא קמא, גם למה אינו מביא מבחינה ב' ומבחינה ג' של הלשון של חציו חייב וחציו זכאי כמו הת"ק התנא קמא. כי הת"ק מדבר מבחינה ב' ומבחינה ג' של האהבה, על דרך שנתבאר לעיל (סעיף ע' ד"ה דבור המתחיל [במילה] הא' וסעיף עב' ד"ה דבור המתחיל [במילה] הב'), ור"א בר"ש ורבי אלעזר בן רבי שמעון מדבר אמנם, מבחינה ד' של האהבה כנ"ל (סעיף עג', ד"ה דבור המתחיל [במילה] מידה), שהיא האהבה הנצחית, דהיינו, גילוי הפנים כמות שהוא באמת, מבחינת הטוב והמטיב לרעים ולטובים.

קיט) ונתבאר שם, שאי אפשר לזכות לבחינת ד', אלא רק בשעה שהוא בקי, ומכיר ויודע כל עסקיו של הנאהב, איך הוא מתנהג עם כל אחרים, אף אחד מהם לא יחסר לו. ולכן, גם הזכות הגדולה שהאדם זוכה להכריע את עצמו לכף זכות, עדיין אינה מספיקה לו לזכות לאהבה השלמה, דהיינו לבחינה ד', כי עתה אינו משיג מעלתו יתברך מבחינת הטוב ומיטיב לרעים ולטובים, אלא מתוך השגחתו יתברך כלפי עצמו, ע"ד הנ"ל על דרך הנזכר לעיל (סעיף קז', ד"ה דבור המתחיל [במילה] ולפיכך), אבל עוד אינו יודע מהשגחתו יתברך באופן הנעלה והנפלא הזה, עם יתר בריות העולם.

ונתבאר לעיל, שכל כמה שאינו יודע כל עסקיו של הנאהב עם אחרים עד אף אחד מהם לא יחסר, עדיין אין האהבה נצחית, כנ"ל (סעיף עג', ד"ה דבור המתחיל [במילה] הב') עש"ה. ולפיכך הוא מחוייב להכריע גם כל העולם לכף זכות, ורק אז מתגלה לו האהבה הנצחית.

Repentance Out of Love and transforming malicious actions into merits in a person who is completely evil

120) And this is why Rav Elazar, son of Rav Shimon says (verses 110-111): "Since the world is judged by the majority, and the individual is judged by the majority [of his actions], etc." But because he is talking about all people, he cannot express himself like *Tana Kama* (the first *Tana*) and thus (lit. that he should) regard them as if half of them are guilty and half of them are innocent; this degree [of half-innocent, half-guilty] comes to someone only after receiving the Revelation of the Face and Repentance Out of Fear, as mentioned above (verses 57, 113). [In other words,] how could he [Rav Elazar] say about the people of the world [that they are half-guilty and half-innocent] when they have not [yet] gained this kind of repentance? Therefore, he may only say that the world is judged according to its majority and that an individual is judged according to *his* majority [of actions].

This means that it is possible to conclude that a person can gain the category of a complete righteous only when he is not [committing any] transgression and has never, ever sinned, and those who failed by committing sins and intentional offences are no longer worthy of gaining the category of completely righteous [people]. Therefore, Rav Elazar, son of Rav Shimon, teaches us that this is not the case, but that the world is judged by the majority [of its actions], as is the case with the individual. This means that [a person] emerges from the category of a middling—that is, after he has done his Repentance out of Fear, as mentioned (verse 88) above, then he immediately gains the 612 Precepts and he is called a middling—meaning half his life is guilty and half his life is innocent, as mentioned above. (verse 113)

And after this, if [the person] adds only one Precept, namely the Precept of Love, he will be considered as if his majority [of actions] are innocent and will [tip the balance] of everything towards the side of innocence. This means that the side (pan) of [his] transgressions is transformed into merits as well, as mentioned in the words of

תשובה מאהבה והפיכת הזדונות לזכיות ברשע גמור

קכ) וזה שאומר ר"א בר"ש רבי אלעזר בן רבי שמעון (סעיף קי'-קיא'), לפי שהעולם נידון אחר רובו, והיחיד נידון אחר רובו וכו'. ומתוך שמדבר מכל העולם אינו יכול לומר כמו הת"ק התנא קמא (התנא הראשון), שיראה אותם כאלו הם חצים חייב וחצים זכאי, כי מדרגה זו מגיעה לו לאדם רק בזמן שזוכה לגילוי פנים, ולתשובה מיראה כנ"ל (סעיף נז', קיג'), ואיך יאמר זה על כל העולם כולו, בזמן שהמה לא זכו לתשובה זו. ולפיכך, מוכרח רק לומר, שהעולם נידון אחר רובו, והיחיד נידון אחר רובו.

פירוש, כי אפשר לחשוב, שאין האדם זוכה לבחינת צדיק גמור, אלא, בזמן שאין לו שום עבירה ולא חטא מעודו, אבל הללו שנכשלו בחטאים וזדונות, כבר אינם ראויים לזכות לבחינת צדיקים גמורים. לפיכך מלמדנו ר"א בר"ש רבי אלעזר בן רבי שמעון, שאינו כך, אלא שהעולם נידון אחר רובו, וכן היחיד. כלומר, שאחר שיצא מבחינת בינוני, דהיינו, לאחר שעשה תשובה מיראה כנ"ל (סעיף פח'), שאז זוכה תיכף בתרי"ב 612 מצוות ונקרא בינוני, דהיינו, מחצית שנותיו חייב ומחצית שנותיו זכאי, כנ"ל (סעיף קיג').

הנה אחר זה, אם רק מוסיף מצוה אחת, דהיינו מצות אהבה, נבחן שהוא רובו זכאי ומכריע הכל לכף זכות, כלומר, שהכף של העבירות נהפכת גם כן לזכויות, כנ"ל בדברי ת"ק התנא קמא (התנא הראשון), ע"ש

161

Tana Kama (the first *Tana*); see here (verses 110-111). Therefore, even if his side [of the scale] is full of transgressions and malicious deeds, they are all turned into merits, and he resembles someone who has certainly never sinned and is considered a complete righteous.

And what has been said is that both the world and the individual are judged by each one's majority [of actions], which means that the transgressions that he did before his repentance are not taken into account at all because they have been transformed into merits. So accordingly, even those who are completely evil, once they have gained Repentance out of Love, are considered completely righteous (see verses 64, 106, 109, 117).

Tipping the balance of the entire world towards the side of merit

121) And this is why it is said that if the individual has performed [the] "one Precept"—referring to [the time] after Repentance out of Fear when only the fulfillment of [the] "one Precept" is missing for him, as was mentioned above (verses 110-111)—"happy is he since he has tipped [the balance] for himself and the whole world towards the side of merit." This means that not only does he merit tipping towards the side of merit for himself, through the Repentance out of Love that he has done, as *Tana Kama* (the first *Tana*) said, but it is also found that he also gets to tip [the balance] for the whole world towards the side of merit.

This means that he gets to ascend in new wondrous insights (lit. perceptions) about the Holy Torah, until it is revealed to him how people of the whole world are bound to gain Repentance out of Love, at which time the same wonderful Providence that he has achieved for himself will be revealed and seen by them as well. And the balance will also be tipped for them towards the side of merit, and then: "Let the sinners be consumed from the Earth, and let the wicked be no more!" (Psalms 104: 35)

(סעיף קי'-קיא'). הרי, שאפילו יש בידו כף מלאה של עוונות וזדונות, נהפכים כולם לזכויות, ודומה ודאי למי שלא חטא מעולם, ונחשב לצדיק גמור.

וזש"א וזה שאמרו שהעולם וכן היחיד נידון אחר רובו, כלומר, שהעבירות שבידו מלפני התשובה, אינן באות בחשבון כלל, כי נהפכו לזכויות. הרי, שאפילו רשעים גמורים, אחר שזכו לתשובה מאהבה, נחשבים לצדיקים גמורים (ראה שוב סעיפים סד', קו', קט', קטז').

הכרעת כל העולם לכף זכות

קכא) ולפיכך, אומר, שאם היחיד עשה "מצוה אחת", כלומר, אחר התשובה מיראה, שאז אינה חסרה לו אלא "מצוה אחת" כנ"ל (סעיף קי'-קיא'), "אשריו שהכריע את עצמו והעולם כולו לכף זכות", כלומר, לא בלבד, שזוכה על ידי התשובה מאהבה שעשה, עד להכריע את עצמו לכף זכות כדברי תנא קמא התנא הראשון, אלא עוד נמצא, שזוכה גם כן להכריע את כל העולם לכף זכות.

פירוש, שזוכה לעלות בהשגות נפלאות בתורה הקדושה, עד שמתגלה לו, איך כל בני העולם כולו, סופם לזכות לתשובה מאהבה, אשר אז גם עליהם תגלה ותראה כל אותה ההשגחה הנפלאה כמו שהשיג לעצמו, וגם המה מוכרעים כולם לכף זכות, אשר אז (תהילים קד, לה') יתמו חטאים מן הארץ, ורשעים עוד אינם וכו'.

And although the people of the world themselves have not yet gained even Repentance out of Fear, nevertheless, after an individual perceives the tipping [the scales] towards the side of merit, which will eventually reach them as well, in a manner that is absolutely clear, then this situation is similar to [the concept (mentioned in verses 76-77):] "You will see your world in your lifetime," which is said about a person who does Repentance out of Fear. And he is amazed and delighted by it [by achieving repentance], as we have said, and it is as if it were already in his hand because whatever is due to be collected can be seen as having been already received, as mentioned above (verse 84 starting with the words: And even though…); study that well.

And here as well, for this individual who perceives the repentance of the whole world, it is considered just as if [people] have already merited achieving Repentance out of Love themselves and that each and every one of them has tipped [the scale] of his own guilts towards the side of merit to the extent that this is sufficient for him to know [the Creator's] dealings with each and every single one from among the people of the world.

And this is why Rav Elazar, son of Rav Shimon, said, "Blessed is he who has tipped [the balance] for himself and for the whole world towards the side of merit" (verses 110-111) because from this point forward, [this individual] knows all the ways of [the Creator's] Providence with each and every created being from the aspect of the Revelation of His real Face, namely, "He Who is good and does good to both the good [people] and the bad." And by understanding this, he has gained the fourth degree of love, which is the eternal love, as was explained (above in verse 73, starting with the words: The second level…).

And Rav Elazar, son of Rav Shimon, just like *Tana Kama*, also warns [this person] that even after having merited tipping [the balance] for the whole world towards the side of innocence, still he should not trust himself until the day of his death because if,

ואף על פי, שבני העולם בעצמם, עדיין לא זכו אפילו לתשובה מיראה, מכל מקום, אחר שהיחיד משיג את ההכרעה לכף זכות העתידה לבא להם, בהשגה ברורה ומוחלטת, הרי זה דומה, לבחינת "עולמך תראה בחייך" (סעיף ע'-ע״ח) האמור כלפי העושה תשובה מיראה, שאמרנו, שמתפעל ומתענג מזה, כמו שכבר היה מושג לו תיכף, משום דכל העומד לגבות כגבוי דמי (סעיף פד' ד״ה דבור המתחיל [במילה] ואע״פ ואף על פי) כל העומד להגבות נחשב כאילו כבר גבוי, כנ״ל עש״ה.

וכן כאן, נחשב לו לאותו היחיד המשיג את תשובת כל העולם, ממש כמו שמכבר היו זכו ובאו לתשובה מאהבה, והכריע כל אחד ואחד מהם את כף חובותיו לכף זכות, עד שמספיק לו לגמרי, לידע עסקיו יתברך עם כל אחד ואחד מבני העולם.

וז״ש ר״א בר״ש וזה שאמר רבי אלעזר בן רבי שמעון (סעיף קי׳-קיא׳), אשריו שהכריע את עצמו ואת כל העולם לכף זכות, שמעתה נמצא יודע, את כל דרכי השגחתו יתברך עם כל בריה ובריה, מבחינת גילוי פניו האמיתיים, דהיינו, הטוב ומיטיב לרעים ולטובים, וכיון שיודע זה, הרי, זכה לבחינה ד' של אהבה, שהיא האהבה הנצחית, כמבואר (לעיל סעיף עג' ד״ה דבור המתחיל [במילה] מידה).

וכן ר״א בר״ש רבי אלעזר בן רבי שמעון כמו הת״ק התנא קמא, מזהירו גם כן, שאפילו אחר שזכה, גם להכריע את כל העולם לכף זכות, מ״מ מכל מקום אל יאמין בעצמו עד יום מותו, ואם חס ושלום יכשל בעבירה

Heaven forbid, he fails [by committing] a single transgression, all his achievements and wondrous goodness will be immediately lost, as it is said: "One sinner loses much goodness" (Ecclesiastes 9:18) as the *Tana Kama* (first *Tana*) said (verses 110-111).

And thus, the difference between *Tana Kama* (first opinion) and Rav Elazar, son of Rav Shimon, has been made clear. *Tana Kama* speaks only about the second and third categories of love, and therefore does not mention the tipping [of the balance] of the whole world. But Rav Elazar, son of Rav Shimon, speaks about the fourth degree of love, which cannot be imagined except through the perception of tipping [the balance] of the whole world towards the side of merit, as explained (verse 119). However, one must still understand how we attain this wondrous perception of tipping the balance of the whole world towards the side of merit.

Explaining the statement of our sages about the obligation to grieve together with the community

122) And we should understand here the words of the sages (Tractate *Ta'anit*, 11a), which are as follows: "We have further learned that when the community is absorbed in grief, one should not say, 'I will go home and eat and drink, and let my soul be in peace.' And if he does so, he is the one on whom the Scriptures say: 'And behold, joy and gladness; slay the oxen and kill the sheep, eat meat and drink wine; let us eat and drink, for tomorrow we shall die.' (Isaiah 22:13) What is written further on? 'And it shall be revealed to the ears of the God of Hosts, and surely it [this iniquity] will not be forgiven for you till you die.' (Ibid. 14)

Up to here, [it talks about] the attribute of the middling. But what does it say about the attribute of the wicked? 'Come, let us take wine, and let us fill ourselves with liquor; and the following day will be like this day.' (Isaiah 56:12) What is written after this? 'The righteous perishes, and no one takes it to heart that because of the evil, the righteous is taken away.' (Isaiah 57:1) So one should be together with the community

אחת, יאבדו כל השגותיו וטובותיו הנפלאות תיכף, כמ"ש כמו שכתוב וחוטא אחד יאבד טובה הרבה וכו', כנ"ל בדברי תנא קמא (סעיף קי'- קיא').

והנה נתבאר ההפרש מהת"ק לר"א בר"ש מהתנא קמא (הדעה הראשונה) לרבי אלעזר בן רבי שמעון, כי הת"ק התנא קמא, שמדבר רק מבחינה ב' ומבחינה ג' של האהבה, לפיכך אינו מזכיר את הכרעת כל העולם כולו. אמנם, ר"א בר"ש רבי אלעזר בן רבי שמעון מדבר מבחינה ד' של האהבה, שהיא לא תצוייר זולת על ידי ההשגה של הכרעת כל העולם כולו לכף זכות, כמבואר (סעיף קיט'), אלא עדיין יש להבין, במה זוכים להשגה הנפלאה הזו, להכריע את כל העולם לכף זכות.

ביאור מאמר חז"ל בהחיוב להצטער עם הציבור

קכב) וצריכים אנו כאן להבין דברי חז"ל (תענית י"א ע"א), וז"ל וזה לשונו, תניא אידך למדנו עוד, בזמן שהציבור שרויין בצער, אל יאמר אדם, אלך לביתי, ואוכל ואשתה, ושלום עליך נפשי, ואם עושה כן, עליו הכתוב אומר (ישעיהו כב, יג'), והנה ששון ושמחה, הרוג בקר ושחוט צאן, אכול בשר ושתות יין, אכול ושתו, כי מחר נמות. מה כתיב בתריה מה כתוב אחרי, ונגלה באזני ה' צבאות, אם יכופר העון הזה לכם עד תמותון (שם, יד').

עד כאן מידת בינונים, אבל במידת רשעים מה כתיב, אתיו בואו ואקחה יין ונסבאה שכר, והיה כזה יום מחר (ישעיהו נו, יב'). מה כתיב בתריה מה כתוב אחרי, הצדיק אבד, ואין איש שם על לב... כי מפני הרעה נאסף

in sorrow, etc. ... "Then he shall merit receiving consolation together with the community." End of quote (of Tractate *Ta'anit*).

123) These words seemingly have no connection to each other. [The tractate] wants to bring proof from the Scriptures that one is obligated to grieve together with the community, but if that is so, what business do we have there of separating and dividing between the attribute of the middling and the attribute of the wicked? Moreover, why does the text explicitly say "the attribute of the middling and the attribute of the wicked" instead of saying, "the middling and the wicked?" Why does it talk about attributes?

And furthermore, from where do we understand that the text [above] speaks of the sin of not taking part in the sorrows of the community? Also, we do not see any punishment relating to the attribute of the wicked, only a reference to what has been said: "the righteous perishes, and no one takes it to heart, etc." But if the wicked have sinned, what has the righteous done that he should be punished? And why would the wicked care whether or not the righteous is taken away?

The attribute of the middling and the attribute of the wicked

124) Indeed, you should know that these attributes of the middling, of the wicked, and of the righteous (*tzadik*) mentioned in this *Braita* do not refer to specific people—rather, all three [attributes] are present in each and every person in the world. This is because these three attributes should be observed in each and every person. During the time of the Concealment of the Face for a person—meaning before he even gains Repentance out of Fear—he is considered to belong to the attribute of the wicked (verse 52).

Later, if he merits Repentance out of Fear (verse 57), he is considered to belong to the attribute of the middling, as mentioned above (verse 62). And then, if he also merits Repentance out of Love, which is the fourth level [of love], namely the eternal love, as mentioned above (verses 64 and

168

הצדיק (שם נז, א'). אלא יצער אדם עם הצבור וכו' זוכה ורואה בנחמת צבור, עכ"ל עד כאן לשון (מסכת תענית).

קכג) ולכאורה אין לדברים הללו שום קשר, כי רוצה להביא ראיה מהכתוב, אשר האדם מחוייב להצטער עצמו עם הצבור, ואם כן מה יש לנו להבדיל כאן ולחלק, בין מידת בינונים למידת רשעים. ועוד, מהי הלשון שמדייק: מידת בינונים, ומידת רשעים, ולמה אינו אומר בינונים ורשעים, ומידות למה לי.

ועוד, מאין משמע, שהכתוב מדבר, בעון שאינו מצטער עצמו עם הצבור. ועוד, שאין אנו רואים שום עונש במידת רשעים, אלא, במ"ש במה שכתוב, הצדיק אבד ואין איש שם על לב וכו', ואם הרשעים חטאו, צדיק מאי עבידתיה מה עשה הצדיק שיענש, ומאי איכפת להו לרשעים, אם הצדיק נאסף.

מדת בינונים ומדת רשעים

קכד) אמנם תדע, שאלו המידות של בינונים ושל רשעים וצדיק שמזכירים בברייתא הזאת, אינם באנשים מיוחדים, אלא, ששלשתם נמצאים בכל אדם ואדם שבעולם. כי בכל אדם יש להבחין ג' המידות הנ"ל, כי בזמן הסתר פנים של האדם, דהיינו, עוד מטרם שזכה אפילו לתשובה מיראה, נבחן אז במידתם של רשעים (סעיף נב').

ואחר כך, אם זוכה לתשובה מיראה (סעיף נז'), נבחן במידתם של בינונים, כנזכר לעיל (סעיף סב'), ואחר כך, אם זוכה גם כן לתשובה מאהבה, בבחינה ד' שבה, דהיינו אהבה נצחית כנ"ל (סעיף סד' ועג'),

73), he is considered as a complete righteous. Therefore, [the sages] did not just say "middling" and "righteous," but [rather] "the attribute of the middling" and "the attribute of the wicked," as explained (verse 122).

Participating in the sorrow of the community

125) Moreover, we must remember that [a person] cannot merit the aforementioned fourth degree of love without first gaining the aspect of the Revelation of the Face, which is destined to appear to the whole world and through which he has sufficient power to tip the balance of all the people in the world towards the side of innocence, as mentioned above in the words of Rav Elazar, son of Rav Shimon (verse 118). And we have already explained that the Revelation of the Face is bound to transform every sorrow and sadness that appeared during the time of the Concealment of the Face, turning them into wonderful delights, so much so that one might be sorry for having suffered so little, as we have explained well (above verse 121 starting with the words: And this is why…); study that well.

This being the case, we should ask: When a person tips his balance towards the side of innocence, surely he remembers all the sorrow and the painful experiences that he underwent during the time of the Concealment of the Face. And so, there is a reality here, where all of [these sorrows] are transformed into wonderful delights for him, as has been said. But when he tips [the balance] of the whole world towards the side of innocence, how does he know the degree of sorrow and painfulness that all the people in the world are undergoing, and thus understand them and [know] how they are tipped towards the side of innocence, in the same way that we have clarified [the situation] regarding the person who tips his own [balance]? (See above, (verse 121) starting with the words: And this is why…).

The aspect (lit. pan) of merit for the whole world should not be missing at the time that [the person] is capable of tipping them towards the side of innocence. [For that to happen] the person has no other way (lit. scheme) but to make sure that he will always feel sorrow in himself empathyzing with the sorrows of the community,

נבחן לצדיק גמור. ולפיכך, לא אמרו בינונים וצדיקים סתם, אלא, מידת בינונים ומידת רשעים, כמבואר (סעיף קכג).

השתתפות בצרת הצבור

קכה) עוד צריכים לזכור, שאי אפשר לזכות לבחינה ד' של אהבה האמורה, אם לא שיזכה קודם להשיג לבחינת גילוי פנים העתיד לבא לכל העולם, שבזה כחו יפה להכריע גם את כל העולם לכף זכות, כדברי ר"א בר"ש רבי אלעזר בן רבי שמעון הנ"ל (סעיף קיח'). וכבר נתבאר, שענין גילוי הפנים, מחייב להפוך כל צער ועצבון שבאו בעת הסתר פנים, ולעשותם לתענוגות נפלאים, עד כדי להצטער על מיעוט היסורים שסבל, כמו שנתבאר היטב לעיל (סעיף קכא ד"ה דבור המתחיל [במילה] ולפיכך) עש"ה.

ומכיון שכן, יש לשאול אדם כשהוא מכריע את עצמו לכף זכות, הוא ודאי זוכר, כל הצער והמכאובים שהיו לו בשעת הסתרת הפנים, לכן יש מציאות, שכולם מתהפכים לו לתענוגות נפלאים כאמור, אך כשהוא מכריע את כל העולם לכף זכות, מאין יודע את מידת הצער והמכאובים שכל הבריות שבעולם סובלים, כדי שיבין אותם, איך הם מוכרעים לכף זכות, באותו האופן שביארנו באדם בהכרעת עצמו, לעיל (סעיף קכא ד"ה דבור המתחיל [במילה] ולפיכך).

וכדי שלא תהיה כף הזכות של כל העולם חסרה, בעת שיהיה מוכשר להכריע אותם לכף זכות, אין לאדם שום תחבולה אחרת, אלא

171

just as he would feel sorrow for his own sorrows. Then the aspect (lit. pan) of guilt of the whole world will be ready within him, just like his own guilt, in a manner that if he merits ruling [tipping] himself towards the side of innocence, he will be able to rule the whole world towards the side of innocence. And then he will merit being a complete righteous.

Interpreting the *Braita* according to: "Surely this iniquity will not be forgiven for you."

126) And through these explanations, the words of the *Braita* can be understood properly: that if a person does not participate in the sorrows of the community, then it is found that even when he gains Repentance out of Fear, which is the attribute of a middling, as mentioned above ((verse 62) starting with the words: And he is also called…), the Scriptures refer to him and speak in his favor, saying (verse 122): "Behold joy and gladness." Meaning that the person has gained the blessing of "You will see your world in your lifetime" (verses 76-78) and sees all the rewards of his actions according to the Precepts—rewards ready for him in the World to Come—surely he is "full of joy and gladness," and he says to himself, "Slay the oxen and kill the sheep, eat meat and drink wine. Let us eat and drink, for tomorrow we die." (verse 122) This means that he is full of great joy because of the reward that is promised to him in the World to Come, and is why he says very gladly, "For tomorrow we shall die," [meaning,] I shall collect my life in the World to Come, since I shall be paid after my death.

But what is written in the following: "And it shall be revealed to the ears of the God of Hosts, and surely this iniquity will not be forgiven to you till you die?" (Isaiah 22:14) This means that the Scripture is scolding [the individual] for the unintentional sins that he has committed because it has been explained that the intentional sins of him who does Repentance out of Fear, are transformed only into unintentional sins, as explained above (verse 121 starting

שיראה, להצטער עצמו תמיד בצרת הצבור ממש כמו שמצטער
בצרותיו עצמו, כי אז, תהיה לו כף החובה של כל העולם מוכנה
בקרבו, כמו כף החובה של עצמו, באופן, שאם יזכה להכריע את
עצמו לכף זכות, יוכל כן גם להכריע את כל העולם לכף זכות, ויזכה
לבחינת צדיק גמור.

ביאור הברייתא ע"פ אם יכופר לכם העון הזה

קכו) ומהמתבאר מובנים דברי הברייתא כהלכתם, שאם האדם
אינו מצטער עצמו עם הצבור, נמצא, שאפילו בעת שזכה לתשובה
מיראה, שהיא מידת בינוני כנ"ל (סעיף סב' ד"ה דבור המתחיל [במילה]
ונקרא), אומר עליו הכתוב (סעיף קכב'), ומדבר בעדו, "והנה ששון
ושמחה", פירוש, שהאדם שזכה לברכה של "עולמך תראה בחייך"
(סעיף עו'-עח'), ורואה את כל שכר המצוה שלו המוכן לעולם הבא, הנה
הוא ודאי "מלא ששון ושמחה", ואומר לעצמו, "הרוג בקר ושחוט
צאן, אכול בשר ושתות יין, אכול ושתו כי מחר נמות" (סעיף קכב').
כלומר, שמלא שמחה גדולה מחמת השכר המובטח לו לעולם הבא,
וזה שאומר בשמחה רבה "כי מחר נמות" ואגבה את חיי העולם
הבא שלי משלם לאחר מיתתי.

אמנם מאי כתיב בתריה מה כתוב אחרי "ונגלה באזני ה' צבאות, אם
יכופר העון הזה לכם, עד תמותון" (סעיף קכב'). כלומר, שהכתוב
מוכיח אותו על השגגות שבידו, כי נתבאר, שהעושה תשובה מיראה
הזדונות נהפכות לו רק לשגגות כנ"ל (סעיף קכא' ד"ה דבור המתחיל [במילה]

with the words: And this is why...). This being the case, since he did not grieve with the community and [thus] cannot merit Repentance out of Love—where his intentional sins would have been transformed into merits (verses 110-111) —it follows of necessity that the unintentional sins he has performed will not be forgiven during his lifetime, so how can he be happy with his life in the World to Come? And this is what the Scriptures [mean] by saying: "Surely this iniquity will not be forgiven," (here, verse 122) namely, the unintentional sins or errors, "till you die," that is, before he dies, since he is being deprived of atonement.

ולפיכך), ואם כך, מכיון שלא ציער עצמו עם הצבור, ואינו יכול לזכות
לתשובה מאהבה, אשר אז הזדונות נהפכו לו לזכויות (סעיף קי'-קיא'),
אם כן הכרח הוא, אשר לשגגות שבידו לא תהיה שום כפרה, בחיים
חיתו, ואיך יוכל לשמוח בחיי העולם הבא שלו. וז"ש זה שאומר הכתוב
"אם יכופר לכם העון הזה" (סעיף קכב'), דהיינו השגגות, עד תמותון,
כלומר, בטרם שימות והריהו נמנע מכפרה.

Chapter Nine
The Good Life Versus The Bad Life

The attribute of the wicked, the middling, and the righteous within each person

127) And the *Braita* goes on to say (verse 122) that "this is the attribute of the middling," meaning that the scriptural passage [above] speaks of the time when one has done Repentance out of Fear onwards, a period during which he is called "a middling," as mentioned above (verse 62). "But of the attribute of the wicked, what has been written?" meaning, what happens from the time [the person] was in the Concealment of the Face, which is called "the attribute of the wicked?" as mentioned above (verse 122). And it was explained that Repentance out of Fear does not correct what the person went through before doing the repentance [at all], and therefore, the *Braita* presents (lit. brings) another scriptural passage about [these people], which is "Come, let us take wine, and let us fill ourselves with liquor; and the following day will be like this day." (verse 122)

The meaning of this [passage] is that those days and years that he has gone through from the time of the Concealment of the Face and that he has not yet corrected (as mentioned earlier verses 80-82) are called "the attribute of the wicked." Those [days and years] do not want him to die because they have no part after death in the World to Come, being the attribute of the wicked. And therefore, during the same time that his attribute of a middling is happy and joyful, [as indicated by] "for tomorrow we shall die," [because] it will gain the life of the World to Come, simultaneously the attribute of the wicked in him does not say so, but says [instead], "and the following day will be like this day." This means that it [the attribute of the wicked in him] wants to be happy and to live in this world forever, since it does not have any part in the World to Come because he has not corrected it, as explained above, for it [the attribute of the wicked in him] cannot be corrected except by Repentance out of Love.

176

פרק תשיעי
הוזיים הטובים והוזיים הרעים

מדת רשע בינוני וצדיק אשר בכל אדם

קכז) ואומרת עוד הברייתא (סעיף קכב'), זו "מידת בינונים", כלומר, שהמקרא הזה מדבר, מעת שעשה תשובה מיראה ואילך, שבזמן הזה נקרא בינוני כנ"ל (סעיף סב'), "אבל במידת רשעים מה כתיב", פירוש, מה יהיה מאותו הזמן שהיה שרוי בהסתר פנים, שנקרא אז "מידת רשעים", כנ"ל (סעיף קכב'). ונתבאר, אשר תשובה מיראה, אינה מתקנת את העבר עליו מטרם שעשה תשובה, ולפיכך, מביאה עליהם הברייתא מקרא אחר (סעיף קכב'), שהוא "אתיו אקחה יין ונסבאה שכר, והיה כזה יום מחר".

פירוש, שאותם הימים והשנים, שעברו עליו מזמן של הסתר הפנים, שלא תיקן עוד אותם כנ"ל (סעיף פ'-פב'), שנקרא "מידת רשעים", הנה הם אינם חפצים שימות, משום שאין להם שום חלק לאחר מיתה בעולם הבא, להיותם מידתם של רשעים. ולפיכך, באותה השעה שמידת הבינונים שבו, שמחה וצוהלת "כי מחר נמות", ותזכה לחיי העולם הבא, הרי יחד עמה, מידת הרשעים שבו אינה אומרת כן, אלא שאומרת "והיה כזה יום מחר", כלומר, שרוצה לשמוח ולחיות בעולם הזה לעולם, כי אין לה עדיין שום חלק לעולם הבא, כי לא תיקן אותה, כמבואר לעיל, שאין לה תיקון אלא על ידי תשובה מאהבה.

177

128) And with this, the *Braita* concludes: "What is written in the following? 'The righteous has perished'" means that the aspect of the complete righteous that this person has to achieve has gone missing from him. '…and no one takes it to heart that due to the evil, the righteous is taken away' (verse 122) means that because the middling one has not grieved together with the public, he therefore cannot gain Repentance out of Love, which transforms malicious actions into merits and misery into wondrous delights, as mentioned above (verses 110-111). Instead, all the unintentional sins and sorrows that he had suffered before he gained Repentance out of Fear are still valid because they still exist from the aspect of the "attribute of the wicked," who still feel sorrow from His Providence. And because of these sorrows that [the attribute of the wicked within him] still feels, he cannot merit being a complete righteous.

And the Scriptures say: "And no one takes it to heart," which means that this person does not take it to his heart "because due to the evil," namely, due to the "sorrows" that he still feels from past times from [the Creator's] Providence, "the righteous is taken away," which means that his attribute of being a righteous is taken away and he will die and depart from the world [while he is] only in the aspect of a middling, as mentioned above. And all this is because anyone who does not feel sorrow together with the public does not get to see the consolation of the public because he will not be able to tip the scale for them towards the side of innocence and [thus] witness (lit. see) their consolation, as explained. And therefore, he will never be able to merit the aspect of a righteous, which has been explained at length above.

The wicked who feel bad think that the whole world, like them, is under negative Providence

129) From all that has been said up to this point, we have had the merit of learning that there is no human being (lit. born to a woman) to whom the following three *midot* (attributes and also levels) mentioned above do not apply: the attribute of the wicked,

קכח) וזה שמסיימת הברייתא, מה כתיב בתרי' מה כתוב אחרי זה, "הצדיק אבד", כלומר בחינת הצדיק הגמור, שהאדם הזה צריך לזכות בו, הנה זה אבד ממנו, "ואין איש שם על לב, כי מפני הרעה נאסף הצדיק" (סעיף קכב'). כלומר, מפני שאותו הבינוני, לא ציער עצמו עם הצבור, ואינו יכול לזכות משום זה לתשובה מאהבה, המהפכת הזדונות לזכויות ואת הרעות לתענוגות נפלאים כנ"ל (סעיף קי'-קיא'), אלא כל ההשגגות והרעות שסבל, מטרם שזכה לתשובה מיראה, עדיין הן עומדות בעינן, מבחינת מדת רשעים, המרגישים רעות מהשגחתו יתברך, ומפני הרעות האלו שעודם מרגישים, אינו יכול לזכות ולהיות צדיק גמור.

וזה שהכתוב אומר, "ואין איש שם אל לב", כלומר, אותו האדם אינו שם אל לבו, "כי מפני הרעה", כלומר, משום ה"רעות" שעדיין מרגיש מזמן שעבר, בהשגחתו יתברך, "נאסף הצדיק", כלומר, נאבדה לו בחינת צדיק, וימות ויפטר מהעולם רק בבחינת בינוני בלבד, כמבואר. וכל זה הוא, שכל מי שאינו מצער עצמו עם הצבור, אינו זוכה ורואה בנחמת הצבור, כי לא יוכל להכריע אותם לכף זכות, ולראות בנחמה שלהם, כמבואר. ולפיכך, לא יזכה לעולם לבחינת צדיק, כנ"ל באריכות.

הרשעים שמרגישים רע חושבים שכל העולם מושגחים בהשגחה לא טובה כמותם

קכט) והנה מכל האמור עד הנה זכינו לדעת, שאין לך ילוד אשה, שלא יעברו עליו ג' המידות הנ"ל, שהן: מידת רשעים, ומידת בינונים,

179

the attribute of the middling, and the attribute of the righteous. They are called *midot* (attributes, levels) because they are derived from the *midot* (levels) of understanding His Providence.

And this is what is said by our sages: "According to the level (*mida*) that one evaluates (*moded*), he is thus being evaluated (*modedim lo*)," (Tractate *Sotah*, 5b) meaning that those who perceive the *mida* (level or evaluation) of His Providence from the aspect of the Concealment of the Face are "evaluated" to be the level/attribute of the wicked—either not completely wicked, corresponding to the One Concealment or completely wicked, corresponding to the Double Concealment (as mentioned above, (verse 124) starting with the word: Indeed…).

And according to their thinking and feeling, the world is being conducted with bad Providence, Heaven forbid, in the same way that they bring evil upon themselves by receiving suffering and pain from [the Creator's] Providence and by feeling only bad all day long. And they bring evil upon themselves even further by thinking that all the people of the world are supervised, like them, through this bad Providence, Heaven forbid. And therefore, those who perceive Providence from the aspect of the Concealment of the Face are called wicked or bad.

And you should understand that this name [wicked] is revealed within them out of the depth of their feeling. It depends on the understanding of the heart [alone] and there is no importance at all to any speech or thought justifying His Providence, when it [the Providence] contradicts the feeling of all the organs and the senses that do not know how to lie like [the thought does] even when forced to.

Therefore, those who are in the level of perceiving this Providence [from the aspect of the Concealment of the Face] are considered to have tipped [the balance] for themselves and for the whole world towards the side of guilt, as mentioned above (verses 110-111) in the words of Rav Elazar, son of Rav Shimon; study that well. This is because of the reason described earlier: that they imagine that all the people of the world are like them—being supervised with bad

ומידת צדיקים. ונקראות בשם מידות, להיותן נמשכות ממידות השגתם את השגחתו יתברך.

וע"ד ועל דרך שאמרו ז"ל, במידה שאדם מודד מודדים לו (סוטה ה' ע"ב) כי המשיגים מידת השגחתו מבחינת הסתר פנים, נבחנים במידת רשעים: או רשעים שאינם גמורים שמצד ההסתר האחד, או רשעים גמורים שמצד ההסתר הכפול (כנ"ל סעיף קכד' ד"ה דבור המתחיל [במילה] אמנם).

ומשום, שלדעתם והרגשתם, מתנהג העולם בהשגחה לא טובה חס ושלום, דהיינו כמו שהם "מרשיעים" את עצמם, שמקבלים מהשגחתו יתברך יסורים ומכאובים ומרגישים רק רע כל היום, והמה עוד "מרשיעים" ביותר, במה שחושבים, שכל בני העולם מושגחים כמותם בהשגחה לא טובה חס ושלום, ולפיכך משיגי ההשגחה מצד הסתר הפנים, מכונים בשם "רשעים".

והבן זה, כי מתוך מעמקי הרגשתם מתגלה בהם השם הזה, ובאבנתא דלבא ובהבנת הלב תלוי, ולא חשוב כלל הדיבור או המחשבה, המצדקת השגחתו יתברך, בשעה שהיא מתנגדת להרגשת כל האברים והחושים, שאינם יודעים לשקר בעצמם מאונס כמותה.

ולפיכך, הנמצאים במידת השגת ההשגחה הזאת, נבחנים שהכריעו את עצמם ואת כל העולם לכף חובה כנ"ל בדברי ר"א בר"ש רבי אלעזר בן רבי שמעון (סעיפים קי'-קיא') עש"ה, שהוא מטעם האמור להיותם

Providence, Heaven forbid, as befits the nature of the Creator, Who is good and does good to the wicked and to the righteous.

More about the degree of the middling and the righteous

130) And those who merit to perceive and feel His Providence from the aspect of the Revelation of the Face in its first degree, which is called Repentance out of Fear (as mentioned above, ((verse 109) starting with the words: And here…and also verse 62), are considered on the level (attribute) of middling because their emotions are divided into two parts, which are called "the two pans of the scale." This is because now that they merit the Revelation of the Face from the aspect of "you will see your world in your lifetime, (verse 76-78)" as mentioned above (verse 117) starting with the words: And the *Tanna* tells…), they have perceived His good Providence at least from this point onwards, which befits His good name, and therefore they have [earned] "the side (lit. pan) of merit (innocence)".

However, all the sorrow and bitter suffering that was deeply engraved into their emotions from all the days and years during which they received the Providence of the Concealment of the Face (verse 80-82) —that is, from past times before they gained the said Repentance [out of Fear]—are still valid, and they are called "the side (lit. pan) of guilt (verse 110)". And they have these two sides (lit. pans) [of the scales] set against each other: From the moment of their repentance and before, the side of guilt is arranged and still valid; and from the moment of their repentance onwards, the pan of innocence is arranged and guaranteed. This means that the moment of repentance is set in [the middle], between (*bein*) the guilt and (*bein*) the innocence, and therefore they are called middling (*beinonim*).

131) And those who merit the second degree of the Revelation of the Face, which is called Repentance out of Love (verse 64), where their malicious actions become merits for them (as mentioned

מדמים לעצמם שכל בני העולם מושגחים כמותם בהשגחה לא
טובה חס ושלום, כראוי לשמו יתברך הטוב ומיטיב לרעים ולטובים.

עוד בדרגות בינונים וצדיקים

קל) **והזוכים** להשיג ולהרגיש השגחתו יתברך מבחינת גילוי פנים
במדרגתו הראשונה, המכונה תשובה מיראה כנ"ל (סעיף קט' ד"ה
דבור המתחיל [במילה] והנה וסעיף סב'), נבחנים במידת בינונים, משום
שרגשותיהם מתחלקים לב' חלקים, המכונים "ב' כפות המאזנים":
כי עתה שזכה ל"גילוי פנים" (סעיף נד'-נו') מבחינת "עולמך תראה
בחייך" (סעיף עו'-עח'), כנ"ל (סעיף קטז' ד"ה דבור המתחיל [במילה] ואומר),
הרי, כבר השיגו לכל הפחות מכאן ואילך, את השגחתו יתברך
הטובה כראוי לשמו יתברך הטוב, ויש להם על כן "כף זכות".

אמנם כל הצער והיסורים המרים שנחקקו היטב ברגשותיהם, מכל
הימים והשנים שקבלו השגחת הסתר הפנים (סעיף פ'-פב'), דהיינו,
מזמן העבר מטרם שזכו לתשובה האמורה, הרי כל אלו עומדים
בעינם, ונקראים "כף חובה" (סעיף קי'). וכיון שיש להם ב' הכפות הללו
הערוכות זו לעומת זו, באופן: שמרגע תשובתם ולפניהם ערוכה
ועומדת בעינה כף החובה. ומרגע תשובתם ולאחריהם, ערוכה
ומובטחת להם כף הזכות. הרי עת התשובה נמצאת להם "בין"
החובה ו"בין" הזכות, ועל כן, נקראים "בינונים".

קלא) **והזכאים**, לבחינת גילוי פנים ממדרגה ב', המכונה תשובה
מאהבה (סעיף סד'), שזדונות נעשים להם אז כזכויות כנ"ל (סעיף
קכא' ד"ה דבור המתחיל [במילה] ולפיכך), נבחנים, שהכריעו את "כף

above, (verse 121) starting with the words: And this is why…), are considered as if they have tipped [the scale from] the side of guilt mentioned above to the side of innocence. This means that all the sorrow and painfulness that had been engraved into their bones while they were under the Providence of the Concealment of the Face is now ruled and tipped to the side of innocence because all the sorrow and sadness has been turned into wonderful and endless pleasure, (as mentioned above (verse 108) starting with the words: This is analogous to…). And they are now called *tzadikim* [plural of *tzadik,* meaning "righteous" or "just"] because they justify (*matzdikim*) His Providence.

132) And we should know that the aforementioned attribute of the middling is also in effect even when the person is under the Providence of the Concealment of the Face, because when [people are] making a great effort in the belief in reward and punishment, a Light of great certainty in the Creator is revealed to them, and they gain, for the time being, the level of the Revelation of His Face, as befits the attribute of a middling. But the disadvantage is that they cannot depend on this attribute remaining permanently because the only way to maintain it permanently is through Repentance out of Fear, (as mentioned above (verse 109) starting with the words: And here…).

Once a person has gained Repentance out of Love, he is given more work in the Torah and its Precepts

133) We should also know that the things we have said regarding the matter of freewill being valid only during the time of the Concealment of the Face, (as mentioned above (verse 53) starting with the words: We should know…), does not mean that after one has gained the Providence of the Revelation of the Face, he is free from toiling and putting effort in the Torah and the Precepts. The opposite is the case: The main work in the Torah and the Precepts properly begins after one has gained Repentance out of Love, because only then is it possible for one to engage with the Torah

החובה" הנ"ל ל"כף זכות", דהיינו, שכל הצער והיסורים שנחקקו בעצמותיהם, בעת שהיו עומדים תחת השגחת הסתר פנים, הוכרעו עתה ונהפכו ל"כף זכות", כי כל צער ועצב נהפך לתענוג נפלא לאין קץ, כנ"ל (סעיף קח' ד"ה דבור המתחיל [במילה] וזה דומה), ונקראים עתה "צדיקים" על שם שמצדיקים את השגחתו יתברך.

קלב) וצריכים לדעת, שמידת הבינונים (סעיף קכג') האמורה נוהגת גם כן, בשעת היות האדם, אפילו תחת השגחת הסתר פנים, כי על ידי התאמצות יתירה באמונת שכר ועונש, מתגלה אליהם, אור של בטחון גדול בהשם יתברך, וזוכים לשעתם, במדרגת גילוי פניו יתברך, במידתם של בינונים. אלא החסרון הוא, שאינם יכולים לעמוד על מידותיהם, שישארו כן בקביעות, כי להשאר בקביעות, אי אפשר, אלא על ידי תשובה מיראה, כנ"ל (סעיף קט' ד"ה דבור המתחיל [במילה] והנה).

אחר שזכה האדם לתשובה מאהבה מוטל עליו יותר העבודה
בתומ"צ בתורה ומצוות

קלג) גם יש לדעת, שמה שאמרנו, שאין ענין הבחירה נוהג אלא בזמן הסתר הפנים, כנ"ל (סעיף נג' ד"ה דבור המתחיל [במילה] וצריכים) אין הכונה, שאחר שזכה להשגחה של גילוי פנים, אין לו עוד שום טורח ויגיעה, בעסק התורה והמצוות, אלא אדרבה, עיקר העבודה בתורה ומצוות כראוי, מתחילה אחר שזכה האדם לתשובה מאהבה, כי רק

and the Precepts out of love and fear, as we are commanded, for "the world was not created but only for the complete righteous." (Tractate *Bracho* 61b)

This is analogous to the king who wished to select all his most loyal and beloved [subjects] in his country for himself and put them to work inside his palace. What did he do? He issued an open decree in the country, saying that whoever wanted to, whether young or old, could come to him and engage in the inner works in his palace. But he took many of his slaves and put them as guards both at the entrance to the palace and on all the roads leading to his palace, instructing them to cunningly mislead all those who approached and to divert them from the road leading to the palace.

Of course, all the people of the country started to run towards the royal palace, but upon arriving, they were misled by the shrewdness of the diligent guards. Many of them overcame the guards and managed to come closer to the door to the palace. But the guards at the door were very conscientious, and whoever came closer to the door was moved and pushed away with great cunning and skill to the point that they returned to where they had come from. And so they came and went back again; and again gained strength, came again and returned, and thus they did again and again for days and years until they became disheartened from trying anymore. And only the most valiant of them, who had enough patience, defeated those guards and opened the door immediately, managing to be received by and see the face of the king, who gave each of them a proper task that suited him best.

And naturally, from then on, they had no more dealings with those guards, who had tried to divert and push them away and had made their life bitter for many days and years, by [forcing them to go] back and forth to the door, because [now] they merited working and serving with respect to the glory of the light of the face of the king inside his palace. And this is also the case in the work of the completely righteous (*tzadik*), since the free will that was valid during the time of the Concealment of the Face surely is no longer valid from the moment he opens the door to perceiving Visible Providence.

אז אפשר לו, לעסוק בתורה ומצוות באהבה ויראה כמצווה עלינו. ולא איברי עלמא, אלא לצדיקי גמירי ולא נברא העולם אלא לצדיקים גמורים (ברכות ס"א ע"ב).

אלא הדבר דומה, למלך, שחשק לבחור לעצמו, כל אוהביו הנאמנים לו ביותר שבמדינה, ולהכניסם לעבודתו בהיכלו פנימה. מה עשה, נתן צו גלוי במדינה, שכל הרוצה כקטן כגדול, יבא אליו לעסוק בעבודות הפנימיות שבהיכלו. אבל העמיד מעבדיו שומרים רבים, על פתחו של ההיכל, ובכל הדרכים המובילים להיכל, וציווה אותם להטעות בערמה את כל המתקרבים להיכלו, ולהדיחם מהדרך המוביל להיכל.

וכמובן, שכל בני המדינה התחילו לרוץ להיכל המלך, אמנם, נידחו בערמת השומרים החרוצים, ורבים מהם התגברו עליהם, עד שהצליחו להתקרב אל פתח ההיכל, אלא ששומרי הפתח היו חרוצים ביותר, ומי שהוא שהתקרב אל הפתח הסיתו אותו והדיחו אותו במזימה רבה, עד ששב כלעומת שבא. וכן חזרו ובאו ושבו, ושוב התחזקו וחזרו ובאו ושבו, וכן חזרו חלילה כמה ימים ושנים, עד שנלאו מלנסות יותר. ורק הגבורים מהם, אשר מידת סבלנותם עמדה להם, וניצחו את השומרים ההם, ופתחו הפתח, זכו תיכף לקבל פני המלך, שמינה כל אחד על משמרתו המתאימה לו.

וכמובן, שמאז ואילך, לא היו להם עוד עסקים עם השומרים הללו, שהסיתו והדיחו אותם ומררו את חייהם כמה ימים ושנים, בהלוך ושוב על הפתח, כי זכו לעבוד ולשמש מול הדר אור פני המלך בהיכלו פנימה. כן הוא הדבר בעבודת הצדיקים הגמורים, שהבחירה הנוהגת בעת הסתר פנים, ודאי אינה נוהגת עוד מעת שפתחו הפתח להשגת ההשגחה הגלויה.

Indeed, one starts with the essence of the [Creator's spiritual] work from the aspect of the Revelation of the Face because this is when one starts climbing up the many rungs of the ladder that is based in the Earth and its top reaches the Heavens. This is the secret of the passage: "And the righteous will go from one triumph to the other." (Psalms 84:8) And this is what is meant by the words of the sages: "that every righteous is burnt by the canopy of his friend" (*Tractate Bava Batra* 7a) because these [ways] of [spiritual] work prepare them for the Will of the Creator, so that His Thought of Creation—which is "to fulfill His created beings with joy" according to His generosity and goodness—will be manifest in them.

Revelation is particularly in the place where there was concealment

134) And it is good to know this Supernal law: that there is no revelation except in a place where there was concealment before. This is also the case with worldly matters, where the void exists prior to the revelation; for example, the growth of wheat is revealed only where it was sown and rotted. And this is also the case in Supernal matters, where concealment and revelation are related to each other, as are the wick and the light that clings to it, because after any concealment that achieves correction, the particular light related to this kind of concealment is revealed due to it. And the light that is manifest gets attached to it like a light to a wick, and you should remember this in all your journeys (in this wisdom).

The saying: The entire Torah consists of the Names of the Creator

135) You should [also] understand what our sages have said: that the entire Torah consists of the Names of the Creator (*Zohar, Ha'azinu*, 281). This is seemingly something peculiar because one can find in [the Torah] many crude things, such as names of the wicked, like Pharaoh and Bilaam and others like them, as well as prohibitions

אמנם, מתחילים בעיקר עבודתו יתברך, שמבחינת גילוי פנים, שאז מתחילים לפסוע על המדרגות הרבות, שבסולם המוצב ארצה וראשו מגיע השמימה, בסוד הכתוב (תהילים פד, ח') וצדיקים ילכו מחיל אל חיל , וכדרז"ל וכדברי רבותינו ז"ל (מסכת בבא בתרא עה, ע"א), שכל צדיק וצדיק נכוה מחופתו של חברו, אשר העבודות הללו מכשירות אותם לחפץ ה', שתתקיים בהם מחשבתו יתברך שבבריאה, שהיא "כדי להנות לנבראיו", כידו יתברך הטובה והרחבה.

גילוי הוא דוקא במקום שהיה הסתר

קלד) ורצוי לדעת החוק העליון הזה, שאין לך שום גילוי אלא במקום שהיה ההסתר. כמו בעניני העולם הזה, אשר ההעדר הוא קודם להויה, כי אין צמיחת החיטה נגלית אלא במקום שנזרעה ונרקבה. וכן בדברים העליונים, אשר ההסתר והגילוי יש להם, יחס, כפתילה והאור הנאחז בה, כי כל הסתר אחר שבא לתיקון, הנה נגלה בסיבתו האור המיוחס למין ההסתר הזה, והאור שנתגלה נאחז בו, כמו אור בפתילה, וזכור זה על כל דרכיך.

במאמר: כל התורה שמותיו של הקב"ה

קלה) ועם זה תבין מ"ש מה שאמרו חז"ל, שכל התורה כולה הם שמותיו של הקדוש ברוך הוא (זוהר הסולם האזינו רמא'). שלכאורה הדבר תמוה, כי מצינו הרבה דברים גסים, כמו שמות של רשעים: פרעה, ובלעם,

and impurities, and cruel curses in the two admonitions (in portions *Bechukotai* and *Ki Tavo*), and the like. So how can we understand that all these [too,] could be the Names of the Creator?

The Torah descended and contracted through many contractions

136) In order to understand this, we have to know that the [Creator's] ways are not our ways because our way is to go from imperfection to perfection, while His way is that all revelations come to us from Perfection to imperfection. In the beginning, the complete Perfection is emanated and emerges from Him, and this Perfection descends from within His Face and rolls down by [means of] one contraction after another through various stages till it reaches the most contracted final stage, which is most appropriate to our material world, and then it is revealed to us here in this world.

137) And from what has been said, you will learn that the Sacred Torah, the excellence of which is without end, did not emanate and come out of Him at once, as it exists before us here in this world, because it is known that the Torah and the Creator are one and the same, but in the Torah of this world, this [unification] is not apparent at all. Not only that, but (see verse 17) whoever studies the Torah Not For Its Own Sake, the Torah becomes for him a potion of death, (as was mentioned above (verse 102) starting with the words: And this is what it is said...)

But as we have mentioned earlier, as [the Torah] emanated from Him in the beginning, it emanated and emerged in complete perfection, namely, according to the aspect of the Torah and the Creator being actually one and the same. And this is why it is called the Torah of *Atzilut* (Emanation), as we have learned (in the Introduction to the *Tikkunei HaZohar* page 3b): that He and His Essence and His causations are One. And afterwards, it came down from the Front of His Face, and contracted through many stages of contraction until it was given from Sinai, where it was written in the same way

וכיוצא בהם, ואיסור, וטומאה, וקללות אכזריות שבב' התוכחות (פרשת בחוקותי ופרשת כי תבוא), וכדומה, ואיך אפשר להבין, שכל אלו יהיו שמותיו של הקדוש ברוך הוא.

שהתורה ירדה ונצטמצמה בצמצומים רבים

קלו) ולהבין זאת צריכים לידע, שלא דרכיו דרכינו, היות שמדרכינו הוא, להגיע מהבלתי מושלם אל השלימות, ומדרכו יתברך באים לנו כל הגילויים, מהשלימות אל הבלתי מושלם. כי מתחילה נאצלת ויוצאת מלפניו השלימות הגמורה, והשלימות הזו יורדת מפאת פניו יתברך, ומשתלשלת בצמצום אחר צמצום, דרך כמה מדרגות, עד שמגיעה לשלב האחרון המצומצם ביותר המתאים לעולם החומרי שלנו, ואז מתגלה הדבר לנו, כאן בעולם הזה.

קלז) ומהאמור תשכיל לדעת, אשר התורה הקדושה, שלגובה מעלתה אין קץ, הנה לא נאצלה ויצאה מלפניו תיכף, כמות שהיא מצויה לעינינו כאן בעולם הזה, שהרי נודע, שאורייתא וקוב"ה חד הוא התורה והקדוש ברוך הוא אחד הם, ובתורה דעולם הזה לא ניכר זה כלל. ולא עוד, אלא (סעיף טז') שהעוסק בה שלא לשמה, נעשית תורתו לו סם המות, כנ"ל (סעיף קב' ד"ה דבור המתחיל [במילה] וז"ש).

אלא כנ"ל, שמתחילה כשנאצלה מלפניו יתברך, הנה נאצלה ויצאה בתכלית השלימות, דהיינו, בבחינת אורייתא וקוב"ה חד הוא התורה והקדוש ברוך הוא אחד הם ממש. וזה שנקרא תורה דאצילות, שאיתא (שמובא בהקדמת תיקוני זוהר דף ג' [פרוש מעלות הסולם, סט]), דאיהו וחיוהי וגרמוהי חד בהון שהוא, חיותו ועצמותו אחד הם. ואחר כך, ירדה מפאת פניו יתברך, ונצטמצמה דרך המדרגה, בצמצומים רבים,

as we have it now in this world, [that is,] as it became vested in the crude Garments that are of the material world.

The descent to this world does not diminish the Torah's value

138) **Still**, you should know that even though the distance between the Garments that the Torah is vested with in this world and those [that it is vested with] in *Olam Atzilut* (the World of Emanation) is immeasurable, as mentioned above (see verse 137); nevertheless, the Torah itself, namely, the Light within those Garments, is not different at all, so there is no difference between the Torah of *Olam Atzilut* (the World of Emanation) and the Torah of this world. This is the secret of the verse: "For I, the Creator, do not change." (Malachi 3:6) Moreover, these crude Garments of our Torah [in our World] of *Asiya* (Action) are not, Heaven forbid, [any] degradation for the Light that covers itself with them [the Garments]. On the contrary, seen from the perspective of the end of their correction, their importance is immeasurably more than any of its purer Garments that are in the Supernal Worlds.

And the reason for this is that the concealment is the cause for the revelation. Because when the concealment is corrected during the time of the revelation, it becomes [a support] for the revelation just like the wick [supports] the light that attaches itself to it, as mentioned above. During [the concealment's] correction, the greater the concealment is, the greater the Light that will be revealed and will be attached to it. So, all these crude Garments that the Torah has assumed in this world do not constitute any lessening of value relative to the Light that vested inside it [the Garments while being in the Torah], rather it is the opposite, as was explained.

The revelation of the Torah occurs precisely in the concealment of this world

139) **And with the following,** Moses had victory over the angels by claiming "Is there jealousy among you? Can the evil intention be found among you?" (Tractate *Shabbat*, 79a) Study that well. This means,

עד שניתנה מסיני, שנכתבה כמות שהיא לעינינו כאן בעולם הזה, בהתלבשותה בלבושים הגסים שבעולם החומרי.

התורה בירידתה לעולם הזה אינה נפחתת מערכה

קלח) אמנם תדע, שאף על פי, שהמרחק שבין לבושי התורה שבעולם הזה, עד הלבושים שבעולם האצילות, הוא לאין ערוך כנ"ל (סעיף קלז'), עם כל זה, התורה עצמה, כלומר, המאור שבתוך הלבושים, אין בו שום שינוי כל שהוא, בין תורה דאצילות לתורה דעולם הזה, שזה סוד הכתוב אני ה' לא שניתי וכו' (מלאכי ג' ו'). ולא עוד, אלא הלבושים הגסים הללו, שבתורה דעשיה שלנו, אינם חס ושלום שום פחיתות ערך אל המאור המתלבש בה, אלא אדרבה, שחשיבותם עולה בהרבה לאין ערוך, מבחינת גמר תיקונם, על כל הלבושים הזכים שלה שבעולמות העליונים.

והוא מטעם, שההסתר הוא סיבת הגילוי, שההסתר אחר תיקונו בעת הגילוי, נעשה לגילוי כמו פתילה לאור הנאחז בה, כנ"ל, וכל שההסתר הוא גדול ביותר, דרכו בעת תיקונו, שיתגלה ויאחז בו האור הגדול ביותר. הרי שכל אלו הלבושים הגסים, שהתורה התלבשה בהם בעולם הזה, אינם כלל שום פחיתות ערך כלפי המאור המתלבש בה, אלא עוד להיפך, כמבואר.

גילוי התורה בהסתר עולם הזה דוקא

קלט) ובזה ניצח משה למלאכים, בטענתו, כלום קנאה יש ביניכם, יצר הרע יש ביניכם (מסכת שבת פ"ט ע"א), עש"ה, דהיינו, כמבואר,

as was explained, that the greater concealment reveals the greater Light. And he showed them that the pure Garments that the Torah covers itself with in the world of the angels are not fit to reveal the greatest Lights, as is possible with the Garments of this world, as was explained.

The explanation of the passage: "Your teacher will not hide himself any more, etc."

140) It has been made clear that there is no change, Heaven forbid, in anything of the Torah of Emanation [when it descends] all the way to the Torah of this world because the Torah and the Creator are one and the same. The entire difference is in the Garments because the Garments of this world conceal the Creator and hide Him, as mentioned earlier ((verse 101) starting with the words: The verse says…). And you should know that because of Him covering Himself with the Torah, He is called "Teacher" (*moreh*), which goes to show you that even during the Concealment of the Face, and even in its aspect of Double Concealment (Concealment within Concealment), (as mentioned earlier (verse 52) starting with the words: And Concealment…), the Creator prevails in the Torah and is enveloped by it.

This is because He is the "*Moreh*" (Teacher) and she is the "*Torah*" (Teaching), except that the crude Garments of the Torah seem to our eyes like wings (*kanaf*), which cover and conceal the Teacher, Who is enveloped by them and is hiding inside them. And indeed, when a person gains the Revelation of the Face, that is, the Repentance out of Love in its fourth degree (as mentioned earlier, (verse 73) starting with the words: The second level…; and (verse 121) starting with the words: And this is why…), it is said about him: "Your Teacher will not hide Himself (lit. *yiknaf*, "will not cover himself by wings") any more, but your eyes shall see your Teacher." (Isaiah 30:20) [This is] because from that moment on, the Garments of the "*Torah*" (Teaching) no longer conceal (*maknifim*) the "*Moreh*" (Teacher), and he (the Creator) is revealed to him forever, because the Torah and the Teacher [the Creator] are one and the same.

194

שההסתר היותר גדול מגלה את האור היותר גדול, והראה להם,
שבלבושים זכים אשר התורה מתלבשת בהם בעולם המלאכים,
אי אפשר שיתגלו על ידיהם האורות היותר גדולים, כמו שאפשר
בלבושים דעולם הזה, כמבואר.

ביאור הכתוב: ולא יכנף עוד מוריך והיו עיניך רואות את מוריך

קמ) **הרי** נתבאר, שאין שום שינוי חס ושלום במשהו, מתורה
דאצילות, שאוריתא וקדוש ברוך הוא חד הוא התורה והקדוש ברוך הוא
אחד הם, עד התורה שבעולם הזה, אלא, כל ההבחן הוא בלבושים, כי
לבושים שבעולם הזה, המה מעלימים להקדוש ברוך הוא ומסתירים
אותו, כנ"ל (סעיף קא' ד"ה דבור המתחיל [במילה] וז"ש). ותדע שעל שם
התלבשותו יתברך בתורה, הוא מכונה בשם "מורה", להודיעך
שאפילו בעת הסתר הפנים ואפילו בבחינת ההסתר הכפול, כנ"ל
(סעיף נב' ד"ה דבור המתחיל [במילה] והסתר), הרי הקדוש ברוך הוא שורה
ומלובש בתורה.

כי הוא יתברך "מורה", והיא "תורה". אלא, שלבושי התורה הגסים
לעינינו המה בחינת כנפים, המכסים ומסתירים את המורה יתברך,
המלובש ומסתתר בהם, אמנם, כשזוכה האדם לגילוי פנים,
בתשובה מאהבה בבחינתה הד' (כנ"ל סעיף עג' ד"ה דבור המתחיל [במילה]
מידה סעיף קכא' ד"ה דבור המתחיל [במילה] ולפיכך) נאמר עליו "ולא יכנף
עוד מוריך והיו עיניך רואות את מוריך(ישעיה ל' כ'), כי מאז ואילך,
אין לבושי ה"תורה" מכניפים ומסתירים עוד את ה"מורה", ונתגלה
לו לנצח כי אוריתא וקוב"ה חד הוא התורה והקדוש ברוך הוא אחד הם.

A commentary on the essay of our sages: I wish they had forsaken Me but had kept My Torah, etc.

141) And this will clarify the words of our sages on the passage: "They have forsaken Me but have kept My Torah," which means: "I wish they had forsaken Me but had kept My Torah because the Light in it would have brought them back to the right path (lit. to good)." (Jerusalem *Talmud*, Tractate *Hagigah* 81a:7) This might seem strange but their intention was that by fasting and performing austerities, in order to find the Revelation of His Face, as it is said: "They seek the closeness to the Creator." (Isaiah 58:2) And the Scriptures speak to them on behalf of the Creator, Who says, "I wish you had left Me because all of your efforts are in vain and for no avail because I am not to be found anywhere except in the Torah; therefore, follow the Torah and look for Me there, and the Light in it will bring you to the right path, and you will find Me," (as explained above (verse 95) starting with the words: And now…,) on the scriptural passage: "Those who seek Me diligently shall find Me," (Proverbs 8:17) study there (verses 41 and 93-94).

ביאור מאמר חז"ל: הלואי אותי עזבו ותורתי שמרו כו'

קמא) ובזה תבין דברי חז"ל, על הכתוב, אותי עזבו ותורתי שמרו
(לפי ירמיהו, טז, יא), שפירשו, הלואי אותי עזבו, ותורתי שמרו,
המאור שבה, מחזירן למוטב (תלמוד ירושלמי מסכת חגיגה פ"א ה"ז
פרק א' הלכה ז'), שלכאורה תמוה. אמנם כונתם, כי המה היו צמים
ומתענים, למצוא גילוי פניו יתברך, כמ"ש כמו שכתוב: קרבת אלקים
יחפצון (ישעיה נ"ח ב'), ואומר להם הכתוב בשם ה', שאומר להם,
הלואי שתעזבו אותי, כי כל יגיעתכם לריק וללא הועיל, משום
שאינני נמצא בשום מקום אלא בתורה, לכן שמרו את התורה, ושם
תחפשו אותי, והמאור שבה יחזירכם למוטב, ותמצאוונני, כמבואר
(סעיף צה' ד"ה דבור המתחיל [במילה] ובזה) בכתוב ומשחרי ימצאונני
(משלי ח' יז') ע"ש עיין שם.

Chapter Ten
The Garment of the Soul

The three aspects: World (*Olam*), Year (*Shanah*), Soul (*Nefesh*)

142) **Now** we can somewhat explain the meaning of the wisdom of Kabbalah in a way that would be sufficient to give us a truthful idea of the nature of this wisdom, so as not to delude ourselves with the false notions [of Kabbalah] that most people imagine in their minds. And it is important that you know that the Holy Torah is divided into four aspects that encompass the entirety of reality. There are three aspects that are considered to constitute the totality of reality in this world, and these are called "World," (*Olam*) "Year," (*Shanah*) and "Soul" (*Nefesh*); the fourth aspect is the way these three aspects of reality co-exist, that is, their nourishment and their conduct, and all their interactions.

143) **Explanation:** The external values of reality, such as the Heavens and the firmaments and the Earth and the seas, etc., mentioned in the Holy Torah, are all referred to by the term "World" (*Olam*). The inner [aspect] of reality, namely the various kinds of men and beasts and animals and the various birds mentioned in the Torah that can be found in those places which are called external, are referred to by the term "Soul" (*Nefesh*).

And the unfolding development [chains of events] within the reality, together with its generations, are [called] cause and effect— an example [being] the chain of the "heads of the generations" mentioned in the Torah, from Adam [all the way] to Joshua and Caleb who came into the land of Israel, where the father is considered as the "cause" relative to the son, who is [considered] the "effect"—thus the aspect of this unfolding development of reality, in terms of cause and effect, is called by the name "Year." And all the ways of existence of all the reality, in terms of both its exterior and interior aspects, as mentioned above, including all the ways they are conducted by and their interactions mentioned in the Torah, are called "the existence of the reality."

פרק עשירי
הלבוש על הנשמה

שלשת הבחינות: עולם שנה נפש

קמב) ועתה אפשר לבאר, מהות חכמת הקבלה באפס-מה, באופן, שיספיק למושג נאמן בטיב החכמה ההיא, שלא להטעות את עצמו בדמיונות כוזבים, שההמונים למרביתם מדמים לעצמם, וצריך שתדע, שהתורה הקדושה, מתחלקת לד' בחינות, המקיפות את כל המציאות, כי ג' בחינות נבחנות בכלל המציאות שבעולם הזה, שנקראים: עולם, שנה, נפש, ובחי"ד *ובחינה ד'* היא, דרכי קיומם של אותם ג' חלקי המציאות, דהיינו, הזנתם והנהגתם וכל מקריהם.

קמג) פירוש, כי החיצוניות של המציאות כמו: השמים והרקיעים והארץ והימים וכדומה, הכתובים בתורה הקדושה, כל אלו מכונים בשם "עולם". והפנימיות של המציאות, דהיינו האדם והבהמה והחיה והעוף למיניהם וכדומה, המובאים בתורה אשר ישנם במקומות הנ"ל שנקראים חיצוניות, הם מכונים בשם "נפש".

והשתלשלות המציאות לדורותיהם, בשם סיבה ומסובב, למשל, כמו ההשתלשלות של ראשי הדורות, מאדם הראשון, עד יהושע וכלב באי הארץ, המובאת בתורה, שהאב נבחן ל"סיבה" אל בנו ה"מסובב" על ידו, הנה בחינת ההשתלשלות הזו של פרטי המציאות, בדרך סיבה ומסובב האמורה, מכונה בשם "שנה". וכל דרכי הקיום של כל המציאות הן מהחיצוניות והן מהפנימיות הנ"ל לכל דרכי הנהגותיהם ומקריהם, המובאים בתורה מכונים בשם "קיום המציאות".

199

Four Worlds: Emanation, Creation, Formation, and Action - from the aspect of stamp and seal

144) And you should know that the Four Worlds referred to in the Wisdom of Kabbalah—*Atzilut* (Emanation), *Beriah* (Creation), *Yetzirah* (Formation), and *Asiyah* (Action)—came out unfolding as a chain of events. They came one out of the other as an aspect of "stamp and seal." This means that everything that is inscribed on the stamp is, of necessity, revealed and comes [to light] in the seal that comes out of [the stamp], no more and no less. This was the case in the chain of evolution of the Worlds, namely how all the four aspects—World, Year, Soul and their existence, as mentioned above—that exist in the World of *Atzilut* (Emanation)—emerged as their form was sealed and appeared also in the [lower] World of *Beriah* (Creation), and then from the World of *Beriah* (Creation) to the [lower] World of *Yetzirah* (Formation), all the way [down] to the World of *Asiyah* (Action).

In such a manner, all the three aspects of reality before us called World, Year, and Soul (*Nefesh*), with all their ways of existence laid out in front of us here in this world, were extended from the World of *Yetzirah* (Formation) and appeared here [in the World of *Asiyah* (Action)]. And the World of *Yetzirah* (Formation) was extended from that which is above it [namely, the World of *Beriah* (Creation)] in such a manner that the source of all these innumerable details in front of our eyes exists in the World of *Atzilut* (Emanation). Not only that, but also those innovations that appear in our world in these days must first be revealed above in the World of *Atzilut* (Emanation).

And it is from there that it [each innovation] comes down and reveals itself here in this world. As our sages have said: "You have no weed that grows Below that doesn't have an [astrological] sign and a ministering angel Above, which hits it and says, 'Grow!'" (*Beresheet Rabbah*, 10:6) And this is the secret behind the passage: "No one lifts a finger Below unless it has been declared Above." (Tractate *Hulin*, 7b) Understand this well.

200

ארבע עולמות אבי"ע בבחינת חותם ונחתם

קמד) ותדע, שד' העולמות הנקראים בחכמת הקבלה: אצילות
בריאה, יצירה, עשיה, בעת שנשתלשלו ויצאו, הנה יצאו זה מזה,
בבחינת חותם ונחתם, כלומר, כמו שכל מה שנמצא רשום בחותם
מתגלה בהכרח ויוצא בדבר הנחתם ממנו, לא פחות ולא יותר. כן
היה בהשתלשלות העולמות, באופן, שכל ד' הבחינות שהם עש"נ
עולם שנה נפש וקיומיהם כנ"ל, שהיו בעולם האצילות, יצאו כולם
ונחתמו ונתגלו דוגמתם, גם בעולם הבריאה. וכן מעולם הבריאה
לעולם היצירה, עד לעולם העשיה.

באופן, שכל ג' הבחינות שבמציאות שלפנינו המכונות עש"נ עולם שנה
נפש, עם כל דרכי הקיום שלהם הערוכים לעינינו, כאן בעולם הזה,
הנה נמשכו ונתגלו כאן מעולם היצירה, והיצירה מן שלמעלה ממנו,
באופן שמקור כל הפרטים המרובים הללו שלעינינו הם בעולם
האצילות. ולא עוד, אלא אפילו אותם החידושים המתחדשים
ובאים היום בעולם הזה, הנה מוכרח כל חידוש להתגלות מקודם
מלמעלה בעולם האצילות.

ומשם בא ומשתלשל ונגלה לנו בעולם הזה. וז"ש חז"ל וזה שאמרו
חכמינו זכרונם לברכה, אין לך כל עשב מלמטה שאין עליו מזל ושוטר
מלמעלה, שמכה עליו ואמר לו גדל (בראשית רבה פ"י פרשה י, ו').
וזה סוד, אין אדם נוקף אצבעו מלמטה, עד שמכריזין עליו מלמעלה
(חולין דף ז' ע"ב), והבן.

The vesting of the Torah in this world through disappearance and concealment

145) And know that the aspect of the Torah vested in the three aspects of reality—World, Year, Soul and their physical existence in this world, as mentioned above (verse 142)—is where we have the prohibited, the impure, and the disqualified that appear in the Revealed Torah, in which the Creator is vested, as explained earlier (verses 101 and 140). This is the secret of "the Creator and the Torah are one and the same" although through disappearance and great concealment, because these material Garments are the wings that cover and conceal Him. And as for the Torah being vested in the aspect of the pure World, Year, and Soul and their existence in the three Upper Worlds of *Atzilut* (Emanation), *Beriah* (Creation), and *Yetzirah* (Formation)—these are called, all in all, "the Wisdom of Kabbalah."

The Wisdom of Kabbalah is the revelation of the Torah of Emanation, Creation, and Formation.

146) Thus, the Wisdom of Kabbalah and the Revealed Torah are one and the same. But while a person experiences the aspect of Providence [referred to] as the Concealment of the Face and the Creator hides in the Torah (as mentioned above, (verse 101) starting with the words: The verse says...), it is considered that he is engaging with the Revealed Torah. This means that he is not capable of receiving any enlightenment from the Torah of *Yetzirah* (Formation), and needless to say, even less so from [the Worlds] above *Yetzirah* (Formation).

But when a person merits the Revelation of the Face, as mentioned above (verse 109) starting with the words: And here...), he then starts engaging with the Wisdom of Kabbalah. This is because the Garments of the Revealed Torah themselves are made pure through him, and his Torah becomes the Torah of *Yetzirah* (Formation), which is called "the Wisdom of Kabbalah."

התלבשות התורה בעולם הזה בהעלם והסתר

קמה) ותדע, שבחינת התלבשות התורה בג' בחינות המציאות:
עולם, שנה, נפש, וקיומיהם שבעולם הזה, החומריים כנ"ל (סעיף
קמב), הנה מכאן נמצאים לנו האיסור והטומאה והפסול, שבאים
בתורה הנגלית, אשר נתבאר לעיל (סעיף קא' וקמ'), שהקדוש ברוך
הוא מלובש בה, בסוד אורייתא וקדוש ברוך הוא חד הוא התורה
והקדוש ברוך הוא אחד הם, אלא בהעלם והסתר גדול, היות והלבושים
החומריים האלו, המה הכנפיים, המכסים ומעלימים אותו יתברך.
אמנם בחינת התלבשות התורה, בבחינת עש"ן עולם שנה נפש הזכים
וקיומיהם, שבג' העולמות העליונים, שנקראים: אצילות, בריאה,
יצירה, המה מכונים בכללם, בשם "חכמת הקבלה".

חכמת הקבלה היא גילוי התורה דאצילות בריאה יצירה

קמו) באופן, שחכמת הקבלה והתורה הנגלית, הם היינו הך, אלא,
בעוד שהאדם מקבל מבחינת השגחה של הסתר פנים, והקדוש
ברוך הוא מסתתר בתורה (כנ"ל סעיף קא' ד"ה דבור המתחיל [במילה]
וז"ש), נבחן, שעוסק בתורת הנגלה, כלומר, שאינו מוכשר לקבל
שום הארה מתורה דיצירה, ואצ"ל ואין צורך לומר עוד מלמעלה ליצירה.

וכשהאדם זוכה לגילוי פנים כנ"ל (סעיף קט' ד"ה דבור המתחיל [במילה]
והנה), אז מתחיל לעסוק בחכמת הקבלה, היות ולבושי התורה
הנגלית בעצמם, נזדככו בעדו, ונעשתה תורתו, תורת היצירה,
שנקראת "חכמת הקבלה".

203

And even for one who gains the Torah of *Atzilut* (Emanation), this does not mean, Heaven forbid, that the letters of the Torah have altered their order, but [rather] that the very same Garments of the Revealed Torah have become purified for him. [These Garments] became extremely pure (lit. transparent), as they have become according to the secret of the passage: "Your Teacher will not hide Himself any more, and your eyes shall see your Teacher," as mentioned above (verse 140), because then the Garments all become "He and His Essence and His causations are One and the same," as mentioned above (140).

The difference between the Wisdom of Kabbalah and the Torah of Emanation on one hand and the Revealed Wisdom on the other is only a matter of the degree of revelation and concealment

147) **In order** to bring [this concept] closer to our understanding, I will give you an example. While the person was in the period of the Concealment of the Face, the letters and the Garments of the Torah were, of necessity, hiding the Creator. This is why he failed through the intentional and unintentional sins that he had committed and [as a result] he was under the rod of punishment, Heaven forbid, of these crude Garments of the Torah, which are the impurities and prohibitions and disqualifications, etc.

However, when he merits the Visible Providence and enjoys Repentance out of Love (verse 64), where his intentional [sins] become like merits to him, then all the evil actions and errors which he committed (lit. failed in) during the time that he was under the Concealment of the Face, have now taken off their very crude and bitter Garments and have covered themselves with Garments of Light and Precepts and merits, those very crude Garments having themselves become merits, (as we have said above (verse 121) starting with the words: And this is why…); study that well. So now they [have taken] the aspect of the Garments that extend from the World of *Atzilut* (Emanation), or *Beriah* (Creation), and they do

ואפילו הזוכה לתורה דאצילות, אין הפירוש חס ושלום, שנתחלפו לו אותיות התורה, אלא, אותם הלבושים עצמם של התורה הנגלית, נזדככו לו ונעשו ללבושים זכים מאוד, שהם נעשו בסוד הכתוב ולא יכנף עוד מוריך, והיו עיניך רואות את מוריך, כנ"ל (סעיף קמ'), שאז נעשו בבחינת איהו וחיוהי וגרמוהי חד בהון הוא, חיותו ועצמותו אחד הם, כנ"ל (קמ').

ההבחן בין חכמת הקבלה ותורה דאצילות לחכמת הנגלה הוא רק במדת הגילוי והעלם

קמז) וכדי לקרב הדבר מעט אל השכל, אתן לך דוגמא למשל, כי בעוד, שהיה האדם בזמן הסתר פנים, הנה בהכרח שהאותיות ולבושי התורה היו מסתירים את הקדוש ברוך הוא, כי על כן נכשל, על ידי הזדונות והשגגות שעשה, ואז היה מוטל תחת שבט העונש חס ושלום, המלבושים הגסים שבתורה, שהם טומאה ואיסור ופסול וכדומה.

אמנם בעת שזוכה להשגחה הגלויה, ולבחינת תשובה מאהבה (סעיף סד'), שהזדונות נעשו לו כזכויות, הרי כל הזדונות והשגגות שנכשל בהם, מעת היותו תחת הסתר פנים, הנה נתפשטו עתה מלבושיהם הגסים והמרים מאד, ונתלבשו בבחינת לבושי אור ומצוה וזכויות, כי אותם הלבושים הגסים בעצמם נתהפכו לזכויות, כנ"ל (סעיף קכא' ד"ה דבור המתחיל [במילה] ולפיכך) עש"ה עיין שם היטב, שהמה עתה בחינת לבושים הנמשכים מעולם האצילות, או בריאה, שהמה אינם

not hide (*maknifim*, "cover as if with wings") the Teacher. Quite the opposite, in fact, [as it is said]: "Your eyes shall *see* your Teacher," as mentioned above (verse 140).

Thus, there is no exchange of anything, Heaven forbid, between the Torah of *Atzilut* (Emanation) and the Torah of this world, that is, between the Wisdom of Kabbalah and the Revealed Torah. The only distinction is with regard to the person who is engaged with the Torah: You [can] have two [individuals] who are engaged with the Torah with regard to the same *Halachah* and literally using one language [terminology], and with all this, the Torah for one will be from the aspect of the Wisdom of Kabbalah and the Torah of *Atzilut* (Emanation), while for the other, it will be the Torah of *Asiyah* (Action) and the Revealed Torah, and understand this well.

The words of Rav Eliyahu from Vilnius regarding the PARDES of the Torah

148) **And by this,** you will understand how rightful the words of the Gaon, Rav Eliyahu from Vilnius (in his prayer book, in the blessings of the Torah) are. He wrote that one should start (studying) the Torah with the *Sod* (secret, concealed), namely, the Revealed Torah of *Asiyah* (Action), which is in the category of the concealed because the Creator conceals Himself in it completely, as mentioned above (verse 41). And afterwards, he should continue to the *Remez* (hint), which means that which has been mostly revealed in the Torah of *Yetzirah* (Formation). And finally, he gets to the *P'shat* (literal, explicit), which is the secret of the Torah of *Atzilut* (Emanation), which is called *P'shat* (literal, explicit) because it has taken off (*nitpashta*) all the Garments that conceal the Creator, as explained.

מכניפים ומכסים על ה"מורה" יתברך, אלא אדרבה, והיו עיניך רואות את מוריך, כנ"ל (סעיף קמ').

הרי, שאין חס ושלום שום חילוף של משהו, בין תורה דאצילות לתורה שבעל פה"ז שבעולם הזה, דהיינו בין חכמת הקבלה לתורת הנגלה, אלא, שכל ההבחן הוא רק בבחינת האדם העוסק בתורה, ושנים עוסקים בתורה בהלכה אחת, ובלשון אחת ממש. ועם כל זה, לאחד תהיה התורה ההיא בבחינת חכמת הקבלה ותורה דאצילות, ולשני תהיה תורה דעשיה ונגלה, והבן זה היטב.

מאמר הגר"א בענין פרד"ס התורה

קמח) ובזה תבין צדקת דברי הגר"א הגאון רבי אליהו מווילנא ז"ל (בסדור [הגר"א], בברכת התורה), שכתב, שמתחילין התורה בסוד, דהיינו, תורת הנגלה דעשיה, שהיא בחינת נסתר, שהשם יתברך מסתתר שם לגמרי כנ"ל (סעיף מא'). ואחר כך ברמז, כלומר, שנתגלה ביותר בתורה דיצירה, עד שזוכה לפשט, שהוא סוד תורה דאצילות, שנקראת פשט, משום שנתפשטה מכל הלבושים המסתירים להשם יתברך כמבואר.

Emanation, Creation, Formation, and Action of Holiness, and their connection to the four aspects of perceiving His Providence

149) And after we have reached this point, we can give some idea and discernment regarding the Four Worlds known in Kabbalah by the names: *Atzilut* (Emanation), *Beriah* (Creation), *Yetzirah* (Formation), and *Asiyah* (Action) of Holiness. And [there are also] the four Worlds: *ABYA*: Atzilut (Emanation), Beriah (Creation), Yetzirah (Formation), and Asiyah (Action) of the *Klipot* (Shells), which are arranged according to the secret of: "one opposite the other." (Ecclesiastes 7:14) in relation to *ABYA* Atzilut (Emanation), Beriah (Creation), Yetzirah (Formation), and Asiyah (Action) of Holiness that was mentioned above.

All these [issues] can be understood from the explanation above (verse 64), about the four aspects of perceiving the Creator's Providence and about the four stages of love. So first, we will explain the four Worlds—*Atzilut* (Emanation), *Beriah* (Creation), *Yetzirah* (Formation), and *Asiyah* (Action)—of Holiness, starting from the lowest (lit. below), from the World of *Asiyah* (Action).

150) We have explained above (verse 19, starting with the words: And here...) the first two aspects of Providence from the perspective of the Concealment of the Face [namely, One Concealment and Double Concealment]; study that well. And you should know that both [aspects] correspond to the World of *Asiyah* (Action), which is why it is stated in the book *The Tree of Life* (Etz Chayim, Gate 48, page 3) that the World of *Asiyah* (Action) is mostly evil, and even the small amount of goodness that is in it is also mixed with the evil, so much so as to be unrecognizable (end of quote).

This means that as far as the One Concealment is concerned (as was mentioned above, verse 50, starting with the words: This was not...), we can understand that it is mostly evil, alluding to the suffering and pain that people feel under this Providence. And as far as the Double Concealment (Concealment within Concealment) is concerned, we find that the good also mixes with the bad, but the good goes completely unnoticed (as mentioned above, verse 52, starting with the words: And Concealment...)

אבי"ע דקדושה, וקישורם עם ד' הבחינות בהשגת השגחתו ית'

קמט) ואחר שבאנו לכאן, אפשר ליתן איזה מושג והבחן, בד' העולמות הנודעים בחכמת הקבלה, בשמות: אצילות, בריאה, יצירה, עשיה, של הקדושה. ובד' העולמות אבי"ע אצילות, בריאה, יצירה, עשיה, של הקליפות, הערוכים בסוד זה לעומת זה (קהלת, ז, יא'), לעומת אבי"ע אצילות, בריאה, יצירה, עשיה דקדושה הנ"ל.

ותבין כל זה, מהביאור הנ"ל (סעיף סד'), בד' הבחינות של השגת השגחתו יתברך (סעיף סד'), ומד' המדרגות של האהבה. ונבאר מתחילה את ד' העולמות אבי"ע אצילות, בריאה, יצירה, עשיה דקדושה ונתחיל מלמטה מעולם העשיה.

קן) כי הנה נתבארו לעיל (סעיף קט' ד"ה דבור המתחיל [במילה] והנה), ב' הבחינות הראשונות של ההשגחה, מבחינת הסתר פנים, עש"ה. ותדע, ששניהם הם בחינת עולם העשיה, כי על כן איתא מובא בספר עץ חיים (שער מ"ח פ"ג), אשר עולם העשיה רובו רע, וגם אותו מיעוט טוב שישנו בו, מעורב גם כן יחד עם הרע, בלי להכירו, עכ"ל עד כאן לשונו.

פירוש, כי מצד ההסתר הא' (כנ"ל סעיף נ' ד"ה דבור המתחיל [במילה] משא"כ) נמשך שרובו רע, דהיינו, היסורים והמכאובים שמקבלי ההשגחה הזאת מרגישים, ומצד ההסתר הכפול נמצא גם הטוב מתערב ברע, ואין הטוב ניכר לגמרי (כנ"ל סעיף נב' ד"ה דבור המתחיל [במילה] והסתר).

The first aspect of the Revelation of the Face is the aspect of the World of *Yetzirah* (Formation), which is why it is stated in the book *The Tree of Life* (Gate 48, verse 3) that the World of *Yetzirah* (Formation) is half bad and half good (end of quote). This means, (as we have seen above (verse 138) starting with the word: Still…), that whoever perceives the first aspect of the Revelation of the Face—the first degree of the Love that Depends on Something— which is called Repentance out of Fear—is called a middling, and half of him is guilty and half of him is innocent, as mentioned above (verse 114).

The second aspect of love—(as mentioned above, (verse 70) starting with the words: The first attribute…), which also Depends on Something, but has no trace of any evil or harm at all in it—and also the third degree of love—(as mentioned above verses 72-73), which is the first degree of Love that Does Not Depend on Anything— both correspond to the World of *Beriah* (Creation). Therefore, it is stated in the book *The Tree of Life* (Gate 48, Ch. 3) that the World of *Beriah* (Creation) is mostly good and less evil, and that minor evil is not noticed; study that well. This means, (as is mentioned above (verse 117) starting with the words: And the *Tanna* tells…) in the commentary of the *Braita*, that because the middling merits [the] one precept [of love], he tips his own balance towards the side of innocence, and for this reason he is referred to as mostly good; namely, the second degree of love.

And the minor unnoticeable evil that is found in the World of *Beriah* (Creation) stems (lit. extends) from the third degree of love, which does not depend on anything, and also [where] one has already tipped the scale for himself towards the side of innocence (verse 110), but has not yet tipped the balance for the whole world (as mentioned above, (verse 119) starting with the words: And it has been explained…). And the conclusion is that the least [amount] of evil is in him because this love is not yet considered eternal, as mentioned there; study that well. Indeed, this minor evil is not noticeable because one has not yet felt any evil or harm even towards others (as mentioned above, (verse 72) starting with the words: The second attribute…).

והבחינה הראשונה של גילוי פנים, היא בחינת "עולם היצירה" ועל כן איתא מובא בע"ח בספר עץ חיים (שער מ"ח פ"ג), שעולם היצירה חציו טוב וחציו רע, עכ"ל. דהיינו, כמ"ש כמו שנאמר לעיל (סעיף קלח' ד"ה ד"ה הדבור המתחיל [במילה] אמנם), שהמשיג הבחינה הראשונה של גילוי פנים, שהיא בחינה א' של האהבה התלויה בדבר, המכונה רק תשובה מיראה, הוא נקרא בינוני, והוא חציו חייב וחציו זכאי, כנ"ל (סעיף קיד').

והבחינה השנייה של האהבה (כנ"ל סעיף ע' ד"ה הדבור המתחיל [במילה] הא'), שהיא גם כן תלויה בדבר, אלא שאין שום זכר ביניהם מהיזק ורע כל שהוא, וכן בחינה ג' של האהבה (כנ"ל סעיף עב'-עג'), שהיא בחינה א' של אהבה שאינה תלויה בדבר, הנה הן שתיהן, בחינת "עולם הבריאה". וע"כ איתא בע"ח ועל כן מובא [בספר] עץ חיים (שמ"ח פ"ג שער מח' פרק ג'), שעולם הבריאה הוא רובו טוב ומיעוטו רע, ומיעוט הרע אינו ניכר, עש"ה עיין שם היטב, דהיינו כמ"ש כמו שכתוב לעיל (סעיף קטז' ד"ה הדבור המתחיל [במילה] ואומר) בפירוש הברייתא שמתוך שהבינוני זוכה למצוה אחת, הוא מכריע את עצמו לכף זכות, שנקרא משום זה, רובו טוב, והיינו בחינה ב' של האהבה.

ומיעוט הרע שאינו ניכר שישנו בבריאה, נמשך מבחינה ג' של האהבה שהיא אינה תלויה בדבר, וגם, כבר הכריע את עצמו לכף זכות (סעיף קיז'), אמנם, עדיין לא הכריע את העולם כולו, (כנ"ל סעיף קיט' ד"ה הדבור המתחיל [במילה] ונתבאר), שנמצא מזה, שמיעוטו רע, כי עדיין אין האהבה הזו, בבחינת נצחיות, כמ"ש שם, עש"ה. אמנם, אין המיעוט הזה ניכר, כי עדיין לא הרגיש שום רע והיזק אפילו כלפי אחרים (כנ"ל סעיף עב' ד"ה הדבור המתחיל [במילה] הב').

The fourth degree of love—love that does not depend on something and is also eternal (as mentioned above (verse 73) starting with the words: The second level… and (verse 121) starting with the words: And this is why…)—corresponds to the World of *Atzilut* (Emanation). And this is what is said in the book, *The Tree of Life* [Gate of Klipot 48:3]: that in the World of *Atzilut* (Emanation), there is no evil whatsoever, and this is the secret meaning of the passage: "Evil may not sojourn with You." (Psalms 5:5) Because one has tipped the [scale] for the whole world towards the side of innocence, love becomes eternal and absolute, and any cover or concealment is forever gone.

This is because [the World of Emanation] is the place of complete Revelation of the Face, according to the secret meaning of the words: "Your Teacher will not hide Himself any more, but your eyes shall see your Teacher" (verse 140), because now one already knows all the Creator's ways of conduct (lit. dealings) with all His created beings, according to the aspect of the true Providence that is manifest from the Name: He Who is good and does good to the evil and to the good, as mentioned above (verse 73).

Emanation, Creation, Formation, and Action of the *Klipot* (Shells) as opposed to Emanation, Creation, Formation and Action of Holiness

151) Through this, you can understand also the four Worlds of *Atzilut* (Emanation), *Beriah* (Creation), *Yetzirah* (Formation), and *Asiyah* (Action) of the *Klipot* (Shells) as they mirror (lit. are arranged against) the Worlds of *Atzilut* (Emanation), *Beriah* (Creation), *Yetzirah* (Formation), and *Asiyah* (Action) of Holiness. This is the secret meaning of: "The Creator has made the one opposite the other" [(Ecclesiastes 7:14)] (verse 149). This is because the Chariot of the *Klipot* of the [World of] *Asiyah* (Action) corresponds to the Concealment of the Face in both its degrees because that Chariot rules in order to cause [every] person to tip the [scale] towards the side of guilt, Heaven forbid.

בחינה ד' של האהבה, שפירושה אהבה שאינה תלויה בדבר, וגם היא נצחית (כנ"ל סעיף עג' ד"ה דבור המתחיל [במילה] מ*י*דה] וסעיף קכא' ד"ה דבור המתחיל [במילה] ואע"פ), היא בחינת עולם האצילות, וז"ש בע"ח וזה שכוב [בספר] עץ חיים [שער הקליפות, שער מח' פרק ג'], שבעולם האצילות אין שום רע כל שהוא, ושם סוד הכתוב לא יגורך רע, כי אחר שהכריע גם את העולם כולו לכף זכות, הרי, האהבה נצחית ומוחלטת, ולא יצוייר עוד שום כיסוי והסתר לעולם.

כי שם מקום גילוי הפנים לגמרי, בסוד הכתוב ולא יכנף עוד מוריך והיו עיניך רואות את מוריך (סעיף קמ'), כי כבר יודע כל עסקיו של הקדוש ברוך הוא עם כל הבריות, בבחינת ההשגחה האמיתית המתגלה משמו יתברך הטוב והמיטיב לרעים ולטובים כנ"ל (סעיף עג').

אבי"ע דקליפה לעומת אבי"ע דקדושה

קנא) ובזה תבין גם כן, בחינת ד' העולמות אבי"ע אצילות, בריאה, יצירה עשיה דקליפה הערוכים לעומת אבי"ע אצילות, בריאה, יצירה, עשיה דקדושה, בסוד זה לעומת זה עשה אלקים (סעיף קמט'). כי המרכבה של הקליפות דעשיה, היא מבחינת הסתר הפנים בב' דרגותיה, שמרכבה ההיא שולטת, כדי לגרום לאדם שיכריע הכל לכף חובה חס ושלום.

And the World of *Yetzirah* (Formation) of the *Klipot* holds the side (lit. the pan) of guilt with his hands, which has not [yet] been corrected in the World of *Yetzirah* (Formation) of Holiness (as was discussed above, verse 121, starting with the words: And this is why…). And thereby, they take control over the middlings, who receive from the World of *Yetzirah* (Formation), as was mentioned above, according to the secret: "The Creator has made the one opposite the other."

And the World of *Beriah* (Creation) of the *Klipot* has the same power to cancel out love that depends on something; that is, to cancel the thing on which that love depends, which is the imperfection of the love of the second degree.

And the World of *Atzilut* (Emanation) of the *Klipot* grips tightly on to that unnoticeable lesser evil that exists in the World of *Beriah* (Creation) through the power of the third degree of love. Even though it is real love that comes from the power of "He who is good and does good to the evil as well as to the good," which is the aspect of [the World of] *Atzilut* (Emanation) of Holiness, still with all of this, because one has not merited in this manner to tip [the scale] of the whole world to the side of innocence, the *Klipah* (Shell) has the power to make that love fail, out of the power of the Providence over others (as mentioned above, (verse 72) starting with the words: The second attribute…).

152) And this is what is said in [the book] *Etz Chaim* (*The Tree of Life*): that the World of *Atzilut* (Emanation) of the *Klipot* (Shells) stands against the World of *Beriah* (Creation) and not the [World of] *Atzilut* (Emanation); study there. This means, as we have said, that in the World of *Atzilut* (Emanation) of Holiness, from which only the **fourth degree** of love is extended, the *Klipot* have no control whatsoever. This is because one has already tipped [the scale] for the whole world towards the side of innocence, and one knows all the dealings of the Creator—including His Providence over all

ועולם היצירה דקליפה, תופס בידיו את כף החובה, שאינה מתוקנת בעולם היצירה דקדושה (כנ"ל סעיף קכא' ד"ה דבור המתחיל [במילה] ולפיכך). ובזה שולטים על הבינונים, המקבלים מעולם היצירה, כנ"ל, בסוד זה לעומת זה עשה אלקים.

ועולם הבריאה דקליפה, יש בידיהם אותו הכח, כדי לבטל את האהבה התלויה בדבר, דהיינו, רק לבטל את הדבר שבו נתלית האהבה, והיינו, הבלתי שלימות, שבאהבה דבחינה ב'.

ועולם האצילות דקליפה, הוא שתופס בידיו אותו מיעוט הרע שאינו ניכר, מכח בחינה ג' של האהבה, שאף על פי שהיא אהבה אמיתית מכח הטוב והמיטיב לרעים ולטובים, שהיא בחינת אצילות דקדושה, עם כל זה, כיון שלא זכה להכריע באופן זה גם את העולם כולו לכף זכות, יש כח ביד הקליפה להכשיל את האהבה, מכח ההשגחה על האחרים (כנ"ל סעיף עב' ד"ה דבור המתחיל [במילה] הב').

קנב) וז"ש בע"ח וזה שכתוב [בספר] עץ חיים, אשר עולם האצילות של הקליפות, עומד לעומת עולם הבריאה ולא לעומת האצילות, ע"ש. דהיינו, כמו שנתבאר, כי עולם אצילות דקדושה, שמשם נמשכת רק **בחינה ד'** של האהבה, הרי שאין שם שליטה לקליפות כלל, היות שכבר הכריע את כל העולם לכף זכות, ויודע כל עסקיו של השם יתברך גם בהשגחתו על כל הבריות, מהשגחת שמו יתברך הטוב והמיטיב לרעים ולטובים, אלא בעולם הבריאה, שמשם נמשכת

created beings—as the Providence of the His Name: "He who is the good and does good to the evil and to the good." But in the World of *Beriah* (Creation) [of holiness]—from which the third degree [of love] comes, which has not yet tipped [the scale] for the whole world—the *Klipot* still have some hold. These *Klipot*, however, are considered the *Atzilut* (Emanation) of the *Klipot* because they stand against the third degree, which is 'love that does not depend on anything', as mentioned above (verse 72). This love is the aspect of *Atzilut* (Emanation).

153) And hereby, the [nature of the] Four Worlds of [*ABYA*] *Atzilut* (Emanation), *Beriah* (Creation), *Yetzirah* (Formation), and *Asiyah* (Action) of the Holiness have been well explained, as well as the *Klipot* (Shells) that constitute the "opposite side" of each and every World. They are the aspect of the void that exists in opposition to the Worlds of Holiness. And they are called the four Worlds of *Atzilut* (Emanation), *Beriah* (Creation), *Yetzirah* (Formation), and *Asiyah* (Action) of the *Klipot*, as explained.

הבחינה הג', שעדיין לא הכריעה את העולם כולו, ועל כן יש עוד אחיזה לקליפות, אלא שקליפות אלו נבחנות לאצילות דקליפה, להיותם לעומת בחינה ג', שהיא האהבה שאינה תלויה בדבר, כנ"ל (סעיף עב'). שאהבה זו היא בחינת אצילות.

קנג) ונתבארו היטב, ד' עולמות אבי"ע אצילות, בריאה, יצירה, עשיה דקדושה, והקליפות שהן בחינת הלעומת של כל עולם ועולם שהם מבחינת החסרון שיש בעולם שכנגדו בקדושה, והם שמכונים ד' עולמות אבי"ע אצילות, בריאה, יצירה, עשיה של הקליפות, כמבואר.

Chapter Eleven
The Practical Wisdom of Truth

The books of the Kabbalah were written for those who have already merited Supernal Understandings

154) These words are enough [to allow] any learner to somehow make sense of the essence of the Wisdom of Kabbalah. And you should know that most of the authors of the books of Kabbalah only meant to write for those readers who have already received the Revelation of the Face and all the Supernal Understandings, as mentioned above. And we should not ask: but if they [the readers] have already gained Understanding, then they know everything from their own insights, so why should they go on studying the books of Kabbalah from others?

Indeed, this question is not a wise one because this is like a person who engages with the Revealed Torah but has no idea about the way this world is conducted in terms of World (*Olam*), Year (*Shanah*), Soul (*Nefesh*) of this world, as is mentioned above, and [who] does not know the various ways of humans and how they conduct themselves and how they interact with others. He also does not know the beasts and the animals and the fowl that are in this world. And could you imagine that such a person would be able to properly understand anything in the Torah? For such a person would turn the Torah [on its head], calling the evil "good" and the good "evil," and would not be able to find either his arms or his legs in anything.

This is the case with the matter at hand, because even though someone merits Understanding—and even if the Understanding is from the Torah of *Atzilut* (Emanation)— he still does not know anything other than [those] things that have relevance for (lit. regard) his own soul and himself. He still has to know—in complete awareness—all three aspects mentioned earlier: World, Year, and Soul, in all situations (lit. their cases) and ways of behavior, so that

פרק אחד עשׂר
וחכמת האמת המעשׂית

ספרי הקבלה נכתבו עבור אלו שכבר זכו להשגות העליונות

קנד) והנה הדברים האלו מספיקים לכל מעיין, שירגיש בדעתו את מהותה של חכמת הקבלה באפס מה. וראוי שתדע, שרוב מחברי ספרי הקבלה, לא התכוונו בספריהם, אלא כלפי מעיינים כאלו, שכבר זכו לגילוי פנים ולכל ההשגות העליונות, כנ"ל. ואין לשאול, אם כבר זכו להשגות, הרי הם יודעים הכל מהשגתם עצמם, ולמה להם עוד ללמוד בספרי חכמת הקבלה מאחרים.

אמנם לא מחכמה שאלה זאת, כי זה דומה לעוסק בתורת הנגלה, ואין לו שום ידיעה בעסקי העוה"ז העולם הזה, בבחינת עולם שנה נפש שבעולם הזה, כמ"ש כמו שכתוב לעיל, ואינו יודע במקרי בני אדם והנהגתם לעצמם, והנהגתם עם אחרים, ואינו יודע את הבהמות, החיות והעופות שבעולם הזה. וכי יעלה על דעתך, שאיש כזה יהיה מסוגל להבין איזה ענין בתורה כהלכתו, כי היה מהפך העניינים שבתורה, מרע לטוב ומטוב לרע, ולא היה מוצא את ידיו ורגליו בשום דבר.

כן הענין שלפנינו, אף על פי שהאדם זוכה להשגה, ואפילו להשגה מתורה דאצילות, מ"מ מכל מקום אינו יודע משם אלא מה שנוגע לנפשו עצמו, ועדיין אמנם צריך לדעת כל ג' הבחינות: עולם שנה

he will be able to understand the matter of the Torah that relate to that World. This is because these matters, in all their details and subtleties, are explained in the *Zohar* and in the true Kabbalah texts that each sage (lit. wise) who comperhends it on his own must contemplate day and night.

The benefits to every person of the study of the Kabbalah

155) **Accordingly,** one should ask why, therefore, did the kabbalists urge every person to study the Wisdom of Kabbalah. There is indeed a great issue here, and it is worthy of making it known to all! There is invaluable virtue for those who engage in the study of the Wisdom of Kabbalah—even when they do not understand what they are studying—since it is by the strong desire and the will to understand what they are studying that the learners awaken upon themselves the Surrounding Lights of their soul. This means that every Israelite person is guaranteed that eventually he will achieve all the wonderful Understandings that the Creator planned in His Thought of the Creation—to bestow pleasure upon all created beings.

And whoever does not achieve this [understanding] in this incarnation will achieve it in the next or the next or the next, etc., until he manages to complete the Thought of the Creator that He had planned for him and this has been explained in the *Zohar*, as is well known. Now, as long as the person does not gain this completeness, those Lights that are going to reach him in the future are considered to be the aspect of the Surrounding Lights. This means that they are standing ready for him, but they wait for the person to merit purifying his Vessel of Receiving, and then these Lights will enter the appropriate Vessels.

Therefore, even when he still lacks (lit. misses) the Vessels, nevertheless, when a person engages with this Wisdom and mentions the Names of the Lights and the Vessels, which, as far as the soul is concerned, belong to him, they immediately shine

ונפש, הנ"ל, בכל מקריהם והנהגותיהם, בתכלית ההכרה, כדי
שיוכל להבין את עניני התורה המיוחסת לאותו עולם, שענינים אלו
בכל פרטיהם ודקדוקיהם, מבוארים בספרי הזוהר ובספרי הקבלה
האמיתיים, שכל חכם ומבין מדעתו מחוייב להגות בהם יומם ולילה.

תועלת לימוד הקבלה לכל איש

קנה) ולפי"ז *ולפי זה*, יש לשאול, א"כ *אם כן*, למה זה חייבו המקובלים
לכל איש ללמוד חכמת הקבלה, אמנם יש בזה דבר גדול, וראוי
לפרסמו, כי יש סגולה נפלאה לאין ערוך, לעוסקים בחכמת הקבלה,
ואף על פי שאינם מבינים מה שלומדים, אלא מתוך החשק והרצון
החזק, להבין מה שלומדים, מעוררים עליהם את האורות המקיפים
את נשמתם. פירוש, כי כל אדם מישראל, מובטח בסופו, שישיג
כל ההשגות הנפלאות, אשר חשב השם יתברך במחשבת הבריאה
להנות לכל נברא.

אלא מי שלא זכה בגלגול זה, יזכה בגלגול ב' וכו' עד שיזכה להשלים
מחשבתו יתברך שחשב עליו, כמ"ש *כמו שכתוב* בזוהר, כנודע. והנה כל
עוד שלא זכה האדם לשלימותו, נבחנים לו אותם האורות העתידים
להגיע אליו, בבחינת אורות מקיפים, שמשמעותם היא, שעומדים
מוכנים בעדו, אלא שהמה מחכים לאדם, שיזכה את כלי הקבלה
שלו, ואז יתלבשו האורות האלו בכלים המוכשרים.

ולפיכך, גם בשעה שחסרו לו הכלים, הנה, בשעה שהאדם עוסק
בחכמה הזאת, ומזכיר את השמות של האורות והכלים, שיש להם
מבחינת נשמתו שייכות אליו, הנה הם תיכף מאירים עליו, בשיעור

upon him to a certain degree, although they shine upon him without incorporating themselves into the interiority of his soul. This is because the appropriate Vessels for Receiving are lacking (lit. missing), as explained. Indeed, the illumination that he receives time and again during his engagement [with the Wisdom of Kabbalah] causes grace to extend to him from Above and bestows upon him an abundance of holiness and purity, which brings him very close to attaining his perfection.

Beware of materializing[2]

156) But there is a strict condition that while engaging in this Wisdom, one should not try to materialize things [the words in the books] through imaginary and material matters because this may constitute a violation, Heaven forbid, of [the Precept]: "You shall not make for yourself a graven image." (Exodus 20:3) In this case, one would actually receive harm instead of benefit (see verse 35). Therefore, our sages warned that one should not study this Wisdom except after the age of forty, or [one can] study it from a Rav [Kabbalist], etc. And all this caution is because of the said reason.

The commentaries "Illuminating Face," "Welcoming Face," and "The Meaning of Words": - the terms of Kabbalah arranged alphabetically

Therefore, with the Creator's help, I have prepared the commentaries "Illuminating Face" and "Welcoming Face," which comment upon [the book] *Etz Chaim* (The Tree of Life) and, which I have prepared in order to save the learners from any materialization.

Indeed, after the first four parts of these commentaries were printed and were disseminated among the learners, I realized that I had not

---

2. For example: thinking that the word "circle" means a phisical circle materializes the kabbalistic idea that "circle" kabbalistically means "Endless."

מסויים, אלא שהם מאירים לו בלי התלבשות בפנימיות נשמתו, מטעם שחסרים הכלים המוכשרים לקבלתם, כאמור. אמנם ההארה שמקבל פעם אחר פעם, בעת העסק, מושכים עליו חן ממרומים, ומשפיעים בו שפע של קדושה וטהרה, שהמה מקרבים את האדם מאד, שיגיע לשלימותו.

זהירות מהגשמת הענינים

קנו) אבל תנאי חמור יש בעת העסק בחכמה זאת, שלא יגשימו הדברים בענינים מדומים וגשמיים שעוברים בזה על לא תעשה לך פסל וכל תמונה חס ושלום (סעיף לה'), כי אז, אדרבה מקבלים היזק במקום תועלת. ולפיכך הזהירו ז"ל שלא ללמוד החכמה כי אם לאחר ארבעים שנה או מפי רב, וכדומה מהזהירות, וכל זה הוא מהטעם האמור.

הפירושים "פנים מאירות" ו"פנים מסבירות", ו"פירוש המלות" – ערכי הקבלה ע"פ סדר הא"ב

ולפיכך, הכינותי בעז"ה את הפירושים פנים מאירות ופנים מסבירות על עץ חיים, שעשיתי, כדי להציל המעיינים מכל הגשמה.

אמנם אחר שנדפסו ד' החלקים הראשונים מביאורים אלו, ונתפשטו בקרב הלומדים, ראיתי בהם, שעדיין לא יצאתי ידי חובת ביאור כמו שחשבתי, וכל הטרחה הגדולה שטרחתי לבאר

finished my task of commentator as I had thought, and [that] all
the great efforts that I had put into explaining and expounding so
that things would be made clear with no difficulty were almost for
nothing. This is because learners do not feel any great obligation to
diligently study the meaning of each and every word before them
and to repeat it numerous times in a way that would be sufficient
for them to remember it well later on in the book every time this
same word shows up again. And out of forgetting the meaning of a
certain word, some things would become confusing. This is because
these concepts (lit. the matters) are so subtle that not having the
meaning of one word would be enough to confuse the entire issue
(lit. matter).

So here, in order to correct this, I have started to write "The Meaning
of Words," arranged alphabetically, of all the words that appear (lit.
are brought) in Kabbalah texts that need commentary. On one side,
I have collected all the commentaries of the Ari and the rest of
the first kabbalists, quoting all that they said about [a particular]
word; and on the other side, I have explained the essence of all
these commentaries and have put together a faithful definition to
clarify the meaning of that word to the point where [this definition]
would be sufficient for the learner to understand [the word] in each
and every place that he encounters it in all the authentic books of
Kabbalah, from the early ones to the latest. And I have done so to
all the words commonly used for the Wisdom of Kabbalah.

And with the help of the Creator, I have already printed the words
starting with the letter *Alef* and also some of the letter *Bet*, and
only from one side, and already they make up close to 1000 pages.
Indeed, because of lack of money, I have stopped the work in its
inception. It has now been more than a year since I discontinued
this important task and only the Creator knows whether or not I will
be able to succeed in [completing the work] because the expenses
are very large and I have no one to help me at the moment.

ולהרחיב, כדי שיתבהרו הענינים בלי קושי, היתה כמעט ללא
הועיל, והיה זה, מחמת שהמעיינים אינם מרגישים את החובה
הגדולה, לשקוד על פירוש כל מלה ומלה המגיעה לפניהם, ולחזור
עליה כמה פעמים, באופן שיספיק להם לזכרה היטב בהמשך הספר
בכל מקום שמובאת שם אותה המלה, ומתוך השכחה של איזו מלה
היו מתבלבלים להם הענינים ההם, כי מתוך דקות הענין, הרי חוסר
פירוש של מלה אחת, די לטשטש להם הענין כולו.

והנה כדי לתקן זה, התחלתי לחבר "פירוש המלות" על פי סדר א"ב,
על כל המלות המובאות בספרי הקבלה שצריכות פירוש: מצד אחד
קבצתי את הפירושים של האר"י ז"ל, ויתר המקובלים הראשונים,
בכל מה שאמרו על אותה המלה. ומן הצד השני, ביארתי התמצית
מכל אותם הפירושים, וערכתי הגדרה נאמנה בביאור המלה ההיא,
באופן שיספיק למעיין להבינה, בכל מקום ומקום שיפגוש אותה
המלה, בכל ספרי הקבלה האמיתיים, מהראשונים עד האחרונים,
וכן עשיתי, על כל המלות השגורות בחכמת הקבלה.

והנה כבר הדפסתי בעזרת השם, את המלות המתחילות באות א',
גם קצת מאות ב', ורק מצד אחד, והם כבר קרובים לאלף דפים.
אכן מחמת חסרון כסף, הפסקתי העבודה בהתחלתה. וזה קרוב
לשנה, שאינני ממשיך עוד בעבודה החשובה הזו, והשם יתברך יודע
אם הדבר יעלה לי עוד, כי ההוצאות מרובות ביותר, ומסייעים אין
לי כעת.

The purpose of the book *The Study of the Ten Sefirot*

Therefore, I have now taken a different route, according to the proverb "you got less you got it!" [less is more] and that is this book: *The Study of the Ten Sefirot* of the Ari. I have prepared a collection of essays from books written by the Ari, especially from his book *Etz Chayim* (*The Tree of Life*). These are all the main essays that have to do with the explanation of the Ten *Sefirot*, and I have placed them at the upper part of each page. Then I have proceeded to make one extended commentary called "Inner Light" and a second commentary called "Inner Vision," which explain each word and each concept (lit. matter) mentioned in the words of the Ari [that appear] in the upper part of the page. I used simple and easy language to the extent that I could.

I have divided the book into sixteen parts, each part being one lesson on a particular topic in the Ten *Sefirot*, with the "Inner Light" explaining mainly the words of the Ari quoted in that lesson, and "Inner Vision" explaining the essence of concept (lit. matter) in general. In addition (lit. on top of these), I have arranged a table of questions and a table of answers covering all the words and concepts that are discussed in that part. After the learner has completed each part, he should test himself to answer every question contained in the table of questions properly.

And after he answers, he should look at the table of answers, in the answer that pertain to that question [same footnote for question and answer], to see if he answered it properly. And even if he knows the answers to all the questions from memory, he should repeat the questions many times over, until they will be as if contained in a box, because then he will be able to remember the word whenever it is needed, or at least remember where it is located in order to find it. "And may it be the Creator's Will that he be successful." (Isaiah 53:10)

מטרת הספר "תלמוד עשר הספירות"

לפיכך לקחתי לי עתה דרך אחרת, ע"ד על דרך תפשת מועט תפשת,
והוא הספר הזה "תלמוד עשר הספירות" להאריז"ל, שבו אני מקבץ
מספרי הארי ז"ל, ובייחוד מספר עץ החיים שלו, כל המאמרים
העיקריים הנוגעים לביאור עשר הספירות, שהצבתי אותם בראש
כל דף, ועליו עשיתי ביאור אחד רחב הנקרא בשם "אור פנימי"
וביאור שני הנקרא "הסתכלות פנימית", המבארים כל מלה וכל
ענין, המובאים בדברי האריז"ל בראש הדף, בפשטות ובלשון קלה,
עד כמה שיכולתי.

וחילקתי הספר לששה-עשר חלקים, שכל חלק יהיה שיעור אחד
על ענין מיוחד שבעשר הספירות, אשר ה"אור פנימי" מבאר בעיקר
את דברי האריז"ל המובאים באותו השיעור, ו"הסתכלות פנימית"
מבארת בעיקר העניין בהקף הכללי. ועליהם סדרתי לוח השאלות
ולוח התשובות על כל המלות ועל כל העניינים, המובאים באותו
החלק, ואחר שיגמור המעיין אותו החלק, ינסה בעצמו אם יוכל
להשיב כהלכה על כל שאלה המובאת בלוח השאלות.

ואחר שהשיב, יסתכל בלוח התשובות, בתשובה המיוחסת לאות
ההיא של השאלה, לראות אם השיב כהלכה. ואפילו אם ידע היטב
להשיב על השאלות מתוך הזכרון, עם כל זה יחזור על השאלות
פעמים הרבה מאד, עד שיהיו כמו מונחים בקופסא, כי אז יצליח
לזכור המלה בעת שיצטרך לה, או על כל פנים יזכור מקומה כדי
לחפש אחריה "וחפץ ה' בידו יצליח" (ישעיהו נג, י').

The Order of the Study

Study first the original [the words of the Ari] (lit. Inner) essay—that is, the words of the Ari printed at the top of the page—to the end of the book. And even though you may not understand, repeat [reading] them a few times, according to the saying: "From beginning to end, the understanding is enhanced." After that, study the "Inner Light" commentary and put effort into it, to the point that you will be able to study and understand the original (lit. inner) essay even without the help of the commentary. And after that, study the "Inner Obsevation" commentary until you understand it and remember it fully. And after all this, test yourself with the table of questions, and after you have answered each question, check the answer that is marked with the same letter as the question; do this with each and every question.

And you should study and memorize and repeat them a number of times until you remember them as well as if they were laid out in a box, because in each and every word of the third part [volume], you must remember the first two parts so that no meaning will be missing. And the worst thing would be that the learner would not even notice what he has forgotten; instead, either things would become confusing for him, or he would arrive at an erroneous meaning for the matter because of his forgetfulness. And of course, one mistake is followed by ten other mistakes, until one comes to a complete misunderstanding and has to drop the study altogether.

סדר הלימוד

למד תחילה את ה"פנים", דהיינו דברי האריז"ל, המודפסים בראשי העמודים עד סוף הספר. ואף על פי שלא תבין, חזור עליהם כמה פעמים ע"ד "מתחילה למגמר והדר למסבר" מתחילה לגמור (לשנן) ואחר כך להבין. אחרי זה, למד את הביאור "אור פנימי", והשתדל בו, באופן שתוכל ללמוד ולהבין היטב את ה"פנים" גם בלי עזרת הביאור, ואחר זה למד את הביאור "הסתכלות פנימית" עד שתבינהו ותזכרהו כולו. ואחר כולם, נסה עצמך בלוח השאלות, ואחר שהשבת על השאלה, הסתכל בתשובה המסומנת באותה האות של השאלה, וכן תעשה בכל שאלה ושאלה.

ותלמד ותשנן ותחזור עליהם כמה פעמים עד שתזכרם היטב כמונחים בקופסא, כי בכל מלה ומלה ממש, שבחלק השלישי, צריכים לזכור היטב כל שני החלקים הראשונים, אף מובן קטן לא יחסר. והגרוע מכל הוא, שהמעיין לא ירגיש כלל מה ששכח, אלא, או שהדברים יתטשטשו בעיניו, או שיתקבל לו פירוש מוטעה בענין, מחמת השכחה. וכמובן, שטעות אחת גוררת אחריה עשר טעויות, עד שיבא לאי הבנה לגמרי, ויהיה מוכרח להניח את ידו מהלימוד לגמרי.

GLOSSARY

613 – The number of Precepts—spiritual actions—which we can do to get spiritually closer to the Light of the Creator. There are 613 Precepts, and all can be found within the *Five Books of Moses*. They are separated into two categories: 248 Precepts of proactive/positive "do" actions, and 365 Precepts of reactive/negative "do not do" actions. Performing both types of Precepts will bring us closer to the Creator. See also: *Halachah*, Precept

Amos – A prophet and contemporary of Isaiah (circa 780 BCE). His prophesies often related to the idea that simply following religious ritual without performing positive actions of caring for our fellow-man actually distances us from the Creator.

Ancient of Days – see *Atik Yomin*

Angel – Frequencies or packets of spiritual energy that constantly roam and move about among us, acting as messengers from the Creator and affecting things that happen in our daily life. We can imagine an angel as being a conduit or channel that transports cosmic energy or thoughts from one place to another or from one spiritual dimension to the other. Angels have no free choice, and each angel is dedicated to one specific purpose. See also: Other Gods

Ari – Rav Isaac Luria, often called "the Ari" or "the Holy Lion." Born in 1534, he died in 1572 in the city of Safed in the Galilee region of Israel. Considered to be the father of contemporary Kabbalah, the Ari was a foremost kabbalistic scholar and the founder of the Lurianic method of learning and teaching Kabbalah. His closest student, Rav Chaim Vital, compiled and wrote the Ari's teachings word-for-word in 18 volumes. These 18 volumes are collectively known as the *Writings of the Ari*. See also: Rav Chaim Vital, *Tree of Life*

Asiyah – see World of Action

Atonement – The act of taking responsibility for our past actions, accepting their consequences, admitting our faults, and vowing to change them. This is an internal action when we try to become *one* with the whole embracing collective consciousness: at-ONE-ment.

Atik Yomin – A term in Aramaic that literally means "Ancient of Days," or "Ancient One," a concept referring to the complete dimension of the *Sefira* of *Keter* (Crown). The word *Atik* has two other meanings: "separated" and "copy," relating to the "blueprint" of the Original Vessel. See also: *Keter*, Ten *Sefirot*, Vessel

Attributes (*Midot*) – Literally meaning "measurements" or "levels," *Midot* refers to the quantity of Light that is revealed through the *Sefirot* which creates different qualities. Exodus 34:6-7 lists the Thirteen Attributes that describe the different aspects of the Creator. See also: Ten *Sefirot*

Atzilut – see World of Emanation

Awe – A term usually related to fear. In Hebrew, however, the words "awe" and "see" have the same letters, which teaches us that the true meaning of awe is related to "seeing" the Almightiness of the Creator rather than fearing it. Awe is often used in the phrase "Awe/ Fear of the Creator." It is only when we "see" the future negative outcome of our past or present actions and perceive the Divine Wisdom that we stand in awe in front of our Maker.

Ba'al HaTurim – Rav Yaakov ben Asher (born circa 1269). He wrote a work on kabbalistic law called *Arba'ah Turim* (*Four Columns*), which dealt with every aspect of spiritual law. This book is one of the most influential and important books of law ever written. He also authored other important commentaries on the *Talmud* and the Five Books of Moses. He died in Toledo, Spain, (circa 1343).

Back – The term used to describe those times when it feels as if the Creator has turned His "Back" on us. When we understand the system of cause and effect but we don't immediately see the good behind a situation we have two choices: to succumb to our doubt and say that the Creator has deserted us, or to choose to understand that everything that happens is part of a bigger picture and we cannot see right now the ultimate good that will come. The sages explain that the period of the Back, although painful to the one experiencing it, always comes right before a period of "face-to-face," which represents complete fulfillment. See also: Concealment of the Face, Face, Revelation of the Face

Beauty – see *Tiferet*

Beit HaMikdash – The Holy Temple, located on the Temple Mount in the old city of Jerusalem. Their spiritual work allowed past generations to rise above the laws of time-space-motion. The sacrifices that were offered on the altar served as a conduit for the people to "sacrifice" their own selfish nature and transform it to being like God.

Beit Midrash – A house of study where kabbalists throughout the ages studied all the secrets of Torah and Kabbalah and other ancient texts with their students or with their teacher,.

Beresheet Rabbah – A part of the *Midrash* that expands upon the events that occur in Genesis. Additionally, it quotes stories from the *Talmud* that relate to the stories in Genesis. See also: *Derash*, *Talmud*

Beriah – see World of Creation.

***Binah* (Intelligence)** – The third of the ten *Sefirot* (levels) that exist in each of the Four Spiritual Worlds. *Binah* is the direct channel that funnels the Light of the Creator through the other levels and into our physical world. *Binah* serves as a store and source of energy—physical, emotional, intellectual, and spiritual—for our whole universe. See also: Ten *Sefirot*, Upper Three, Worlds

Body – The Lower Seven *Sefirot*: *Chesed* (Mercy), *Gevurah* (Judgment/Might), *Tiferet* (Beauty), *Netzach* (Eternity/Victory), *Hod* (Glory), *Yesod* (Foundation), and *Malchut* (Kingdom). These seven *Sefirot* are called the Body (Heb. *Guf*) because they relate to the physical manifestation of action, which is done by the body. The Upper Three *Sefirot* (*Keter, Chochmah,* and *Binah*) are called the Head because they represent the potential aspect: the thoughts and ideas. See also: Head, Lower Seven, Ten *Sefirot,* Upper Three

Book of Formation (*Sefer Yetzirah*) – The earliest known book of kabbalistic knowledge and wisdom. Written by Abraham the Patriarch some 3800 years ago, it deals primarily with the intrinsic power within the Aramaic-Hebrew letters and the stars, and how they affect us in this world. All the secrets of Creation that eventually were revealed are considered to be concealed in this book.

Braita – Words of wisdom from the kabbalists of the 2nd century CE that do not appear in the *Mishnah.* The spiritual laws that were compiled into one compendium in the 2nd century CE were called the *Mishnah*; all other words of wisdom of the kabbalists of that time, the *Tanna'im,* that were not compiled into the *Mishnah* were called *Braitas,* meaning literally "external" or "excluded." Just like the *Mishnah,* the *Braitas* discuss in more detail the laws mentioned in the Five Books of Moses. See also: *Mishnah, Tanna'im*

Braita DeRav Yishmael – A *Braita* that explains 13 rules that Rav Yishmael compiled. These rules were designed for the clarification of the Torah and for making deductions from the Torah that have ramifications in law. See also: *Braita*

Chassid – A term used for anyone who devotes his or her entire life to sharing with others, performing acts of mercy, and acting without judgment or criticism.

Chesed (**Mercy**) – The fourth of the ten levels (*Sefirot*) that exist in each of the Four Spiritual Worlds. *Chesed* is the absolute representation of the Right Column energy, the positive pole of the spiritual energy which is sharing. The Chariot (*Merkavah*) for the *Sefira* of *Chesed* is Abraham the Patriarch. See also: Lower Seven, Ten *Sefirot*

Chochmah (**Wisdom**) – The second of the ten *Sefirot* (levels) that exist in each of the Four Spiritual Worlds. A level of energy where the end result of the most complicated process is known at the very beginning.

Chronicles, Book of – One of the 24 books comprising the Bible. Chronicles describes and reviews the events that happened in the *Books of Samuel* and *Kings*, adding minor details and acting as a supplement to *Samuel* and *Kings*.

Clothing – All spiritual energy like the Lightforce of the Creator needs to be concealed in order to be revealed; this concealment is referred to as clothing. Our thoughts, words, and actions are clothing for the Lightforce of the Creator. Our body is the clothing for our soul. The Torah is the clothing for the Creator. Clothing is also referred to as garments.

Concealed Torah – Aspects of the Torah whose meaning is hidden, also called the Secrets of the Torah. Concealed Torah is essentially a reference to the Wisdom of Kabbalah. One reason that Kabbalah is referred to as the Concealed Torah is because it is concealed from the immediate and literal understanding of the Torah. Another reason is that the Creator is concealing Himself in the Torah. See also: *Sitrei Torah*

Concealment of the Face (*Hester Panim*) – Those moments of chaos and pain in our life so strong that it is as if the Creator is not there (i.e., that He has concealed His Face). The Face of the Divine refers to the clear and evident revelation of Goodness of Providence in people's life. The Revelation or Concealment of· the Face is a relative experience that depends on the level of consciousness of the person; it mainly refers to man's ability to "see" the Divine Wisdom and to understand the ultimate good that is the principal motive of Divine Supervision. When man is not capableof understanding what is going on "behind the scenes," due to lack of merit, then it can be considered as if Providence is hiding its Face from him. Concealment of the Face enables free choice. See also: Back, Merit, Providence, Revelation of the Face

Contraction – see *Tzimtzum*

Correction – see *Tikkun*

Crown – see *Keter*

Derash – One of the four ways to interpret every word and sentence in the Torah. *Derash* is the underlying understanding of the lessons we can apply in our daily life from each section of the Torah. *Derash* is the homiletic exposition in contrast to *Peshat*, the literal interpretation. See also: *PARDES*, *Peshat*

Deuteronomy, Book of – The fifth book of the *Five Books of Moses*, also known as *Devarim* (lit. words). *Deuteronomy* details the review given to the Israelites by Moses of the 40 years they had spent in the desert. This entire book takes place in the time-span of one month, ending in Moses' death and in the Israelites' entry into the land of Israel.

Double Concealment (Concealment within Concealment) – State of being when the chaos and pain is so strong that a person completely loses his faith in the goodness of the Creator and shifts to heretical thoughts and actions. Compare with Concealment of the Face. See also: Concealment of the Face

Ecclesiastes, Book of - One of the 24 books comprising the Bible. *Ecclesiastes* is narrated by King Solomon who calls himself "*Kohelet*, son of David and king in Jerusalem," and its main focus is a reflection on the meaning and purpose of life and on the best way of living.

Eternity/Victory – see *Netzach*

Evil Inclination – Each and every person always has two inner voices that guide him to do everything, whether positive or reactive; the Evil Inclination is the voice that pushes us to be reactive and negative. It is sometimes referred to as Satan, which in Hebrew simply means "adversary." The Evil Inclination is our internal opponent that always tells us to act selfishly and reactively.

Etz Chaim – see Ari, *Tree of Life*

Exile – A state of existence where we are less connected and less in tune with the Light, a state where chaos rules and miracles are rare; this state was brought about by the destruction of both Holy Temples. The Hebrew word for "exile" is *Galut*, which also means "to reveal" because this state of existence will change permanently once we reveal the wisdom of Kabbalah, spread it to everyone, and thus change the world.

Exodus, Book of – The second book of the *Five Books of Moses*. Also known as *Shemot* (lit. Names), it details the Israelites' exodus from Egypt and some of their experiences in the desert. The book is called Names because it contains the 72 Names of the Creator.

Face – The nature of the Creator is to share and bestow good. When we are connected to,   experience and are aware of the goodness of the Creator, it is called the Face of the Creator. See also: Back, Concealment of the Face, and Revelation of the Face

For Its Own Sake – Doing something just for the sake of revealing the Light, without any personal agenda or ulterior thought behind it. This term is commonly said about the study of the Torah and the Precepts. In Hebrew, it is called *Lishma* (lit. For Its Own Name). See also: Not For Its Own Sake, Precept

Foundation – see *Yesod*

Gate of Introduction – An introduction to all the major secrets of Kabbalah, written by the great kabbalist Rav Yehuda Ashlag. Oftentimes, kabbalists would title chapters or volumes of their books with the words "Gate of…" because a gate is a doorway, and the knowledge the books reveal is our doorway to the Creator.

Gemarah – An in-depth commentary on the *Mishnah*, which is an explanation of the laws in the *Five Books of Moses*. The *Gemarah* contains discussions between our great sages regarding these laws along with many stories of the sages themselves. See also: *Mishnah*, *Talmud*.

Genesis, Book of – The first book of the *Five Books of Moses*. Also known as *Beresheet*, *Genesis* details the events that happened from Creation until Jacob and his family moved to Egypt, ending in the death of Joseph the Righteous. *Genesis* contains some of the best-known biblical stories, including Adam and Eve, Cain and Abel, Noah's Ark, the Tower of Babel, and the journeys of Abraham, Isaac, and Jacob.

Gevurah **(Judgment/Might)** – The fifth of the ten levels (*Sefirot*) that exist in each of the Four Spiritual Worlds. *Gevurah* is the direct representation of Left Column energy. The Chariot for the *Sefira* of *Gevurah* is Isaac the Patriarch. See also: Lower Seven, Ten *Sefirot*

Glory – see *Hod*

Habakkuk – A prophet of the Israelites (circa 600 BCE). He is one of the 12 Minor Prophets who have a book named after them in the 24 Books of the Torah. Habakkuk died as a child and was resurrected by the prophet Elisha.

Halachah – Any spiritual law of the universe that is based on the 613 Precepts. The later Talmudic laws, as well as customs and traditions, is called *Halachah*. The literal meaning of *Halachah* is "the path" because *Halachah* is a way of connecting to the path of life through the actions that we do. For those who want to follow a spiritual quest, *Halachah* is a system of instructions for what to do, how, and when. See also: 613, Precept, *Talmud*

Head – The Upper Three *Sefirot*: *Keter* (Crown), *Chochmah* (Wisdom), and *Binah* (Intelligence). These three *Sefirot* are called the Head (Heb. *Rosh*) because they relate to the potential state in the creation of everything, which is done by the head (thinking before manifesting an idea), whereas the Lower Seven *Sefirot*: *Chesed*, *Gevurah*, *Tiferet*, *Netzach*, *Hod*, *Yesod*, and *Malchut* are called the Body because they represent the phases where manifestation takes place. See also: Body, Ten *Sefirot*

He Who knows all mysteries – The Lightforce of the Creator.

Hod (Glory) – The eighth of the ten levels (*Sefirot*) that exist in each of the Four Spiritual Worlds. *Hod* is an additional connection to the energy of the Left Column, although less intense than *Gevurah*. The Chariot for the *Sefira* of *Hod* is Aaron the High Priest. See also: *Gevurah*, Lower Seven, Ten *Sefirot*

Intelligence – see *Binah*

Intentional – A category of a negative action. When we are aware that what we are doing is wrong and we still do it, the action is put under the category of Intentional (*Zadon*), and we are held directly responsible for whatever effect comes our way. Intentional refers to a premeditated act of negativity, one that we do even though we know it is wrong and destructive. See also: Unintentional

Isaiah – One of the greatest prophets (circa 740 BCE) who preached for social justice based on understanding the Providence of the Creator. As a kabbalistic prophet, he urged people to reconnect to spirituality rather than dogmatic religion. Isaiah prophesized the end of days where there would be peace on Earth and a reality where "a wolf shall dwell with a lamb."

Israelite – A code name for anyone who is following a spiritual path and who is working on his or her negative traits and constantly striving to transform them to positive ones. Israelites are people who take upon themselves the responsibility for spreading the Light, putting other people's needs before their own, following the spiritual rules of cause and effect, and not taking the Torah literally but rather as a coded message.

Jeremiah – A prophet who lived in the time of the destruction of the First Temple (586 BCE). He constantly warned the Israelites that their wrongdoing and injustice to their fellowman would lead to destruction. In exile, however, his prophecies were of consolation. Jeremiah wrote the Book of Lamentations.

Jerusalem Talmud – The version of the *Talmud* that was taught in the region of Israel; it differs oftentimes in minor details with the *Babylonian Talmud*. See also: *Talmud*

Job – A righteous man in biblical times whose piety and selflessness prompted Satan to test his virtue with terrible physical suffering, both within and without. Job never succumbed to the pain, always staying true to the Creator, and was ultimately rewarded, double and triple, what he had lost. The *Book of Job* deals with the question of why good people suffer and evil people prosper.

Judgment/Might – see *Gevurah*

Keter **(Crown)** – The first and highest of the ten levels (*Sefirot*) that exist in each of the Four Spiritual Worlds. *Keter* emphasizes the ultimate connection to the Lightforce of the Creator and is the seed level of every spiritual and physical dimension. See also: Ten *Sefirot*, Upper Three, Worlds

King David – The second king of Israel (reigned circa 1010–970 BCE), but the first from the tribe of Judah. Chosen by God and anointed by the prophet Samuel, David was not only a great warrior who expanded his kingdom but also the composer of the *Book of Psalms*. King David is the Chariot of the *Sefira* of *Malchut* (Kingdom), thus representing the physical reality where we need to fight for survival on one hand and be spiritual on the other. King David is the seed of the future Messiah. See also: *Malchut*, Ten *Sefirot*

King Solomon – The third king of Israel (reigned circa 970 – 931 BCE) and the son of King David. King Solomon built the First Temple in Jerusalem. He was the wisest man to ever live, mastering all aspects of wisdom in the world. His name in Hebrew, *Shlomo*, means "completion" or "wholeness" as well as "peace," and in his time, there was no war anywhere on the planet.

Kingdom – see *Malchut*

Klipot – see Shells

Lower Seven – In each of the Four Spiritual Worlds there are ten levels or *Sefirot*. The lower seven *Sefirot* are *Chesed* (Mercy), *Gevurah* (Judgment/Might), *Tiferet* (Beauty), *Netzach* (Eternity/Victory), *Hod* (Glory), *Yesod* (Foundation), and *Malchut* (Kingdom). Collectively, the Lower Seven *Sefirot* represent the six directions: south, north, east, up, down, and west. See also: Body, *Chesed*, *Gevurah*, *Hod*, *Malchut*, *Netzach*, Ten *Sefirot*, *Tiferet*, *Yesod*

***Ma'aseh Beresheet* (Process of Creation)** – A concept referring both to the creation of the world in six days, as described in *Genesis*, and also to the study of the Ten *Sefirot*. The greatest kabbalists were able to tap into *Ma'aseh Beresheet* and could perform miracles for others in need, miracles that defied the laws of nature that were established in the Procces of Creation.

Maimonides – see Rambam

***Malchut* (Kingdom)** – The tenth and lowest of the ten levels (*Sefirot*) that exist in each of the Four Spiritual Worlds. *Malchut* represents manifestation and our physical world as well as every physical connection we make. The Chariot for the *Sefira* of *Malchut* is King David. See also: Lower Seven, Ten *Sefirot*

Mercy – see *Chesed*

Merit – In Hebrew, this word is *Zechut*, which is derived from the root word of "pure," meaning that when we transform our selfish nature into one of selflessness and sharing with others, we become pure. In doing so, we will attain the "merit" of a spiritual lifeline, which will come back when we most need it to remove the chaos, pain, and suffering we are experiencing

Messiah – Often described as a person, the concept of Messiah simply means a collective consciousness of humanity where everyone cares about others' needs ahead of their own, in this way emulating the complete selflessness of the Light. The concept of death (in health, business, relationships, or anything else) cannot exist within the realm of this consciousness.

Middling – Someone who is half-righteous and half-wicked. If we were to place all his or her spiritual actions in one pan of a scale and all his or her negative actions in the other, the pans would be evenly balanced. Most of us are at this level, where neither our spiritual nor our negative actions outweigh the other. When we view ourselves this way, every action that we do suddenly becomes magnified. Doing a positive action tips the scale to the side of peace, happiness, prosperity, and fulfillment; doing a negative action tips the scale to the side of chaos, pain, and suffering. In both cases, the scale tips not just for us, but for the whole world as well. See also: Scales

Midrash Rabbah – The complete collection of the *Midrash*—explanations and more detailed accounts, poetic reflections and homilies—of each of the *Five Books of Moses*. See also: *Beresheet Rabbah*

Mishnah – A six-volume explanation of the spiritual laws in the *Five Books of Moses*. Each of the six volumes deals with a specific category of law. The *Mishnah* was originally an oral teaching, passed on from teacher to student everywhere. However, following the destruction of the Second Temple, Rav Yehuda HaNasi collected all the *Mishnahs* and placed them in categories and volumes in a written format. The *Mishnah* was composed by *Tannaʾim*, kabbalists living in Israel between the years 200 BCE to 200 CE.

Mount Sinai Revelation – The event (circa 1300 BCE) where the Israelites, by achieving total unity, received the Torah on Mount Sinai in the desert. The Israelites experienced immortality, mind over matter, and the reality existing beyond the five senses.

Nachmanides – see *Ramban*

Netzach (**Eternity/Victory**) – The seventh of the ten levels (*Sefirot*) that exist in each of the Four Spiritual Worlds. *Netzach* is an additional connection to the energy of the Right Column, although less powerful than *Chesed*. The Chariot for the *Sefira* of *Netzach* is Moses. See also: *Chesed*, Lower Seven and Ten *Sefirot*

Nitzavim, **Portion of** – The Torah, aside from being composed of the *Five Books of Moses*, is further divided into 54 weekly portions that make up the *Five Books*. The portion of *Nitzavim* is the 51st portion, found toward the end of the *Book of Deuteronomy*.

Not For Its Own Sake – A concept also known as *Lo Lishma*, it refers to a spiritual action that is done with a hidden agenda, where you are trying to get something for yourself alone. See also: For Its Own Sake

Numerical Value – There are 22 Hebrew letters, each with a numerical value ranging from 1 to 400, , which when combined produce words and phrases with their own numerical values. Words or phrases that have the same value are usually another form of providing us with spiritual insight for our lives through the Torah. The main sources for deciphering these combinations are *Sefer Yetzirah* (*Book of Formation*), the *Zohar*, and the *Writings of the Ari*. See also: *Book of Formation*

Oral Torah – Any section of the wisdom of the Torah that was not given to the Israelites on Mount Sinai as the Written Torah, but instead was taught orally by the Creator to Moses, who in turn transmitted it to the Israelites. This wisdom continued to be taught orally, eventually being written down as the *Mishnah* and *Talmud*. See: *Mishnah*, Mount Sinai Revelation, *Talmud*, Written Torah

Other Gods – There are two systems in life: the system of spirituality and purity; and the system of negativity, the Other Side. Our actions (and words) create energy and angels that can belong to either system, depending on the nature of the action. If it is a positive action, these angels help us. If it is a negative action, it creates a negative angel, referred to as "Other Gods," because it belongs to the Other Side. See also: Angel

Side of Guilt – see Scales

Side of Innocence – see Scales

PARDES – Every word and letter in the Torah can be understood in four different ways: *Peshat*, the simple and literal meaning; *Remez*, the allegorical meaning behind the word, metaphors that stand for a higher meaning; *Derash*, the in-depth explanation and homiletical meanings; and *Sod*, the secrets behind the words, where the Wisdom of Kabbalah comes from. The first letter of each type creates the word *PaRDeS,* which means "orchard."

Partzuf – A complete spiritual structure of the Ten *Sefirot. It* represents the Head, the Upper Three *Sefirot*—potential; and the Lower Seven *Sefirot,* the Body—actual. See also: Body, Head, Lower Seven, Ten *Sefirot*, Upper Three and Worlds

Peshat – The simple meaning behind the words of the Torah, the literal meaning of the stories and events. *Peshat* is considered the cornerstone for the other three ways of understanding the Torah. See also: *Derash, PARDES, Remez, Sod*

Precept – One of the 613 spiritual actions we can do in order to connect to the Light of the Creator. There are two types of Precepts: those between man and his fellowman, and those between man and the Creator. In Hebrew, the word for Precept is *Mitzvah*, meaning "unity" or "bonding" because the Precepts create unity between the Creator and us. See also: 613, *Halachah*

Proverbs, Book of – One of the 24 Books of the Bible. The *Book of Proverbs* was written by King Solomon and deals with life lessons.

Providence – Everything that happens on this Earth is led by Divine Providence. The *Zohar* tells us that even every blade of grass has its own individual angel that tells it to grow. In short, every action or event happens with the express oversight of the Creator Himself, and no matter how bad things may seem to us, the Light of Creator is there. See also: Revelation of the Face, Concealment of the Face .

Psalms, Book of – One of the 24 Books of the Bible. The *Book of Psalms* was written by King David as songs and poems that teach us about life and about one's personal relationship with the Creator.

Many prayers are based on *Psalms*, and the *Zohar* often quotes this book.

Rabba – A great Rav and kabbalist whom the Talmud mentions as being from the third generation of *Amora'im*, who were sages who lived in Israel and Babylon between the years 200 and 500 CE.

Ramban – Also known as Nachmanides or Rav Moshe ben Nachman. A 13th century Spanish kabbalist, he wrote an extensive commentary on the Torah, *Talmud* as well as *Sefer Yetzirah* (*Book of Formation*), and authored a prayer meditation called *Igeret HaRamban* (the Letter of the *Ramban*), which we say at least once a week in the morning. He died in 1270 in Israel.

Rambam – Maimonides. A Rav, scholar, philosopher, and physician who was born in Spain (circa 1135), and died in Egypt (circa 1204). Also known as Rav Moshe ben Maimon, he wrote the *Mishneh Torah* (a second Torah), a compilation of 14 books about every single aspect of *Halachah*. His thoughts strongly influenced all philosophical thinking through his major book: *Moreh Nebuchim* (a guide for the perplexed). See also: *Halachah*

Rashbam – Rav Shmuel ben Meir, born circa 1085, died circa 1174. A French *Tosefist* and student and grandson of *Rashi.*, he authored commentaries on the *Talmud* and the Torah, even completing *Rashi's* commentary on the *Talmud* that Rashi himself could not finish in his lifetime. See also: *Rashi, Tosefot*

Rashi – Rav Shlomo Yitzchaki (1040 – 1105), a Rav and commentator on the *Talmud* who lived in France in the 11th century. His commentaries on both the Torah and *Talmud* are still to this day considered the cornerstone for the rest of the commentaries of the *Talmudic* scholars who followed him. He clarified the simple meaning of both the Torah and the *Talmud*; at the same time, his commentaries form the foundation for some of the most profound analysis and mystical teachings. See also: *Talmud, Tosefot*

Rav Ami – One of the fourth-generation *Amora'im* (sages of the *Talmud* who lived between the years 200 and 500 CE). He lived in Babylon and taught Rav Yosef and Rava before moving to Israel.

Rav Hanina ben Dosa – A *Tanna,* a kabbalist sage of the 1st century CE, a miracle worker, rain producer and a student of Raban Yochanan ben Zakai. The *Talmud* quotes God as saying: "The whole world in sustained due only to the holiness of Rav Hanina while few fruits a week are enough to sustain Rav Hanina."

Rav Chaim Vital – The closest and greatest student of the Ari. Blessed with an incredible memory, he was able to write everything the Ari taught him during the two years they were together before the Ari passed away, resulting in the 18-volume set of the *Writings of the Ari.* See also: Ari

Rav Elazar ben Shimon – Son of the author of the *Zohar,* the great kabbalist Rav Shimon bar Yochai. Around 2000 years ago, Rav Elazar and his father hid in a cave for 13 years from the Romans, and that is where they revealed the Wisdom of the *Zohar.*

Rav Hai Gaon – Born in 939, he was the last of the *Ge'onim* (commentators on the Torah and *Talmud* who lived circa 585 to 1038 CE), but about him it is said: "Although he was last [of the *Ge'onim*] in time, he was first in greatness." He died in 1038.

Rav Isaac Luria – see Ari

Rav Meir – One of the *Tanna'im* (authors of the *Mishnah*), student of Rav Akiva. Known also as *Ba'al HaNes* (Miracle Maker), he lived in the beginning of the second century CE after the destruction of the Second Temple and was, together with Rav Shimon bar Yochai, one of five surviving students of Rav Akiva who did not perish in the great plague. The name "Meir" (lit. Illuminator) is actually a sobriquet given to him because he illuminated the eyes of everyone with his teachings. See also: *Tanna Kama*

Rav Shimon bar Yochai – the Master Kabbalist and author of the *Zohar,* the foremost work of kabbalistic knowledge. He was a *Tanna*

of the second century, and student of Rav Akiva. He received his Divine knowledge from Moses and Elijah the prophet while hiding in a cave with his son, Rav Elazar. For Rav Shimon bar Yochai, the limitation of time, space and motion did not exist.

Rav Yosef Karo – A great kabbalist and sage, and author of the *Shulchan Aruch*, a condensation of *Beit Yosef* (his earlier commentary on the *Talmud*) and the most widely used book of *Halachah* today. He lived in Safed in the 16th century, during the time of the Ari. See also: Ari, *Halachah*, *Talmud*

Remez – The hidden meaning behind the words in the Torah. See also: *PARDES*.

Repentance (*Teshuvah*) – Meaning literally "to return," repentance should be understood as a change of thought and action to correct a wrong we have done. By doing so, we change our consciousness: We take responsibility and own up to our past mistakes, thereby removing whatever chaos and pain we might face as a result in the future. Thus "return" back to the future.

Revealed Torah – The simple literal meaning of the written Torah, *Mishnah*, and *Talmud*. See also: *Mishnah*, Revealed Wisdom, *Ta'amei Torah*, *Talmud*

Revealed Wisdom – Any part of the Wisdom of Kabbalah whose meaning is accessible and easy to understand. See: Revealed Torah, *Ta'amei Torah*

Revelation of the Face – A reference to the moments of time when the Creator is "revealed" to us, pain and chaos disappear, and we experience the endless goodness of the Creator. Revelation of the Face is when we suddenly realize that the Creator has always been there, just hiding, and now He is revealed. It is when we see the big picture behind everything. See also: Concealment of the Face, Face

Reward and Punishment – Code words for the basic universal law of cause and effect. The Creator does not punish or reward us for our behavior. Our actions simply create an effect, or consequence that comes back to us in the same degree, good or bad, depending on whether our action was positive or negative.

Righteous (*Tzadik*) – A person who is completely devoted to working on transforming his negative traits and to sharing unconditionally with others. The *Midrash* also tells us that this is a person whose positive actions outweigh his negative actions.

Rishonim (lit. the Firsts) – The great commentators on the *Mishnah* and *Talmud* who lived between the 11th and 15th centuries CE. Two of the most prominent *Rishonim* are *Rashi* and the *Tosefot*. See also: *Mishnah, Rashbam, Rashi, Talmud, Tosefot*

Rosh Hashanah – A two-day event that marks the beginning of the kabbalistic year. It is a cosmic window in time where we can plant positive seeds for the future, affect our entire year positively, and have the opportunity to rewrite our destiny. The *Midrash* teaches us that this is the New Year because it is when man was created during the Six Days of Creation, thereby representing the "birth" of all the souls of humanity. *Rosh Hashanah* always falls on the first day of the month of *Tishrei* (Libra).

Ruach – Of the five levels that make up the soul, *Ruach*, which means "Spirit," is the second from the bottom. It is an additional part of our soul that enters us when we reach Bar/Bat Mitzvah (age 13 for a boy, 12 for a girl), and it activates our free will to choose between Light and darkness.

Sages – A term used to refer to kabbalists from the time of the Second Temple. These were all very wise sages who left us with deep wisdom and many lessons to be found in the *Mishnah,* the *Talmud,* and the *Zohar.*

Samuel, Book of – A two-part volume that is included in the 24 Books of the Bible. It deals with the prophet Samuel and the reign of the first two kings, King Saul and King David, who were both anointed by him. Samuel was considered the last of the judges and first of the major prophets of Israel.

Scales - A metaphysical device for measuring the value of all our actions that we have done in the past. On one pan of the scale are our positive/proactive actions; this pan is called the pan (side) of merit or pan (side) of innocence. On the other pan are our negative/reactive actions and this pan is called the pan (side) of guilt.

Shells (*Klipot*) – Evil husks created by mankind's negative deeds. It is a metaphysical negative covering that hides the Light of the Creator from us and gives it to the Negative Side. It also latches on to the sparks of Light when we fail to act on a positive impulse or action, or when we perform a selfish or negative action. See also: Concealment of the Face

Sitrei Torah – The concealed wisdom of Kabbalah and the Torah. All secrets and teachings of Kabbalah and the Torah can be divided into two categories: *Sitrei Torah* and *Ta'amei Torah*. Literally meaning "Secrets of the Torah," *Sitrei Torah* refers to the Wisdom of Kabbalah that is concealed from most everyone; it can only be revealed to select kabbalists by Divine revelation through a teacher, an angel or Elijah the Prophet. See also: Concealed Torah, Revealed Torah, Revealed Wisdom, *Sod, Ta'amei Torah*

Sod - One of the four ways to interpret every word and sentence in the Torah. *Sod* is the Secrets of the Torah, the Wisdom of Kabbalah. See also: *PARDES*

Surrounding Light – A term used in the study of the *Ten Luminous Emanations*. There are two forms of Light: the Inner Light—the Light that we reveal by our actions; and the Surrounding Light—all the rest of the Light that has the potential to be revealed in our life. This Surrounding Light pushes us to grow and reveal this potential Light.

Ta'amei Torah – The revealed wisdom of Kabbalah and the Torah. All secrets and teachings of Kabbalah and the Torah can be divided into two categories: *Sitrei Torah* and *Ta'amei Torah*. Literally meaning "Taste or Meaning of the Torah," *Ta'amei Torah* refers to the teachings of the Torah where there is a clear and understandable explanation for each connection we make in our daily life through studying and performing the Precepts. These teachings are usually not concealed and are made known to everyone. See also: Revealed Torah, Revealed Wisdom, *Sod, Sitrei Torah*

Talmud – A written compendium of the explanations and commentaries by kabbalists of the 3rd to 7th centuries CE on the laws in the Five Books of Moses regarding ethics, customs, and history. It includes the *Mishnah*, the *Gemarah*, and the *Tosefot*, as well as commentaries by *Rashi* and many other commentators. It is referred to as the *Babylonian Talmud* or the *Jerusalem Talmud*. See also: *Gemarah, Jerusalem Talmud, Mishnah, Tosefot*

Tanna Kama – The term used when dealing with different opinions in various *Mishnahs*. Literally, this phrase in Aramaic translates as "the first author," which refers to the first opinion brought down in a *Mishnah*. If the author (first opinion) is not mentioned by name in the *Mishnah*, then the *Tanna Kama* is most likely Rav Meir, the *Ba'al HaNes*. See also: *Mishnah*, Rav Meir

Tanna'im – The term for the kabbalists of the 1st and 2nd centuries CE (singular, *Tanna*). The spiritual teachings of the *Tanna'im* were compiled into many volumes of the *Mishnah*. See also: *Mishnah*

Ten *Sefirot* – The ten levels of consciousness present in each of the Four Spiritual Worlds. The Ten *Sefirot* Are: *Keter* (Crown), *Chochmah* (Wisdom), *Binah* (Intelligence), *Chesed* (Mercy), *Gevurah* (Judgment/Might), *Tiferet* (Beauty), *Netzach* (Eternity/Victory), *Hod* (Glory), *Yesod* (Foundation), and *Malchut* (Kingdom). They are ten Vessels that reveal the Light; the greater the desire, the higher the level of consciousness that is revealed. See also: *Binah, Chesed, Chochmah, Gevurah, Hod, Keter,* Lower Seven, *Malchut, Netzach, Tiferet, Yesod,* Upper Three, Vessel, Worlds

Ten Luminous Emanations - The study of the emanations of the Sefirot from the Endless down to our physical world, compiled into seven volumes. This study is vital for any deep understanding of the *Zohar* and the way our universe functions. Written by Rav Yehuda Ashlag, founder of The Kabbalah Centre.

Teshuvah – see Repentance

This World – The physical world that we live in, where we are subject to the laws of cause and effect and bound by the limitations of time, space, and motion. Also called the 1 Percent Reality and the illusionary world. See also: World to Come, World of Action

Tiferet (Beauty) – The sixth of the ten levels (*Sefirot*) that exist in each of the Four Spiritual Worlds. *Tiferet* emphasizes the ultimate representation of the Central Column, since this *Sefira* is found between *Chesed* and *Gevurah*, the two representatives of the ultimate Right (Mercy) and Left (Judgment) Columns, respectively. The Chariot for the *Sefira* of *Tiferet* is Jacob the Patriarch. See also: *Chesed*, *Gevurah*, Lower Seven, Ten *Sefirot*

Tikkun (Correction) – We came to this world to "correct" the selfish aspects of our nature and to transform ourselves into "beings of sharing." Thus, everything we experience in life—good or bad—is a *Tikkun* process by which we correct, cleanse, and elevate our souls. The purpose of this process is to bring every human being, along with the entire universe, to perfection. Also known as karma and the purpose of reincarnation.

Tikkunei HaZohar – Literally "Corrections to the *Zohar*," this book addresses the same general subject matter as the *Zohar*, but it is written as 72 commentaries on the first word of *Genesis* (*Beresheet*). *Tikkunei HaZohar* discourses upon teachings specifically directed to the Age of Aquarius. This is the first learning that Rav Shimon bar Yochai received in the cave. See also: Rav Shimon bar Yochai, *Zohar*

Torah – The *Five Books of Moses*. Sometimes the entire body of biblical study, including the *Five Books of Moses*, the 24 other Books of the Bible, the *Mishnah*, the *Talmud*, and Kabbalah, is referred to as *Torah*.

Tosefot – A compilation of commentaries on the *Gemarah* (*Talmud*). *Tosefot* means "additions" and they were authored by more than 100 sages. Foremost among these sages was the grandson of *Rashi* (Rav

Shmuel ben Meir, also known as the *Rashbam*) who wrote most of the commentaries, which take the form of critical and explanatory comments. See also: *Gemarah, Rashbam, Rashi, Talmud.*

Tractate – The *Talmud* and *Mishnah* are each split into six sections, each of which is further divided into subsections called *Masechet* or Tractates. Each subsection is given a name to describe the topic of discussion.

Tractate *Avot* (Fathers) – Also known as *Pirkei Avot* (*Lessons of Our Fathers*), this is one of a very few Tractates in the *Mishnah* that does not have a *Gemarah* commentary on it. This Tractate consists of ethical moral principles and wise sayings to live by.

Tractate *Bava Batra* (Last Gate) – This Tractate discusses damages and business relating to agricultural affairs as well as a person's responsibilities and rights as an owner of rural property (fields, irrigation, pits, etc.).

Tractate *Bava Kama* (First Gate) – This Tractate discusses damages and compensation relating to property or personal belongings. The laws that are covered in this Tractate are found in Exodus 21:18-19 and 21:24-22:5.

Tractate *Bava Metzi'ah* (Middle Gate) – This Tractate discusses civil matters such as property and usury. It also examines a person's obligation to guard lost objects that have been found as well as delineating a person's legal obligations vis-a-vis property that has been entrusted to him.

Tractate *Berachot* (Blessings) – This Tractate discusses the prayers we say every day as well as the blessings we say throughout the day over food and drink.

Tractate *Hagigah* (Holiday) – This Tractate discusses the three harvest holidays (*Pesach, Sukkot, Shavuot*) as well as the travel to Jerusalem and the sacrifices for these holidays.

Tractate *Hulin* (Mundane) – This Tractate discusses the laws of ritual slaughtering of animals for consumption.

Tractate *Kidushin* (Betrothal) – This Tractate discusses the laws pertaining to the betrothal of a woman.

Tractate *Makkot* (Punishments) – This Tractate discusses the laws of the courts and the punishments they can impose on those who have committed wrongdoings.

Tractate *Megilah* (Scroll) – This Tractate discusses the laws pertaining to reading and understanding the Scroll of Esther. It also examines the general laws of Purim, and includes laws concerning the weekly Torah readings.

Tractate *Niddah* (Menstruation) – This Tractate discusses the laws of *niddah* (menstruation) for both married and unmarried women. The main focus of the discussion is sexual matters and purity.

Tractate *Psachim* (Passover) – This Tractate discusses the sacrifice offering of *Pesach* (Passover) as well as all the laws regarding this holiday.

Tractate *Rosh Hashanah* (New Year) – This Tractate discusses the laws of *Rosh Hashanah* (the New Year holiday), along with important rules concerning the calendar year, *Rosh Chodesh* (the inauguration of each month), and the laws of *Shofar*.

Tractate *Sanhedrin* (Assembly) – This Tractate discusses criminal law, its proceedings, and its punishments. This Tractate is noteworthy as a precursor to the development of modern-day common law principles.

Tractate *Shabbat* (Sabbath) – This Tractate discusses the laws of *Shabbat*.

Tractate *Ta'anit* (Fasting) – This Tractate discusses the laws of fast days and the proceedings and prayers involved.

Transgression – Also referred to as sin or iniquity. These are all code words for one thing: a disconnection from the Light of the Creator and a connection to darkness, chaos, pain, and suffering.

Etz HaChayim (*Tree of Life*) – The first four volumes in the 18-volume set of the *Writings of the Ari*, written by Rav Isaac Luria (the Ari). They contain the main teachings of the study of *Ten Luminous Emanations*. See also: Ari, Rav Chaim Vital, Writings of the Ari

Tzadik – see Righteous

Tzimtzum (**Contraction**) –Voluntary rejection or restriction of the Divine Light in the Endless World due to the concept of Bread of Shame and the Vessel's desire to be independent and God-like. In the lower physical world the restriction--if not done voluntarily--is imposed. Restriction constitutes one of the basic rules by which this mundane reality operates.

Unintentional – A category of a negative action. A transgression or sin that is performed by accident, without knowing or without premeditation, is called Unintentional. See also: Intentional

Upper Three – The term used to refer to the first three *Sefirot*: *Keter* (Crown), *Chochmah* (Wisdom), and *Binah* (Intelligence). Out of the Ten *Sefirot*, these three are on the highest plane of existence. See also: *Keter, Chochmah, Binah*, Head, Ten *Sefirot*

Ve Zot HaBrachah, **Portion of** – The Torah, aside from being composed of the *Five Books of Moses*, is further divided into 54 portions that make up the *Five Books*. This portion is the last portion in the Torah and deals mainly with the blessings Moses gave to the 12 tribes of Israel before he passed away.

Vilna Gaon – Rav Eliyahu ben Shlomo Zalman of Vilnius (1720 – 1797), a great kabbalist and sage who lived in the 18th century; he was also known by the acronym, HaGra. He wrote kabbalistic commentaries which number some eighty volumes on the Torah, *Talmud* and *Midrash*. In his prayer book, the Vilna Gaon wrote that understanding the Torah starts when we study its secrets. See also: Rav Yosef Karo

Wisdom – see *Chochmah*

Wisdom of Truth – Another term for the Wisdom of Kabbalah, so called because truth is something that is neither subjective nor inconsistent. Truth is a constant and does not change because of human influences.

Worlds (*Olamot*) – A term used in the study of the *Ten Luminous Emanations*. There are five *Sefirot*, five channels that bring the Light down to this mundane reality. When the channels are filled with Light we call them Worlds. Every World represents a different level of consciousness that is related to a level of veil that covers the Light. The word *olam* in Hebrew means "disappearance," referring to the fact that only when the Light is concealed a reality can be revealed. The worlds are: **Primordial Man** (*Adam Kadmon*), **Emanation** (*Atzilut*), **Creation** (*Beriah*), **Formation** (*Yetzirah*), and **Action** (*Asiyah*). See: *Partzuf*, World of Action, World of Creation, World of Emanation, World of Formation,

World of Action (*Asiyah*) – The lowest (from above downwards) of the Five Spiritual Worlds that emerged after the *Tzimtzum* (Contraction) of the Vessel in the Endless. The World of Action is the dimension where the least amount of Light is revealed. This enables human beings to exercise their free will in discerning between good and evil. This World is also related to the *Sefira* of *Malchut* (Kingdom) and is referred to as the Tree of Knowledge of Good and Evil. See also: *Malchut*, *Tzimtzum*, Worlds,

World of Creation (*Beriah*) – The third (from above downwards) of the Five Spiritual Worlds that appeared after the *Tzimtzum* (Contraction). It is related to the *Sefira* of *Binah* (Intelligence) and is a universal energy store. See also: *Binah*, *Tzimtzum*, Worlds,

World of Emanation (*Atzilut*) – The second (from above downwards) of the Five Spiritual Worlds that appeared after the *Tzimtzum* (Contraction). In this high and most exalted World, the Vessel is passive in relation to the Light, allowing the Light to flow without any agenda. It is related to the *Sefira* of *Chochmah* (Wisdom). See also: *Chochmah, Tzimtzum,* Worlds,

World of Formation (*Yetzirah*) – The fourth (from above downwards) of the Five Spiritual Worlds that appeared after the *Tzimtzum* (Contraction). Whereas in the lowest World (Action), evil is the predominant force, in the World of Formation, goodness is the predominant force. It is related to the *Sefira* of *Zeir Anpin* (Small Face) and to the energy of the Shield of David. See also: *Tzimtzum,* Worlds.

World to Come – A realm where only happiness, fulfillment, love, and joy exist—the 99 Percent Realm of the Light of the Creator. The kabbalists explain that the World to Come exists in each and every moment of our lives. Every action of ours creates an effect that comes back to us either for good and for bad, and through the way in which we live our lives, we can create worlds according to our design. World to Come is commonly referred to as the reality of life-after-life. See also: This World

Written Torah – The *Five Books of Moses* that were given to the Israelites on Mount Sinai and all the teachings found within. See also: Mount Sinai Revelation, Oral Torah

Yesod (Foundation) – The ninth of the ten levels (*Sefirot*) that exist in each of the Four Spiritual Worlds. *Yesod* is the ultimate representation of sustenance and abundance. The Chariot for the *Sefira* of *Yesod* is Joseph the Righteous, who provided sustenance and abundance from Egypt to the whole world during a famine, as described in the Book of Genesis. See also: Ten *Sefirot*, Lower Seven,

Yetzirah – see World of Formation

Zohar – Written by the great sage Rav Shimon bar Yochai, this 23-volume work is the basis and source of all the teachings of Kabbalah we have today. See also: Concealed Torah, Rav Shimon bar Yochai, Revealed Wisdom, Wisdom of Truth

More Books That Can Help You Bring
the Wisdom of Kabbalah into your Life

The Wisdom of Truth: 12 Essays by the Holy Kabbalist Rav Yehuda Ashlag
Edited by Michael Berg

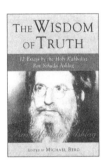

All of the essential truths of Kabbalah are encapsulated in these thought-provoking essays by arguably the most profound mystic of the 20th century. Originally published in 1984 as Kabbalah: A Gift of the Bible, and long out of print, this is a new translation from the Hebrew, edited and with an introduction by noted Kabbalah scholar Michael Berg.

Beloved of My Soul
By Michael Berg

This book is a rare glimpse into the relationship between Kabbalist Rav Yehuda Tzvi Brandwein and his beloved student Rav Berg, the present leader of the Kabbalah Centre. Through the 37 letters presented here, written from Rav Brandwein to Rav Berg between 1965 and 1969, we gain deep insights into loving spiritual lessons from teacher to student. We see their involvement goes beyond spiritual studies, and relates to all aspects of the practical material world. In these passages, we discover Rav Brandwein was connected with Rav Berg with all his soul and might. The letters are presented without a filter of interpretation, allowing readers to leave with answers—and more questions—and a yearning for greater wisdom.

Secrets of the Zohar: Stories and Meditations to Awaken the Heart
By Michael Berg

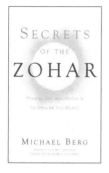

The *Zohar*'s secrets are the secrets of the Bible, passed on as oral tradition and then recorded as a sacred text that remained hidden for thousands of years. They have never been revealed quite as they are here in these pages, which decipher the codes behind the best stories of the ancient sages and offer a special meditation for each one. Entire portions of the *Zohar* are presented, with the Aramaic and its English translation in side-by-side columns. This allows you to scan and to read aloud so that you can draw on the *Zohar*'s full energy and achieve spiritual transformation. Open this book and open your heart to the Light of the *Zohar*!

Immortality: The Inevitability of Eternal Life
By Rav Berg

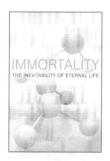

This book will totally change the way in which you perceive the world, if you simply approach its contents with an open mind and an open heart.

Most people have it backwards, dreading and battling what they see as the inevitability of aging and death. But, according to the great Kabbalist Rav Berg and the ancient wisdom of Kabbalah, it is eternal life that is inevitable.

With a radical shift in our cosmic awareness and the transformation of the collective consciousness that will follow, we can bring about the demise of the death force once and for all—in this "lifetime."

The Zohar

Composed more than 2,000 years ago, the 23-volume *Zohar* is a commentary on biblical and spiritual matters written in the form of conversations among teachers. It was given to all humankind by the Creator to bring us protection, to connect us with the Creator's Light, and ultimately to fulfill our birthright of transformation. The *Zohar* is an effective tool for achieving our purpose in life.

More than eighty years ago, when The Kabbalah Centre was founded, the *Zohar* had virtually disappeared from the world. Today all this has changed. Through the editorial efforts of Michael Berg, the *Zohar* is available in the original Aramaic language and for the first time in English with commentary.

The Kabbalah Centre

The Kabbalah Centre is a not-for-profit organization dedicated to bringing the wisdom of Kabbalah to the world. The Centre has existed for more than 80 years, but its teaching lineage extends back to the 16th century and even further back to the Zohar, more than 2,000 years ago.

The Kabbalah Centre was founded in 1922 by Rav Yehuda Ashlag, one of the greatest kabbalists of the 20th Century. When Rav Ashlag left this world, leadership of The Kabbalah Centre was handed/given over to his student, Rav Yehuda Brandwein. Before his passing, Rav Brandwein designated Rav Berg as director of The Kabbalah Centre. Now, for more than 40 years, The Kabbalah Centre has been under the direction of Rav Berg, his wife Karen Berg, and their sons, Yehuda Berg and Michael Berg.

The mission of The Kabbalah Centre is to make the practical tools and spiritual teachings available to everyone as a way of creating a better life.

Local Kabbalah Centres around the world offer lectures, classes, study groups, holiday celebrations, services and community activities including neighborhood volunteer projects. To find a Centre near you, visit to www.kabbalah.com.

Student Support

The Kabbalah Centre empowers people to take responsibility for their own lives. It's about the teachings, not the teachers. But on your journey to personal growth, things can be unclear and sometimes rocky, so it is helpful to have a coach or teacher. Simply call 1 800 KABBALAH (1.800.522.2252) toll free.

Kabbalah University

Be in the center of Kabbalah activities anytime and anywhere through Kabbalah University (www.ukabbalah.com). Kabbalah University is an online resource center and community offering a vault of wisdom spanning 30 years, and rapidly growing. Removing any time-space limitation, this virtual Kabbalah Centre presents the same courses and spiritual connections as the physical centers, with an added benefit of live streaming videos from worldwide travels. As close as a click of your finger, for a low monthly access fee, it's open 24/7.

Stay current with historic lessons from Rav Berg and inspiring talks with Karen. Delve deeper into Michael Berg's teachings and journey with Yehuda Berg to holy sites. Connect with world renowned Kabbalah instructors sharing weekly *Zohar* and consciousness classes that awaken insights into essential life matters such as: relationships, health, prosperity, reincarnation, parenting, and astrology. Check out the library, including hundreds of spiritual topics going back more than four decades. A richer world awaits your presence at ukabbalah.com.

כִּי-מָלְאָה הָאָרֶץ, דֵּעָה אֶת-יְהוָה, כַּמַּיִם, לַיָּם מְכַסִּים

"…for the Earth will be full of the knowledge of the LORD
as the waters cover the sea." (Isaiah 11:9)

To Rav and Karen, Yehuda and Michael, and
all the teachers and chevre of The Centre.
May our work remove, for us all, space and lift
the curtain to *Etz Chayim*—the true reality.